A FORTUNATE LIFE

JOHN WILLIAMS

Copyright © 2018 John Williams and Christopher J Williams

All rights reserved.

ISBN: 978-0-6481438-4-0

Forward

January 2018, Cairns, Australia

Christopher J Williams here, author of *Seconds from Impact* and *Rendition*. I am John Williams' nephew and have the pleasure of introducing his autobiography.

Like John, I was born in Liverpool and spent years in Southport and also in Plymouth before coming to Australia at at 15. John left school early and signed onto the Merchant Navy in the early 50s and, later, when he was in Australia, he decided to jump ship and try life in Australia. As he'd never returned to England while I'd been growing up, we'd never met. Mum and Dad had talking about emigrating to Australia, but had not done anything about it.

In 1976, my grandfather, Joe Williams, whom I had only met once when I was around 9 or so, fell ill in Canberra, where he had been living with my grandmother, Margaret, since the early 1960s. My father, Joe, flew out to be with his father, but he had passed just before Dad could see him.

His sister, Maggie, was also living in Canberra as she had married a Brazilian Diplomat, Miguel de Almeida Ozorio, who was the Ambassador to Australia at the time and they lived in a fine house on acreage in Red Hill, with three of my cousins, Patricia, Marcos and Carlos. Dad was a Civil Servant who working the Department of Trade and, while in Canberra helping the family cope with his own father's death, he struck a deal with Miguel and commenced working at the Brazilian Embassy, as a Trade Advisor.

Meanwhile, Mum put our house near Plymouth on the market, arranged for removal of our stuff and booked us onto a plane. 'Us' was me, my younger brother, Neil, and Janet, my elder sister by two years. I recall it was a stressful time for all, but particularly Mum, selling cars, getting us onto a train to London, etc, etc. It was my first plane ride, Australia was beaches and who knew what, and I was getting out of a private, male only school. So I was excited, even if Janet, who was leaving a boyfriend behind, was not entirely enthusiastic about the trip. (She went back to Plymouth after a year, came back with new man a few years later, and has been here ever since, and with the same, good man, Jim Anstey.)

I remember clearly my new uncle John, who cut a dashing, energetic figure as he bundled us all into a big Holden Kingswood and took us to a flash hotel in the Eastern Suburbs of Sydney. I remember being in awe of everything in Sydney, particularly the sky scrapers and we also met John's second wife, Brownyn, and a wide circle of their friends.

In due course, I finished school in Canberra and joined the public service, the Army Reserve and then the Regular Army. This was the early 1980s. Prior to that, we saw John and his wife Bronwyn, regularly, either when they came to Canberra, or we got in the car and travelled the Hume Hwy to Sydney to stay in their quirky terrace house in Birchgrove.

As my own adult life went forward and John's experienced turbulence, eventually separating from his wife, I started to take the opportunity that he provided by having a flat in Double Bay, which overlooked the harbour. I remember it was a good place to meet girls and he even set me up (well I might add) on a couple of occasions. We got on pretty good, despite the almost 30 years between us. He was still a good looking man and we went out on the town on occasion and had some good times together.

When I first got married in 1990, I saw him again, but less often, as he had moved to Melbourne. I was starting to travel with work by then, so did take opportunity to stay with him, or at least have a drink, while I was there.

Later, there was a long period without contact, perhaps only through phone calls relayed to me by Mum or Dad. In part, he'd moved to Adelaide, but also because I didn't need him, had my own family and life, full of its own ups and downs.

Somewhere around 2010, my Aunt Maggie travelled to Australia to stay with my Mum and Dad in their home near Bateman's Bay in NSW. John, who was living in Adelaide at the time, in a hostel and subject to the rules of a guardian, appointed by the Public Trustee, was invited to come to the reunion. Problem was, everyone underestimated quite how difficult a train journey was when you are in your late 70s.

By the time John got to Sydney, a friend he'd met in Adelaide, Paul, had offered him a flat to stay in and, instead of getting on a train and travelling down the coast to meet his brother and sister, he had a bit of conniption in a pub (hard to say more about it) and ended up in St Vincent's hospital. After a couple of weeks, his son helped to negotiate for his plane travel back to Adelaide and he never got to see his sister before she returned to Brazil.

Fast forward a couple of years and there I was at my Mum's funeral in 2014, seeing John again, after almost 20 years. We embraced and started a dialogue about getting him to move to Cairns, where I'd only recently settled after 30 years of working in the public sector. Six months later after negotiating with his guardian and his son, Christopher, I finally got him a plane ticket and he travelled to Cairns.

That trip was not without incident, however, as I received a call from the airline in Sydney, saying that he'd missed his connection. I pulled out my visa card and we got him into a room at one of the nearby Airport hotels and a seat on a plane for the following day.

I remember waiting for him at the airport and, he duly arrived and strolled through the gate with a backpack containing about 7 items of clothing. I said to him, where was his suitcase and he grinned at me and said he had everything he needed...

Sadly, Dad passed ten months after Mum, a sudden, haemorrhage in his brain and he never woke up. By that time, John was living independently in a flat nearby in Edge Hill and starting his new life. As he has trouble managing his money, I have an enduring power of Attorney for John and have been paying his bills and rationing out the balance of his money, most of which he spends on cigarettes! (Not that I can preach on this subject.)

Eventually, I realised that he hadn't been managing on his own and that I'd been turning a blind eye to his not eating properly and not keeping his place clean. John took some time to understand that he needed full time care, and he's now living in a nearby nursing home, where the staff look after him very well and he is something of a minor celebrity.

John had previously published the book under the title, the Fortunate Life of a Vindicatrix Boy, and asked me to see if I could help him create an eBook. Well, he'd lost the original manuscript so I tried scanning it and converting it to text. Hours and hours I spent and then I tried to get the full manuscript back from Amazon but John had lost his links to Amazon as he no longer had the email or phone accounts to prove who he was. Eventually I was able to solve this and I've been able to resurrect and rewrite the book together with some new pictures. The book is basically as it was finished in 2005, with the addition of my forward, rewording some parts, and the inclusion of an afterword, which John has written. I hope you enjoy his life story.

As a final aside, all the royalties from this book will go to assist John in his final years and for as long as I continue to care for him.

Onto the book, and, as 'the lads' once sang:

Welcome, welcome to the Mystery Tour

DEDICATION

This book is dedicated to all the crews of Allied merchant vessels who served in World War II, enabling so many of us to enjoy fortunate lives at sea and ashore. I trained at the *Vindicatrix* Training School in Sharpness, England, after signing on with the Merchant Navy and I give a special tribute to those fine young Vindi boys who sadly lost their lives or were injured at sea.

During World War II, many Vindi boys served on ships in the Atlantic and Arctic supply convoys that were the lifelines of the Allied campaign in Europe. Of all the World War Two convoy routes, the most dangerous were the Arctic convoys. Ships carrying supplies to the Russian ports of Archangel and Murmansk had to track the hostile coastline of Nazi-occupied Norway.

These convoys had to contend with deadly submarines together with surface vessels and aircraft from Norwegian ports. During the Arctic summer they travelled in 24 hours of daylight for up to 15 days and in winter faced violent storms and gales. The worst losses suffered by a single Arctic convoy were 23 of 34 ships from convoy PQ17 in July 1942.

Crews on convoy ships had a routine for precious sleep that was dictated by the cargo they carried. With general cargo they could sleep below because they might have time to get on deck before a ship sank, with iron ore they slept on deck for if a torpedo hit, sinking was fast and when carrying a load of fuel, they slept below decks because a direct hit meant oblivion.

The last major British deployment of a large fleet of merchant vessels was in the Falklands war. It was the only way to despatch and supply an army 8000 miles away with no airstrips available. It comprised ocean liners including *QE2* and *Canberra*, oil and water tankers, refrigerated cargo ships and even a Row-Row ferry fitted with bow doors, on which the crew kept a wary eye.

THIEVES IN THE NIGHT

He was standing there braced hard against the hatch, flashlight doused, removing a steel locking bar from a small wooden hatch cover, the top canvas already rolled back. "It's cargo we're after, lads, for all the crew to share. You're the smallest two aboard, so you've been chosen. We're only interested in the good stuff, cigarettes, tobacco, grog and the like," he said as he handed us the flashlight, two sheath knives and two baling hooks.

"I'll have to drag the cover back over, but I'll be waiting here when you get back up," he added, as he guided us into the blackness of the hold. No chance to protest, no time to question; we were the chosen ones – modern Oliver Twists – thieves in the night, slithering, crawling down into the dark, cavernous hold, squeezing between loosely packed boxes and crates. Holding tight the precious flashlight, knives and baling hooks firmly tucked into our belts, our hearts pounding and lungs gasping in the murky darkness.

Slipping, falling, sliding as the tramp steamer *Coulgarve* pitched and rolled.

Before I left my home in Liverpool and entered the ranks of the Vindi boys who trained aboard the TS *Vindicatrix* Sea Training School at Sharpness in Gloucester, I had heard lurid tales about the golden rivet, as had Dave the cabin boy. We were relieved to learn we were only to be thieves that night in the stormy Atlantic. As a Vindi boy I had learned to take the word of an officer seriously, especially after my moonlight swim from the *Vindicatrix* with a group of other trainees. Dripping wet and shivering, we had stood "under the clock" for what seemed like an eternity. It was punishment for not taking officers too seriously. "Under the clock" was standard punishment for errant trainees as they spent their last week in training aboard the *Vindicatrix*, formerly a three-masted steel sailing ship.

She'd had two previous names – *Arranmore* and *Waltraute* – before being moored as *Vindicatrix* in a backwater of the Sharpness-Gloucester canal.

Arranmore or Arainn Mhor is an island off the coast of Donegal, Ireland and *Waltraute* is the name of a famous Wagner opera character. Originally moored on the Thames, the *Vindicatrix* was moved to Sharpness in early 1939 because of fears that she could become a target for German bombers.

All those who trained on the *Vindicatrix* during war or peacetime became known as Vindi boys. While she escaped the ravages of World War II, sadly many of the boys who trained on her became casualties. Many a Vindi boy went to an early watery grave as German submarines wrought havoc on Atlantic and North Sea and Arctic convoys.

My night swim was not the first time I had been in trouble in a canal, but more of that later.

I thought I was in bigger trouble on the *Coulgarve* when on my first trip to sea we had been woken two nights out of Rotterdam as our ship ploughed erratic furrows in a hostile sea. A flashlight was shining in our faces as we stirred in our warm, cosy bunks, and a gruff voice, straining to be heard above the ocean's roaring, sang out "On your feet, you two – you're coming with me." We recognised a junior officer in his twenties, stoutly built, short cropped hair, stern and impatient, beckoning us up on deck. We dressed hurriedly in the cramped, lurching space and followed him out into the cold, moonlit night. Clutching the portside gunwale, we edged our way forward along the heaving wet steel deck. As the *Coulgarve* lurched to starboard, we let go our vice like grip, and threw ourselves on to the top of a cargo hatch. The officer removed the steel locking bar, lifted the canvas sheet, pulled back a wooden hatch cover and beckoned us into the black hole. We dropped on to the cargo stack and began slithering down the cracks between the crates and boxes.

Our fears subsided with each rewarding find. Cartons of Lucky Strike and Camel cigarettes, pipe tobacco, finely decorated porcelain jars of assorted Dutch liqueurs, bottles of Johnnie Walker Scotch and boxes of American basketball boots. The officer was there waiting as we made our assaults on our personal Everest; seagoing porters, laden with all manner of supplies; three tortuous ascents in all. No Atlantic storm, no matter how violent, could wake us once, exhausted, we had regained the sanctuary of our bunks. The ship's cook woke us; he couldn't wait to get his bloody basketball boots, and the galley's daily supply of potatoes, those bloody potatoes, sacks and bloody sacks of them.

Potatoes had loomed large in my early years, as I helped my father grow them in the back garden of our modest council house, picked countless hampers of them on cold mornings at nearby farms for pocket money and hungrily devoured them chipped and fried with battered fish religiously every Friday night. In strongly Catholic Liverpool, Friday night was fish and chips night for everyone, even us Protestants.

Friday could also see a night sky ablaze, stabbing searchlights, bursting shells and dashing tracers, as lumbering German bombers and buzzing RAF fighters locked horns. It was a big adventure for a seven-year-old on the fringe of war – close to the dead, the dying, not fully aware of what it was; scared, excited, like your first fireworks show – spectacular. Glowing hot shrapnel bounced at my feet as we stood outside our house in Longview, an outer suburb of Liverpool. Some nights I trailed closely behind my father on Air Raid Precautions duty; sometimes I was bundled hastily over low garden hedges to the high-pitched whine of bombs dropping close. My father had spent an eternity in the trenches of World War I, laying and repairing wires for field telephones with shells bursting all around him.

Coming through that, he seemed indestructible, talking of it as an adventure: seeing Europe, stealing chickens; tough Australian troops and attractive French girls.

Our family was lucky; we survived the black years of two world wars. Our council housing estate was eight miles from Liverpool on the perimeter of the sprawling Merseyside city, the road behind us the boundary of the vast country estate of Lord Derby, where the

Luftwaffe sometimes dropped their bombs haphazardly as they fled the heavy flak criss-crossing the city sky.

Liverpool in the 1940s – no mean city

Dodging and weaving over the outer suburbs, they ditched their lethal payloads before turning for the long and dangerous run home. Many of the bombs fell harmlessly in empty fields and coastal waters.

The good lord's estate was a cut above ours, but we had the best of both worlds. Family and neighbours were as close as the council houses we lived in. They stood in neat rows of four, with sitting room and kitchen downstairs and bedrooms upstairs. Each had a postage-stamp back and front garden and a neatly trimmed privet hedge. In our backyard stood a mangle for squeezing excess water out of the weekly wash, and in which kids sometimes got their fingers caught – which could explain the name. Outer suburbia had few motor cars; trolley buses and trams provided regular, comfortable transport. In a world so compact and orderly, it was difficult to comprehend the destruction and chaos sweeping Europe.

I survived the Battle of Britain, but not the battles of Lord Derby's estates or the perils of household air raid shelters. One of his Lordship's barbed wire fences produced a scar above my right eye and from our indoor steel shelter came a broken collarbone.

The fences were there not to repel the feared German invaders but to keep the lads of Longview from his Lordship's lush apple orchards. A nine mile stone wall surrounds the 2500 acre estate and residence, Knowsley Hall, and its scenic lake.

The Longview lads had dashed through dark, mysterious green woods, across shallow ponds and streams, with a hostile gamekeeper in pursuit, shotgun in hand. Diving head first between the lower strands of the barbed wire fence, I misjudged the gap. The gamekeeper refrained from discharging his two barrels of bird shot in our direction, so we escaped to lick our wounds and eat the few crisp, sweet apples we had salvaged during our scramble through the woods.

The woods were where we caught tadpoles, climbed trees and raided birds' nests, piercing the tiny eggs with sharp thorns and gently blowing the embryo out to leave the fragile eggshell intact to display on a bedroom shelf. Frogs were fun to catch, and we delighted in making them jump by tickling their backsides with a piece of straw or twig. Tadpoles were transported home in jam jars to watch their development into frogs.

If we were there today we would have more than gamekeepers to contend with – we could be chased by lions, tigers, cheetahs, buffalo or elephants. In 1971 Knowsley Safari Park was opened to the public by the eighteenth Earl of Derby, the first safari park built close to a large city.

Motorists travel along a five-mile roadway through the estate with most of the animals roaming free in what is now one of Liverpool's major leisure attractions. I wouldn't think the kids from Longview Estate would still be climbing the wall, but who knows. We were lucky kids, city born but country bred, and the woods were our sanctuary from the ugly war that was tearing the rest of the world apart.

At home we had three air-raid shelters, the corrugated iron Anderson shelter covered by a mound of earth in the back garden, a steel cage structure inside the house that doubled as a dining table, and the backyard entry tunnel that cut through the ground floor of our house and that of our next door neighbours. Anticipating Hitler's territorial ambitions, Britain had started producing the Anderson shelter, named after the Lord Privy Seal, Sir John Anderson, as early as February 1939.

By the time war started in September, the ARP had installed one and a half million of the shelters.

The Anderson was the first to be distributed in our neighbourhood, but it afforded only minimal protection. Eventually it was replaced by the large, square steel cage in which my brother, sister and I slept with rubber Mickey Mouse gas masks always at the ready.

As the war dragged on we found the safest place was the backyard entry tunnel, with its arched brick roof.

My broken collarbone was self-inflicted. After climbing onto the plate steel top of the table shelter I dived off head first. I had just started school swimming lessons at the local pool and was practising diving. It's the only bone I've broken, but I've been leaping headlong into things ever since.

The Anderson shelter came in handy as a hutch for our two pet Angora rabbits, Bubble and Squeak, whose names belied their nature. When expecting a litter, they ferociously chased stray cats and once attacked my father's ankles when he ventured too close. From then on he gave them a wide berth when tending his vegetable garden. Father grew potatoes, peas, turnips, carrots and rhubarb for the family table, while I made a few shillings a day picking potatoes and peas for the wider community.

For a few months I worked in the city fruit and vegetable markets, consigning endless sacks of potatoes to greengrocers. Father's rhubarb was exceptional, thanks to the local traders' horse-drawn carts. Our house was in a row of five, and there was an honour system between neighbours. If a horse relieved itself in front of your house, you got to spade the spoils on to your rhubarb patch. The horses were kind to father's rhubarb and to mother's roses. Later in life I wondered if that's what had created the distinctive Liverpool accent. That nasal sound, from wrinkling your nose as you shovelled up the fresh manure.

Longview boys and girls were an adventurous lot, although sex was still in the closet; there was no sex education at school, no condoms, no Masters and Johnson, no television, and nobody talked about sex on radio. Sex started and finished with the fleeting kisses of "postman's knock", just as it did in the Saturday afternoon movies. Girls were sweet, innocent, and inviolate. There was furtive whispering about "feeling", but no more. Like Lord Derby's apples, girls were the forbidden fruit, fresh skin shiny and glowing, to be admired, but not consumed. At 12 years, none of us knew why girls gave us goose bumps, except Roy, who was one of the best 'feelers' in the gang. He'd felt more girls than the rest of us had kissed. He may have gone further, but we never did find out.

To find out more about girls, some of us joined a local tap-dancing school, and we performed in concerts at working men's clubs throughout the North of England. Speeding through the Lancashire night in a darkened bus, bodies got closer than 'postman's knock'. Hands started to roam, but only in a nice way, a sort of tentative feel. While we tap danced and fondled our way around the country giving concerts at Working Men's Clubs, Roy continued 'feeling' his way round Liverpool. I had dreams of making the big time like my hero Donald O'Connor. That was not to be, but I would make it onto the stage in a different role and play a small but significant role with the biggest Liverpool act of all time The Beatles.

For the moment I was struggling with the most important thing in my life – my education. It had been a big surprise to most people, including me, winning a scholarship to Wade Deacon Grammar school in Widnes; the most surprised being my headmaster. I had not been good at studying, never seemed to concentrate much, and just thought a lot about travelling the world. I often felt the sharp pain of a well-aimed blackboard eraser.

Today I suppose I might have been diagnosed with ADD – Attention Deficit Disorder, sometimes called hyperactivity. Some doctors have said that 50 years ago children who couldn't concentrate at school and were under-performing for their intellect would leave and work on a farm, in my case a tramp steamer. As a child in the 1940s I happily accepted the proposition that an occasional swift kick up the backside was the most effective prescription for most of us. Even being hit by a well-aimed blackboard eraser was an acceptable reminder of the need for order. When I topped the marks for the scholarship examinations, everyone I knew thought it was odd.

The school ordered a recount, but it still came out the same, so off I went to Widnes each day on a bus crowded with girls. A few other lads travelled on the bus each day from Longview to Widnes, but we were heavily outnumbered by the girls. Through sheer weight of numbers they sexually harassed the boys. With our short trousers it was easy for them and we were often groped, but we simply regarded it as part of our education.

Girls weren't the only thing on our minds. Tobacco was another forbidden fruit; we smoked acorn pipes packed with used cigarette butts off the street. Filter tips had not been invented then, so the unsmoked butts were filled with tobacco. When the filter tip arrived it was the down-and-outs who picked butts off the street who lost out.

We played soccer and cricket in the street with two bricks for goalposts or the base of a concrete lamp post as the stumps, and between times there were steam trucks, snowmen, snowball fights, ice slides and radio. Radio was a Godsend in Liverpool during the war, keeping us in touch, keeping us in hope, keeping us entertained.

When the war finished, the docks were still there, with the overhead railway, Pier Head, the ferries to New Brighton, the Mersey Tunnel, Lime Street and the Liver Bird, but we could see right through the middle of the city. It was as if someone had pushed a giant egg slice straight through it, scraping up many of the city's poor who took the brunt of the bombing.

When the wailing sirens stopped we were among the lucky ones who went on with life.

We dreamed up projects like the Longview Olympic Games in which 6 everyone got to carry the torch. It's a wonder we didn't set fire to the entire estate with those bundles of flaming newspapers. We ran in relays handing them to each other, and then chucking them away as they got too hot to carry. We staged track and field events in the street and everyone got a medal of some description, mostly decorated foil caps from milk bottles.

Parents were not amused when we stripped our bicycles down to speedway rig, but we built a real cinder race track and invited some of the country's top speedway stars to the official opening ceremony. We ruined a lot of tyres and shoes, but it was fun, and it took our minds off girls for a while.

Bikes were our great escape. We rode up behind steam trucks, grabbed hold and let the truck drag us along. Sometimes we just ran up, grabbing a rail at the back of the truck, throwing our feet up onto a metal bar and hanging on. Getting off was tricky, with gravel rash a constant hazard. I was dragged around often in Liverpool, once with near fatal consequences, when swimming in the Liverpool-Leeds canal that ran alongside Aintree racecourse, home of the Grand National Steeplechase. I dived into the canal soon after a string of barges had passed by, unaware that a cable was dragging behind the last one. The cable caught around my feet and, terrified, I was dragged along underwater; close to panic, somehow I managed to pull clear of the cable, struggle back to the surface and gulp in some air.

My lucky escape did not deter me from going to sea, although the Merchant Navy was not my original choice. After seeing Gunga Din at a Saturday afternoon matinee I aspired to be an Army drummer boy, bravely leading troops into battle in some far-flung corner of the Empire. At the Army recruiting office I was given enlistment papers for my parents to sign, but they managed to talk me out of it and, as a compromise, suggested the Merchant Navy. As it turned out, they probably would have been happier with a drummer boy, for the British Army was a safer place to be, and they would have seen a lot more of me. In the Merchant Navy I was aboard a floating time bomb in a war zone, came close to sinking, ran aground several times, was shot at, crewed on a troopship, watched a number of old hands go "troppo" and spent a lot of time in sleazy bars and brothels.

In the late 40s, girls were not allowed to become Army drummers, do National Service or go to sea, so my sister Margaret also took up tap dancing. She became a talented dancer and singer and later appeared in a number of theatrical productions. When she became principal dancer at Murray's Cabaret in London, she met her husband to be, a Brazilian diplomat. The subsequent attentions of the Fleet Street paparazzi forced them to flee the country, but that's a later story.

Twelve weeks' training at the TS *Vindicatrix* Sea Training School enabled over 70,000 teenage boys to go to sea aboard British merchant vessels during war and peace from 1939 to 1966. Boys had to pass a tough medical and for many the training course was their first time away from home. During wartime the boys were kitted out in navy jerseys and oilskins which were later replaced by two-piece navy serge suits. I joined the ranks of the 'Vindi boys' in 1951. Vindicatrix deck boys wore blue shirts and catering boys white; on their uniform shoulders deck boys had a red flash with Merchant Navy and catering boys a blue one. Deck boys trained in boat handling, signalling, compass steering, knotting, splicing, cleaning brass and scrubbing decks. Catering boys learned how to make bunks, clean cabins, prepare vegetables, set tables and serve food.

The Vindicatrix – a start of life for many a promising lad

In the shore camp there were wooden accommodation huts, stores, offices, sick bay, parade ground and vegetable garden. These were encircled by a wire fence with guard hut and reception manned 24 hours a day. A nearby Mission to Seamen provided recreation facilities including snooker, darts and table tennis. There were boxing tournaments and monthly dances. The *Vindicatrix* finally went to the wreckers in January 1967 after proudly living up to her Latin name, 'She who vindicates'. The 'ship with three names' has been bobbing up in my life from the time I set sail on my first voyage on the *Coulgarve* in July 1951 through to April 2004. *Coulgarve* was a tramp steamer of 2946 tons, built by Lithgow Ltd in Glasgow. I was not aware at that time that Lithgow Ltd was a firm founded in 1918 from Russell & Co – builders of the *Arranmore* in 1893. Russell & Co had a brilliant reputation, constructing no less than 500 square-rigged sailing vessels. W I Lithgow became sole partner in Russell & Co in 1912, and after the name changed Lithgow built up its own reputation.

Arranmore sailed under the Red Ensign for 17 years and when sold and renamed *Waltraute* flew the German flag for 10 years. *Arranmore* had been sold to a German shipping line and as *Waltraute* saw World War One service as a submarine training base and a POW prison before the British reclaimed her and she became *Vindicatrix*.

The Arranmore just after she was built in 1893

Six years after *Arranmore* was launched the vessel was nearly lost in a strong gale in Algoa Bay off Port Elizabeth, South Africa. Algoa Bay records high winds often and today attracts windsurfers from around the globe. *Arranmore* was riding out the gale, but another Russell & Co vessel, the steamer Mashona, severed *Arranmore*'s both anchors and dragged her spare anchor overboard.

The gale drove *Arranmore* onto the beach by midnight, but incredibly all of her crew managed to scramble to safety. At first *Arranmore* was considered a total loss, but fortunately her hull remained intact and she was eventually salvaged. However, twelve years later, Mashona was wrecked and the next vessel to carry that name, the Royal Navy Tribal class destroyer HMS Mashona, was sunk by German aircraft off the coast of Ireland in May 1941.

Having the same shipbuilder was not the only thing that *Coulgarve* and the ship with three names had in common. *Arranmore*'s maiden voyage in 1893 lasted 18 months and in that time she circumnavigated the globe. My first voyage aboard *Coulgarve* was meant to be three months, but it lasted 15 months. We didn't circumnavigate the world, but we sailed around the same distance in the Atlantic and Pacific Oceans and the Caribbean and North Seas.

Arranmore first sailed to Australia in 1904 and as I write this in the Semaphore Library I am only a few yards from the signal station that greeted and farewelled her as she sailed into and out of Port Adelaide. All that remains of the signal station is the time ball tower by which *Arranmore* would have rated its chronometer. Erected in 1875, the tower was used to signal the hour of 1pm each day, but with the advent of time wireless signals in 1932 the practice was discontinued. For nearly three years I had coffee every morning at the Café Saltwater next to the time ball tower, unaware of the local connection with the ship with three names.

*

I began my life at sea as a galley boy in a crew of twenty-four. *Coulgarve* sailed from Swansea to Amsterdam and Rotterdam, to take on cargo for the West Indies and I shared a cabin with Dave, another first-tripper from Birkenhead. The cabin was nine feet long, five feet wide and not much over head height for an average teenager. It had two bunks and two small cupboards, with additional storage space under the bottom bunk. The cabin was sparse, but cosy on stormy nights, and there were many of those, and a lifetime of other experiences to come. We had signed on for a voyage of some three months. Heading out of the Channel for our Atlantic crossing, we were not to know we would not see Mother England again for fifteen long months.

As we set about finding our sea legs, time was of little concern. Sailing across a stormy English Channel aboard a small tramp steamer is not really the best way to find your sea legs. I would have preferred something slightly larger, like Queen Mary or Queen Elizabeth. It would not be long before I would echo those thoughts during a dramatic event in the Caribbean.

Holland would be my first experience of a foreign country – that is, if you don't count Wales. Many people spoke English in Wales, which was not that far from Liverpool and I would sometimes ride my bike there on weekends. Family holidays were spent in Wales, and as a boy scout I had camped at Llandudno in the lush, rolling green hills.

Once, by chance, returning from a concert at Gwyrch Castle, I fell in love with a Welsh girl. It was love at first sight outside the fish and chip shop where we had stopped for supper and we made small talk and exchanged names and addresses; telephones were a rarity then.

Our troupe had performed at the ancient castle that day as a curtain raiser to public sparring exhibitions by British boxing champion Randolph Turpin.

I met that Welsh girl one more time on the banks of the River Dee, between Liverpool and Wales, but my best mate Tom Pearce was leaving that night to join a ship and I had promised to see him off at Lime Street station. I was getting close to losing my virginity in an England-Wales union in the new mown hay along the riverbank, but I reluctantly had to dash off to catch a bus to farewell Tom. In a quantum leap from 'postman's knock' and foreplay in the hay, the spoils went to the Dutch, not to the Welsh. She was an overweight middle-aged prostitute in an Amsterdam brothel who showed little interest as I pumped away my virginity. Not at all impressive, but for the older crew of the *Coulgarve* I had made the team.

We had left behind the Dutch coast and were steaming out of the Channel into the Atlantic and a long crossing to the West Indies by way of Madeira, when the junior officer woke Dave and me and sent us down into the cargo hold.

"God, we might get trapped down here and get eaten by rats," I said to Dave. "What a way to go on our first trip." Dave said nothing. 'He's too shit frightened to talk,' I thought.

We managed to squeeze through small gaps between cases of all shapes and sizes, gasping in the dank, oppressive hold. Clutching cartons of American cigarettes, Dutch liqueurs and American basketball boots, it seemed much easier making our way back to the deck. It was to be the first of many such trips for the benefit of all the crew. We spent carefree nights on deck, happily guzzling the liqueurs and tossing the beautiful porcelain bottles overboard so there would be no evidence of our illicit activities.

Shipping companies said the introduction of steel containers would make shipping and cargo handling more cost efficient, but security must surely have been one of the main reasons. If the crews of other cargo vessels around the world were like ours, a veritable mountain of cargo was disappearing, and that's not accounting for the wharfies who were equally adept. We accepted the junior officer's assurance that there was a set percentage in the cargo manifest for pilferage, and it was covered by insurance. Liqueurs, luxury soap, cigarettes and baseball boots coming out of war-devastated Europe; who knows where it came from? Black markets were flourishing at the time, fortunes were being made and the destinations of many cargoes were bastions of exploitation. What was wrong with a little petty larceny?

I made my first Atlantic crossing peeling potatoes, sipping liqueurs, peeling potatoes, smoking Lucky Strikes and peeling more potatoes. The officers and crew of *Coulgarve* were a mixed bunch from England, Ireland, Scotland, Wales and Canada. The married ones would feel the strain of the long voyage, but for Dave and me it was a big adventure and time was of no consequence.

I peeled sacks and sacks of potatoes, and washed mountains of pots and pans, while Dave served hundreds of meals, and scrubbed interminable sections of wooden decking. Our boredom with this routine was relieved when we were occasionally allowed to swap duties. Madeira would be our first port of call, then the tropical island of Barbados. I wondered if the liqueurs and cigarettes in the hold would last long enough for the rightful owners to enjoy one or two. I spent many relaxing hours at the ship's bow watching porpoises and dolphins playfully leaping and diving ahead of *Coulgarve* like packs of hounds leading a hunt. At times some of them seemed to touch the bow instinctively, as though to keep us on course.

While sailing peacefully into the tranquil Caribbean, en route to Barbados, there was a loud explosion below decks, bringing *Coulgarve* to a dead stop shortly after midnight. We had been sleeping soundly in our cabin directly over the engine room. Only the cook, stark naked as we were, beat us onto the main deck. As clouds of hissing steam spurted menacingly into our cabin, I had fallen out of my bunk, colliding heavily with Dave as we rushed for the door. While we were frantically dashing onto the deck, the Chief Engineer was rushing down the ladder into the steam-filled engine room. His first concern was for those in his engine room crew.

Later, we learnt that the engine was a new Swedish type, unfortunately still in its experimental stages. Without any warning a cylinder head had disintegrated. Fortunately there were no casualties and the situation was not as bad as it first appeared, so we returned to our cabins and dressed.

Coulgarve – I boarded her as a boy and came home a man. (Note the Coulgarve was renamed the Dunolly in 1956. This picture would have been taken before 1960 as she sank when a Tsunami wave hit her after an earthquake struck in Chile.)

As things transpired, we found we were close to the rocky shoreline of Barbados with a lifeless engine. Our floating home was drifting in the wrong direction so we quickly donned life jackets and hurried to emergency stations as the ship's radio operator appealed for any vessel in the vicinity to come to our aid.

Decades later, it seems an appropriate time to again recall Rudyard Kipling and an extract from 'The Ship That Found Herself':

Song of the Engines

We now, held in captivity,
Spring to our labours nor grieve!
See now, how it is a more blessed,
Brothers, to give than to receive!
Keep trust, wherefore ye were made,
Paying the duty ye owe;
For a clean thrust and the sheer of the blade
Shall carry us where we should go.

No such thrusting blade for us as, with the first grey light of dawn, we were perilously close to the rocks and about to abandon ship.

Fortunately the Canadian passenger liner *Lady Nelson* made a timely appearance and took us in tow.

Set stunningly in the blue Caribbean, the lush island of Barbados had a typical colonial mix of wealthy whites and poverty-stricken blacks. Ironically, the smiles were on the wrong faces – the faces of the exploited. Many of the white expatriates were in a permanent state of homesickness on this island of the gentry. It was a paradise to be lost.

I fell under the influence of a heady combination of rum and cola, calypso music and women. No drummer boy had aspired to the exotic and erotic delights that I was experiencing at the tender age of fifteen.

The exciting, sensual rhythms of the Caribbean were the beat of a different drum for me: silvery flying fish darting over the gently rolling waves, the acrobatic dolphins, the frolicking native women with their glistening black bodies. I was discovering places with romantic sounding names like Curacao, Trinidad and Maracaibo Lakes.

Curacao reminded me of our earlier port of call, Madeira, a magical island with clusters of splendid white villas set on steep hills around a sparkling blue harbour. Vivid green palms and masses of brightly coloured tropical flowers clung to the steep slopes. 'Have some Madeira, my dear' seemed to echo from those affluent picture postcard hills. In stark contrast, a knock on the door of a dilapidated waterfront shack and a couple of packets of cigarettes could buy you grandmother, mother or daughter. Having only thought intermittently then of social injustice, I settled for mother, a strikingly beautiful woman in her mid-thirties – a passionate introduction to Spanish women.

Did anyone ever venture down from those sedate hillside villas to sample such delights? Somewhere between Madeira and Curacao we discovered Cashmere Bouquet soap in the cargo and the crew overindulged, using one bar a shower then tossing them overboard. We left a bubbling soapy trail from Madeira to Barbados and on to Curacao. When it was found that the local women generally preferred the soap to American cigarettes, the crew became more austere in their showering. The Maracaibo Lakes graphically highlighted another kind of exploitation as, dotted around the vast

Venezuelan waterway, Shell oil rigs greedily sucked out liquid black gold.

The intervening years have seen oil flow wherever a drill has been sunk in a country which has enormous resources, but more than its share of poverty.

After the balmy weather of the Caribbean, the Maracaibo Lakes brought us close to the Equator and extremely hot, humid weather, with rarely the hint of a breeze in the surrounding dense green jungles. We found some relief in the air-conditioned social clubs that were a necessity for the oilmen and their families stoically carving out another outpost of the Shell empire. Mainly European, they found Venezuela an uncomfortable posting, and a cold beer at night in the cool, comfortable clubs was a welcome change from the unrelenting tropical heat. The steamy lakes would give us a taste of what lay ahead of us up the Orinoco River.

Return trips north to America's cooler climate were a welcome relief as signs of 'troppo' were already ominous with some of the crew. There were occasions when I helped officers restrain distressed crew members. As the months rolled on, married crew were particularly upset with our extended term at sea. They had told their families it was only going to be a three month trip, but the shipping company just kept accepting new charters.

Cape Hatteras, on the eastern seaboard of the US, is a notorious ships' graveyard. As *Coulgarve* first steamed north past the famous landmark she pitched and rolled violently, and we all said a silent prayer for Swedish engineers. The storm's fury seemed a reasonable price to pay for my first glimpse of New York, the magnificent city of the Saturday afternoon matinees. The Statue of Liberty was breathtaking from the deck of a small tramp steamer.

In my enthusiasm to get the right angle on the symbolic white statue I dropped my camera overboard. The Manhattan skyline was colossal and the Empire State building awesome. American servicemen in World War II said Liverpool reminded them of New York and we could see some similarity in the docks and the Manhattan River entrance, and Coney Island was a bit like New Brighton, but that's where it finished. Liverpool seemed like a village beside this colossus of wealth and power.

"Jack Dempsey's Bar; could he really be there?" Sure enough when we got ashore and located his bar there was the boxing legend pulling beers for the crew.

From Dempsey's bar we went on to the dazzling neon lights of Times Square and to Broadway the beat of Fred Astaire and Donald O'Connor who I had seen perform at the Liverpool Empire Theatre, and waited for hours at the stage door to catch a glimpse of a real tap dancer. No such luck in New York, he was out of town.

Central Park, Fifth Avenue: such opulence, such style; in which high rise apartment tower were the wealthy sugar barons of the Caribbean? We had carried their sweet spoils from Cuba to America, and I had seen the exploitation of the workers on the docks and when Fidel Castro's guerrillas toppled the last, and some say the worst, of the Cuban dictators, Fulgencio Batista, in the late 50s, I found no difficulty understanding.

Cuba exported sugar in large hessian sacks and one night on a wharf in Havana three of us tried together to lift a sack and found it impossible. We had watched each of the Cuban wharf labourers carry a sack at a time on his shoulders up the gangway over and over. It was an incredible feat of strength, but their lifespan – their working lifespan – was around ten years for the lucky ones. They barely made enough to live, let alone anything for their old age, an old age that began, and sometimes ended, in their early 30s in a corrupt and worthless system, crying out for social justice. Drinking rum and cola; working for the Yankee dollar!

To see at first hand how America treated its own blacks explained a lot to me about exploitation. For the black and white buddies of World War II, it was back to reality and segregation in 1945, and America was not alone, as I was to discover. After seeing black and white GIs together in Liverpool, I found it difficult to accept segregation and whenever we went ashore in American ports we would sit with blacks in segregated buses and go into 'blacks only' drugstores and bars. That was the irony. As visiting merchant seamen we could go and sit with the blacks and only the odd white drunk would bother us. Most people, including the cops, just thought we were odd.

Sadly, attitudes often take generations to change and while the exploitation of Cubans had begun to stir my teenage social conscience, for now the bright, flashing lights of Broadway and the vastness of New York had me spellbound. There were to be other American cities like Philadelphia, Baltimore, Galveston, and New Orleans and, thanks to that experimental Swedish engine, Miami. Not many tramp steamers made unscheduled stops at Miami – not many had experimental Swedish engines. It looked so unreal: the endless, neat rows of hotels, apartments and sunbaked beach lovers, a stunning contrast to the grimy industrial cities around our regular US ports of call like Philadelphia and Baltimore. For several months we steamed between the wealthy cities of the eastern seaboard of the United States and the poverty stricken nations of Central America.

The seas off the coasts of Costa Rica, Nicaragua, Honduras, Guatemala, Panama and El Salvador were a calm and glassy contrast to the Atlantic and our lines trailing over the stern yielded a plentiful supply of the large Bonito fish for the galley.

As we steamed backwards and forwards through the Panama Canal, the major issue for the crew was venereal disease. We had frequent 'short arm inspections'. Drop your trousers and flash it. Inexplicably, Dave and I always passed successfully, unlike many of the older hands, some of whom seemed to have a new dose every time they dropped their trousers. We all went to the same bars and brothels, but Dave and I just seemed to be lucky. For centuries gonorrhoea and syphilis have been rife in Central America and, along with Yellow Fever, were the scourge of the Panama Canal during its incredible construction. On *Coulgarve* we travelled through the Panama Canal many times in both directions, but we were always in awe of it. From locks to lakes and surrounding dense jungle it's like travelling along a giant fold-out tourist card.

In an astonishing display of American-Anglo affection, the pleasant, matronly nurse, who was closely inspecting my vital parts in Panama, invited me home to meet her daughter. Was it an invitation extended in the knowledge that I was 'clean', or a motherly attempt to keep me out of those brothels? I never did find out, nor did I care as I enjoyed a home-cooked meal, the first in a long time, and a rare chance to talk to a girl. Whatever happened to short-arm inspections? When 3,000 American sailors descend on the city of Perth in Western Australia, have they all flashed it before leaving ship? With AIDS in epidemic proportions do they all have blood tests before arrival? Do

American tourists returning home from Central America, South America and the Caribbean have to flash it at Kennedy Airport?

During a welcome break from what had become routine journeys through the Panama Canal, we headed south with holds packed with supplies and a deck cargo of trailers for American mining camps up Venezuela's Orinoco River. The Orinoco, which lies just south of the Caribbean island of Trini20 dad, has a fascinating history. As early as 1530 the Spanish were claiming that the legendary city of Eldorado was situated in "The Kingdom of Gold" on the shores of a lake in the basin of the river. This led to many expeditions to the highlands of Guiana. Part of Sir Walter Raleigh's 1595 manuscript map from his expedition up the Orinoco survives, showing 'that mighty, rich and beautiful Empire of Guinea, and that great and golden city which the Spaniards call Eldorado and the naturals call Manoa.' Frenchman T. de Bry's 1599 copperplate map shows the lake with strange creatures such as headless men and fearsome armed women. Maybe this mythical history explains why signs of 'troppo' became more obvious on *Coulgarve* when we reached the Orinoco.

Earlier, off the Central American coast, a drunk Canadian seaman jumped overboard fully clothed, but fortunately, through a porthole, a crew member saw him hitting the water. The Canadian thought we were still in port, but *Coulgarve* was many miles off the coast; it was a calm night; he was a good swimmer and we were able to stop, turn around and recover him alive and well, still singing. Sadly, that was not the case with the Dutchman John Demeyne who complained about being hypnotised before jumping overboard from *Arranmore* back in 1903, never to be seen again. That would be the fate of a passenger on another vessel that I crewed on.

The mighty Panama Canal

We got a foretaste of 'troppo' on the bridge when officers had difficulties with charts and tides and our vessel ran aground on a sandbar in the entrance to the Orinoco. On an earlier trip up the river, we had rammed a number of wharves. After we ran aground for a second time at the river entrance, we began to wonder if 'troppo' was claiming another victim. When an officer had one of the ship's lifeboats lowered, got into it and floated off down the river, we knew he had finally lost the plot.

As I sat on deck at times trying my best to communicate with the indigenous cargo handlers who lived aboard during our river voyages, I would never have dreamed how later in life through my sister I would connect so strongly with Brazil which loomed large south of the Orinoco. That Rio de Janeiro would become as familiar to me as Liverpool.

North of Venezuela, in Central America, corruption was rampant, so Dave and I were not surprised when a Nicaraguan Customs official asked what we could bring off the ship for him to sell locally. He said he would split the proceeds with us, so we asked what he thought would be easy to sell and profitable. He thought for a while then said mantequia (butter), one of a smattering of Spanish words we knew. It was a tall order, for the cook kept a padlock on the refrigeration compartment, the cook and the Chief Steward had the only keys.

The cook liked a drink, which was understandable. Working all day in a coal-fired galley in the tropics, especially kneading dough for the daily bread, gives anyone a big thirst. Getting the butter out of the refrigeration compartment was one thing; getting it ashore was another. We had successfully managed to smuggle some items ashore, despite the watchful eyes of the officer of the watch, and officials on shore.

One of our more ingenious schemes had been with rolls of suit cloth that we had found in the cargo. From a roll we had cut off three long lengths that we considered would be the right dimensions for several suits, and before dressing to go ashore, we wrapped ourselves tightly in the lengths of material. In a number of shallow-water ports *Coulgarve* stood offshore, while barges took the cargo ashore. To get ashore with the cloth, we had to go by small boat, and we had rolled the material around each other too tightly. It was all right standing upright, but going down the gangway, getting into the boat and sitting down was tortuous.

"It's a good job those Egyptians were dead when they were mummified," Dave said. "They could never have walked with all that wrapping."

Amazingly, nobody realised we had so much under our clothes. We found a local tailor close to the waterfront and he took the cloth and obligingly made out receipts for purchase of suits. After only one overnight fitting the suits were not the perfect fit, but it was a profitable venture. We got the suits and the tailor got enough cloth for several more.

Once, when the *Coulgarve* crew was running low on soap, we had gone down into a cargo hold in port in daylight as armed guards patrolled the decks. Others distracted the guards while we ducked out of a companion way and dropped down into the hold and grabbed a large box of Cashmere Bouquet. When the coast was clear, one of the crew alerted us. We quickly emerged from the hold clutching the spoils and dodged back into the companion way.

Stealing butter involved a bolder scheme. "Get the cook drunk and while you're with him, we'll break the padlock," suggested Dave. The refrigeration compartment was the size of a small bedroom, with an outer chiller section and an inner freezer where I had spent many an hour making ice cream. I never got too cold because it was easy to work up a sweat churning ice cream by hand, but I always made sure someone other than the cook knew I was in there, just in case he put that padlock on. We found a bottle of rum and set out to get the cook drunk. It took some time, but eventually he fell asleep, and it must have been a deep sleep, because they made one hell of a noise breaking that padlock off with a fire axe. The cook woke with a start, but dropped off again after I said "It's those bloody locals dropping cargo again." Dave and a deck boy grabbed several large cartons of butter, closed the fridge door, latched it, and took away the broken padlock. We hoped the cook would think he had mislaid the padlock.

It was late at night, and we managed to slip unnoticed down the gangway into the small, darkened shed where the customs officer was waiting. In exchange for the butter he handed us a sizeable wad of local money and we headed into town to one of the local bars. Mostly small timber shacks with tin roofs, the bars offered sultry, dark-haired women, mainly of Spanish Indian blood, for a drink, a dance or sex.

Nazis on the run from Europe ran some of the bars. Thousands of Hitler's henchmen escaped down the "rat lines" through Italy then by submarine and boat to Central and South America where they landed on remote sections of the coast and used money and guns to create safe havens. On several occasions we ran into drunken Germans, and one fired shots at us as we were travelling into a town on flat top railway rolling stock. *Englische Schwein* was not a difficult phrase to translate as the shots rang out and we crouched down low on the slow moving banana train.

To wander off alone in Central America could have proved fatal, for like sex, life was cheap. The exciting atmosphere of the bars, fiery Spanish music and the strong scent of cheap perfume were intoxicating. Some bars had small bedrooms, running directly off the bar, not too far to walk or stagger.

Big wooden ceiling fans whirred noisily overhead, but not enough to chill the hot, humid air, which accelerated our intake of rum and coke, and we discovered the harsh realities of 'brewer's droop', which recognises no age limit, only the level of alcoholic consumption. Even the dedicated bar girls could not overcome it. Nature, of course, has a mind of its own and some nights we got totally drunk and performed like prize stallions.

Rum and coke was one thing, drugs another. Nobody offered us drugs for our own consumption, but one Nicaraguan bartender suggested we might like to take a small package to a friend in the US. "You'll get paid handsomely," he said. Declining the offer, we couldn't help noticing the large photograph of Robert Mitchum adorning the bar, and I wondered if he was the 'friend'. Police and federal narcotics agents had earlier arrested the 31-year-old movie star with 20-year-old starlet Lila Leeds, in a late raid at her Hollywood cottage, and seized a quantity of marijuana cigarettes.

On *Coulgarve* the only thing we became addicted to was bananas which, with coffee and sugar, made up a major part of our cargo on return trips to US east coat ports. Like their Cuban Latin cousins, the wharf labourers of Central America bore a heavy load, humping giant stalks of bananas as tall as themselves. It was easy to divert one into a cabin in return for a packet of cigarettes, more than they got for a full day's labour. To many people, bananas are just another fruit, but in wartime and post-war Liverpool they were a rarity; thus, every year in our Christmas stockings was a present – an apple, an orange and a banana. The apple was not an uncommon sight, thanks to Lord Derby, but oranges normally came in tinned, reconstituted juice and bananas only in Christmas stockings. On the *Coulgarve* we pigged out on bananas and got quite ill, but unlike rum and coke, bananas never gave us brewer's droop; at least, I don't think so.

At sea there was plenty of overtime, so we worked long hours and scraped and painted cabins and decks. It was vital to supplement my monthly income of eight pounds, with four pounds a month of it going directly to my parents by tradition. Four pounds a month plus overtime may not seem much money, but in Central America and the Caribbean then it was a fortune.

*

The funnel and stern flag colours on the *Coulgarve* changed constantly as we picked up new charters for a variety of international companies. She was a tramp who could be tarted up for anyone who had the money as she plied her trade between the US and the Caribbean, backwards and forwards through the Panama Canal, to Central America, and finally back home, by way of Canada. We had forgotten what cold was until *Coulgarve* sat close to ice-bound in the port of Newcastle on Miremichi Bay in the state of New Brunswick which fronts the Gulf of St Lawrence. When we headed home through mountainous seas around the top of Scotland our deck cargo became a nightmare load. Rogue waves swept timber from the deck like matchsticks as we ploughed through a raging storm and we huddled below decks, playing music and cards, and pretending not to be scared.

When the sea abated it took a more precious cargo, contraband from our foraging down the cargo holds, which we had managed to cram into the storage space under the bottom bunk. In New York we had sat nonchalantly on the bunk, wide-eyed and innocent, as Customs officials inspected the cabins; one of them pointedly winking at us as he pinned an all-clear notice on the door. I'm sure he knew we were sitting on more than our backsides.

Coming into West Hartlepool in England, the Chief Steward told us our backsides would get kicked if we were caught with anything. Customs officers were going to check out the whole ship. He had kindly let us fill up our kitbags with canned and packaged food to take home, where wartime food rationing was still in force. After his warning about Customs, we had to empty our kitbags, put all the food back, then go up on deck and toss overboard cartons of American cigarettes, bottles of perfume and liqueurs and other goods pilfered during our fourteen months away. It was poetic justice.

The saving grace was the two bottles of excellent Jamaican rum that I had acquired legitimately. Customs regulations allowed for the import of one full bottle, plus a second one, if part consumed. Taking a swig from one of them, I replaced the top, as we headed into port.

There was much cursing and swearing when we discovered that the news about Customs had been a false alarm; they were nowhere to be seen when we berthed, so we rushed back to the Chief Steward and refilled our kitbags with food. With one more swig of rum, I hoisted my kitbag and was off ashore to catch the train to Liverpool. I arrived back in England in 1952 wearing American Levi's jeans, cowboy boots, broad cowboy belt, tartan shirt, white tee shirt and an American gabardine casual jacket. Fashion hasn't changed much in my 70 years.

It was difficult finding my family then; they had moved across the Mersey to Ellesmere Port, where my father worked for Shell as a cooper – the traditional trade of barrel making. Wooden barrels were still in use for some Shell products, although the advent of metal containers was turning coopering into a dying art. Since crossing the Channel to the horrors of World War I, my father had made several trips back to Europe with my mother. Constantly around the docks checking and repairing barrels, he yearned to travel further a field, but approaching 50, and having little money, believed he'd missed his opportunity and could only watch the ships come and go.

Later, with my mother and the rest of my family, he was to travel extensively. He had been hoping he would see me sail back into Liverpool, but was at work when I got home to Ellesmere Port. On my next trip, when I sailed directly into Liverpool on the tanker *Athelknight* in April 1953, he was on the job again, but I celebrated my birthday with him the next day.

On the train I had drunk most of the remainder of the open bottle of rum to fortify myself against the cold English weather. Lime Street Station made me nostalgic for home and for steam trains. Steam trains were exciting and romantic and for as long as I could remember I had been a dedicated train-spotter, religiously keeping a diary of different trains hurtling along the tracks to distant, exciting destinations, pedalling my bike for miles to railway tunnels, standing on the roadway above and watching in awe as thunderous trains bathed in billowing clouds of steam flashed by below.

Steam trains have shaped the destinies of millions of people. I have had flirtations with motor cars, but steam trains have been a lifetime love. Sadly, motor vehicles have irreparably damaged our environment and it is difficult to understand motorists sporting environmental messages in the rear windows of the very vehicles that are threatening the future of mankind.

'Save the whale', 'Save our forests', 'Quit smoking', in motor cars belching out toxic fumes that daily pollute our cities and take their toll of people. If the world ran out of oil tomorrow there would be a non-polluting vehicle on our streets in no time. Could it be time to bring back steam? Not the coal fired variety of course. I travelled by steam train to Wales on holidays, on my first visit to London and when I went to sea; now I'm steaming into Lime Street after 14 months away with thoughts of the young men from two World Wars arriving in Lime Street by steam train on their journey home.

Had they taken her away? Walking briskly out into the cold Merseyside winter I found Maggie May was alive and well – dozens of 'Maggies' standing in dozens of shop doorways, thighs parted for hundreds of randy customers. God bless the randy Yanks who got five minute knee-tremblers for bundles of money, shiny silk stockings or Lucky Strike Cigarettes.

Sampling the delights of brothels in so many places around the world tempted me to try the home-grown stuff, right there and then. Some time later I might, but first to the ferry across the Mersey and Ellesmere Port. "It was fucking good" was my quick response to my mother's "How was the trip, son?" Delighted with the return of her long-lost son, she may not have heard me. It was perfectly natural; in the world I had lived in for fifteen months, fucking was not just a word; it was a way of life. In Liverpool, circa 1952, using the word in mixed company was quite radical, if not outrageous; to your mother, unpardonable.

Chairman Mao Off the Bow

Many thoughts crossed my mind that day in 1952 when we sailed out of Liverpool on the tanker *Athelknight* – thoughts of Vindi boys my age sailing out of Liverpool on Atlantic, North Sea and Arctic convoys during World War II, some just clearing the Mersey before being blown to hell by a torpedo from a lurking U-Boat. What I didn't know then was that *Athelknight* was a name with two ships and it had spelt tragedy for some Vindi boys on the first *Athelknight*, including four from my home town.

On May 27, 1942, *Athelknight* was out of convoy southeast of Bermuda when she was torpedoed. Under fire from the deck of the U-boat *U172*, the crew abandoned ship. In two lifeboats they eventually reached safety, but the toll was five gunners and the four Liverpool crew members. After 28 days SS Empire Austin picked up survivors from one lifeboat and deck officer Douglas Crook navigated the other lifeboat more than 1000 miles to an island near Antigua.

Crook later told how the U-boat had provided those in the lifeboat with supplies and a bucket. The U-boat commander was the legendary Carl Emmermann, who sank many British vessels including the 23,456-ton P&O troopship *Orcades*. During 1940–1942 *Orcades* carried troops to all theatres of war. On a return voyage from South Africa to Liverpool in October 1942 she fell victim to a U-boat pack led by Emmermann and Crook was awarded an MBE for exceptional bravery and leadership during the epic voyage. Within a few months of my joining her, the second *Athelknight* was involved in a bloody conflict in China.

A floating bomb – Athelknight

I spent six months on *Athelknight*, a 9087-ton tanker, built in 1948 by Sir John Laing & Sons in Sunderland. Like her predecessor, *Athelknight* carried molasses, but in early 1952, after sailing to the Philippines, Java and Sumatra, *Athelknight* was assigned to join a growing stream of tankers carrying fuel for the US Seventh Fleet.

When we were ordered to San Diego in California to load fuel for the Americans, I realised how hazardous life could be for the deck crew. They had to enter the tanks and use powerful high-pressure hoses to clean out all traces of molasses. It was dirty and dangerous work and slippery hoses sometimes broke loose, knocking unwary sailors out cold, and it felt good to be a steward.

When he was defeated on the mainland, Chinese Nationalist leader Chang Kai-shek had flown the coop, scarpered to Formosa and dropped the 'Bamboo Curtain'. It was the time of the Chinese revolution and Nationalist leader Chang Kai-shek had flown the coop; scarpered to Formosa and dropped the "Bamboo Curtain". When the main forces of Chiang Kai-shek retreated to Taiwan in 1949 after their defeat by Mao Zedong's communist forces, fighting continued in Yunnan and other remote parts of China. Mao proclaimed victory in October 1949 in Beijing, but Kunming, the provincial capital of Yunnan, did not fall until December that year.

As with Marcos many years later, the United States had given Chang Kaishek an assisted passage and he had cleaned the place out before leaving. Unlike Imelda Marcos, Madam Chang Kai-shek took her shoes with her. Uncle Sam was prowling the China Straits to ensure that Chiang did not get too badly mauled. I was to find out later that the US backed the Nationalist dictator to the tune of $4 billion, as he turned Formosa into a police state and ruled it by terror.

Mao Zedong's Communist regime assumed power in Peking on October 1, 1949, and Britain had recognised his People's Republic of China on October 26. Now I was aboard this British tanker flying the American flag and carrying US Navy fuel. As we sailed up the China Straits to Formosa; we knew we were sitting ducks, but we had no option. It was an eerie feeling, knowing that at any time a well-aimed bomb from a Communist aircraft could blow us to smithereens. No way to let the pilot know we were Brits, unless I painted 'Good on yer Mao' on the deck.

Since 1949, Chinese Communist aircraft had blown several tankers out of the water and the Americans sent a carrier-based aircraft over each day to see if we were still around. Each day at 1 pm a US fighter would fly low over *Athelknight*, dip its wings and disappear, and we imagined him reporting back: "That goddamn Limey tanker's still in one piece". I thought I'd like to meet one of those guys some day. Eventually my wish would be granted.

After what seemed an eternity running the Chinese blockade, we headed into port to be greeted by a huge sign 'Welcome to Free China' right alongside 'Drink Coca Cola'. We were back in rum and coke territory and we needed buckets of it. Displaced persons flew the American flag for Chiang and British citizens recognised Mao. No shore leave for two days and nights, while Chinese Nationalist propaganda reverberated from banks of sound blasters around the harbour, as we nervously watched an action replay of the Blitz in the skies overhead. It was a port we couldn't wait to leave.

Eventually, Fremantle in Western Australia would have a similar ranking. Whenever *New Australia* berthed in Fremantle, there was more blood spilt than we saw in Formosa. All-out war, with running brawls on the wharf between crew off *New Australia* and sailors from the naval vessels stationed there. It was just one of those things that happened; nobody seemed to know why. If you wanted to get to the pub you had to run the gauntlet.

Ocean liners are fun; tankers can be terrifying. Just getting them from port to port in peacetime can be hazardous. They have a nasty habit of breaking their backs. We spent many a terrifying moment on upper decks, watching the bow disappear under huge waves, then slowly shudder back to the surface with torrents of frothy water cascading from her, knifing back into the next wave in a seemingly desperate attempt to stay afloat, challenging and defying the ocean's might, metal plates creaking and groaning under the pressure of the surging waves.

We would stand there spellbound, not daring to think too much. The crew quarters and facilities on *Athelknight* were superior to those of *Coulgarve*, but on the debit side we did not get to stay as long in port. In the bustling Japanese port of Nagoya, some of the crew did spend more time ashore than they were allowed, and sailing was delayed while they were rounded up from bars and brothels. After our perilous voyage through the China Straits it was understandable. We worked hard and we played hard.

It was my only visit to Japan, my most lasting memory being of the gentle, delicate Japanese women in the ancient castle town that was born in Japan's feudal age. Much of Nagoya's past and its present were destroyed by US bombing during World War II. Nagoya today is an example of Japan's rise from the ashes and it is now a high-technology centre in automobiles, aviation, machine tools, fine ceramics and robotics manufacture.

The allied occupation forces were still in Japan following the horrific end to the war in the Pacific, and prostitution was rife when *Athelknight* sailed into Nagoya. Unlike authorities in Central America and the Caribbean, the occupation forces maintained strict controls on venereal diseases. If a Japanese bar girl showed you her identity card, it meant she had a clean bill of health.

Gentle massage and endless cups of fragrant tea permeated a passionate night for me with an exquisitely delicate young woman. It was a fleeting but pleasant glimpse of a complex society. I was not to know then that one day I would be working secretly with the Prime

Minister of Japan on a project that would benefit Nagoya, while I was being tailed by a CIA agent.

My time aboard the *Athelknight* was an exciting, sometimes scary experience. When we sailed back to Liverpool, I was glad to see the Mersey River and eager for my voyage to end. As we were slowly rounding the Birkenhead dock entrance, I leapt the few feet to the dockside and hurried off with hardly a backward glance. I was soon to enter a different world, the world of the ocean liner, the final chapter in my eventful time at sea. An abrupt ending to my seagoing career would change my life dramatically. Much later I would be a member of an Australian syndicate bidding $6 million for the P & O liner *Oriana*.

*

The New Australia

Southampton was the home port of *New Australia*, a 22,424 ton Shaw Savill liner with a chequered career.

Built in Newcastle by Vickers-Armstrong in 1931 as Monarch of Bermuda, she was a ship with three funnels, catering for 830 first class passengers in cabins with private facilities. World War II abruptly changed all that and she was converted to a troopship. The first contingent of 962 troops must have thought it was Christmas when they were quartered in the luxury cabins. Then she went to Liverpool and had her luxury facilities torn out so she could carry 1385 troops. They do that sort of thing in Liverpool.

During the war, she was chosen to carry the bulk of Britain's bullion, valued at £690 million, to Canada for safe keeping, and in the process survived a torpedo attack after losing her cruiser and destroyer escort. After the war she was being refitted for passenger service when she was gutted by fire. Following a complete refit, including a new superstructure with only one funnel, she was renamed *New Australia* in 1949 and chartered by the British Board of Trade for the migrant run to Australia. .

New Australia continued on migrant and troop runs until 1957 and the following year was sold to the Greek Line which renamed her *Arkadia*. The vessel was converted for Atlantic crossings and cruises for first class and tourist passengers. She made one final voyage to Australia in 1963 before finally going to the breakers in 1996. On each trip on *New Australia* we went via the Suez Canal, but I never did get to see the Pyramids. What I did see as we made our way along a waterway, so unlike the scenic Panama, was the dreadful treatment of Arabs that continues to pervade many parts of the Middle East.

I often saw passengers and crew drop garbage over the side on to Arab hawkers selling souvenirs. The hawkers would send souvenirs up the side of the ship in a basket on the end of a rope they had slung up and often the basket would be thrown back at them without the money for the souvenirs. Passengers frequently yelled abuse at them for no reason.

Robbing and abusing Arabs has long been a sport for many Westerners who, like the Romans before them, have also robbed Egypt of many of its great relics and treasures. Only now are some of them being returned. The mass shipment of mummies from Egypt was a travesty: not only were mummies used for entertainment at fashionable London dinner parties, but great quantities of them were once used as fuel on American rail roads. Not that the locomotive drivers were happy about the practice. Mummies apparently did not burn well, and a most uncomplimentary song was written about that at the time. How would we feel if someone dug up our ancestors for railway fuel? O from England to Singapore on *New Australia* we carried regulars, national servicemen and officers' wives, who were segregated from the troops. Some of the crew formed liaisons; the women waited till the night before we came into port before sleeping around. The next day I watched as they rushed down the gangway to meet their husbands on the dock; knowing that only a few hours before one had been in a bunk with one of my mates. I asked one of the older guys why they had waited so long.

"It's easy; if they get pregnant they can say it was their husband." On a troop run home we had a motley crew of heroes and villains, including Bill Speakman VC and some of the crew from HMS Amethyst which had been shelled and disabled up the Yangtze River in April 1949. Later, it would be recounted in the book and film The Yangtze Incident. On April 20 Chinese Communist forces deliberately attacked the Amethyst on China's Yangtze River. Amethyst was trapped between Nanking and Shanghai, with her commanding officer and many other crew dead, but her remaining crew courageously battled their way to freedom.

Also on board *New Australia* were SAS paratroopers fresh from the Malayan jungles. A group of them called me aside and said: "You look out for us and we'll look out for you." I asked them what they meant.

"It's open bar tonight. Slip us a few free drinks and if a fight starts we'll look out for you." I told them it was a deal and that turned out to be a wise decision. Just off Singapore a brawl erupted in the lounge and I was suddenly surrounded by my new-found SAS friends. So many troops were arrested that the Masters at Arms ran out of cells. While everyone was rationed to two beers a day for the remainder of the voyage to Southampton, I was always able to scrounge extra supplies for the SAS. Apart from the 'protection', it was worth it to hear about their wild escapades, particularly the nights they played hide and seek with live ammunition.

"We were getting bored because we couldn't find any Commies, so we chased each other round the jungle just firing at everything that moved. It was a good night, some of us got hit, but nobody got killed." I had my first contact with the Australian Army in 1953 when we brought troops home from Korea.

By order of King George VI, all members of the 3rd Battalion Royal Australian Regiment are entitled to wear the United States Presidential Citation, a unit Victoria Cross with a blue watered silk ribbon inside a frame of gold silk, on both upper sleeves of their uniform.

The Citation was awarded to the Australians for turning back a major Chinese offensive near Kapyong in April 1951. Eighty miles south of Seoul, the Chinese forces came up against the British Gloucesters on the Imjin River and the Americans, Australians and Canadians on the Kapyong and the Chinese practically annihilated the Gloucesters. While suffering heavy casualties, the Australians and Canadians managed to withdraw.

The US citation says: "The seriousness of the break-through on the central front had been changed from defeat to victory by the gallant stand of these heroic and courageous soldiers."

On the voyage to Sydney I worked as a steward in the Australian officers' mess, which was the ship's library converted. We got large tips from the free-spending Aussie officers, who were happy to be alive and going home.

From May to December 1953 we took many migrants from Southampton to Australia, where I have lived since 1953, but I have never met one of them since.

It was due in part to a migrant passenger that I jumped ship. Barbara, a tall blonde teenage English rose was travelling with her parents and they kept a watchful eye on her. Occasionally, we managed to spend a few moments alone and decided we could make a good team. Barbara left the ship in Fremantle, but after jumping ship in Sydney, I headed straight for Brisbane at the other end of the continent. I had had the opportunity of having a good look at Australia first-hand and knew a lot about Australians.

*

From time to time, my father had told of his experiences fighting along side the Aussies in World War I. Maybe I was destined to go to Australia; fate could have decreed it, somewhere near Ypres, Pozieres, Villers-Bretonneux or the Somme.

"I thought my number was up many times," my father told me, "Jerry threw everything at us and it was mostly the Aussies who turned him back." He said that the Aussies had been wild buggers, and they used to frighten shit out of 'Jerry' with their bayonet charges. Hence, whenever I knew the Aussies were alongside us, I felt safe; they used to inspire all of us. They were big buggers, all of them seemed to be about eight feet tall – at least, they seemed that way to Jerry. They didn't give a damn. I miss my father.

When I saw Australians during World War II, I understood what he meant; they all appeared to be over six feet tall, but it didn't appear that way on arriving in Fremantle for the first time. The Aussies around the Fremantle waterfront were a motley bunch, some were tall, but many of smaller build.

Of course, they were not all home-grown Aussies. It was the height of the post-war migration boom, and they came from everywhere, Greeks, Italians, Poles, Latvians, Czechs, Yugoslavs, Estonians, English, Irish, Scottish and Welsh. Although Perth was only a few miles away I never got there while I was on the *New Australia*, so my view of Western Australia was distorted. Fremantle was a remote outpost then. Completely transformed for the 1987 defence of the America's cup, it now has some of Australia's best restaurants, hotels and tourist facilities, particularly for boating and fishing enthusiasts.

Hostilities during Australia's historic defence of the America's Cup off Fremantle were mostly a war of words. They say that everyone is famous for at least five minutes, and maybe the Fremantle defence was famous for too long. The battle on the water was one-sided, and many Australians were glad to see Dennis Connor win.

Sydney was a city that looked better with every trip on the *New Australia*; no matter how often you sail in through Sydney Heads, the magic remains. People argue over which is the more beautiful, Sydney or Rio de Janeiro. I'd say Sydney has the most beautiful harbour, but Rio is easily the most beautiful city. The mountains around the city of Rio provide a dramatic backdrop, with Sugarloaf and its precarious cable cars and Corcovado – the statue of Christ – looming splendidly through the clouds. Both cities, along with Liverpool, have dominated my life. Thousands of people got their first glorious view of Sydney harbour from the decks of *New Australia*.

While the vessel was contracted to carry British migrants on assisted passage to Australia, on return journeys it embarked a mixture of weird and wonderful types. Many migrants didn't have two coins to rub together, so we didn't expect any tips, but occasionally were surprised.

The crew gave the biggest tips, which we paid in advance to the cooks before we left Southampton. We didn't fancy the food served to the migrants, so we bribed the cooks and ate like lords. The first thing we did when we boarded in Southampton was hand a bundle of money to the cooks. I don't know if this was a widespread practice, or if it continues today. If the migrants had known, there would have been a mutiny. While they were eating mutton dressed as lamb chops, we were tucking into roast turkey. Food aside, for most of the migrants it was the trip of a lifetime.

On my first voyage on *New Australia*, my cabin mate, an Irish lad named Danny, suggested that as few officers and crew knew us, we should put on our best gear and masquerade as passengers. Masters at Arms were there to uphold the law, which included keeping the passengers and crew separated socially, but at this stage they would not have recognised either of us. We put on our best gear, sat in the lounge and enjoyed several beers and chatted to some of the passengers. We got away with it for the first two nights, but eventually the Masters at Arms caught up with us and we got a dressing down from the chief steward.

We were not so keen to mix with the passengers on the return trip to Southampton and in fact we asked for danger money to work with them. There were escape clauses in various agreements between originating countries and Australia. If diagnosed as mentally ill within two years of arrival, a migrant remained the responsibility of the originating country and had to go back there. *New Australia* was the only way back for some 'loony' British migrants, some genuinely mentally ill, others who had gone just a bit strange and the rest of them taking the cheap way home by feigning illness. 'Make out you're a nut case, they'll ship you home and you don't have to pay the ten quid back.' After isolating a section of the ship's accommodation, workmen installed special doors and other fittings to maintain a secure environment. We had one suicide, a woman who somehow managed to squeeze out of a porthole. Leprosy victims were the saddest return passengers as we took them to Malta, home of some of the world's finest facilities for the treatment of leprosy. We never found out if we were carrying them because they had contracted leprosy during their first two years as migrants, or whether they were simply going to Malta for treatment.

*

KGB agents hustle Evdokia Petrov to Mascot airport (Wikipedia)

The most notorious passengers to travel to England on *New Australia* were two KGB agents. It was five months after I had jumped ship. No airline or shipping company wanted to transport the agents, who had tried to bustle Mrs Evdokia Petrov out of Australia on a London-bound BOAC flight in that violent scene dramatically captured by newsreel and newspaper photographers at Darwin Airport on April 20, 1954. Earlier that night about 2000 screaming, struggling people had frantically battled to prevent the KGB taking Mrs Petrov, the wife of Russian defector Vladimir Petrov, aboard an aircraft in Sydney. Eventually police and airline officials managed to get her on board, but it was a different story in Darwin, where local police prevented the KGB agents and Mrs Petrov from leaving the country.

Subsequently, with her husband Vladimir, she was granted political asylum and I heard later that the chief steward himself had to look after the KGB men, as none of the crew would have anything to do with them.

I was 19 when I jumped ship in Sydney in December 1953. It was the year of the coronation of Queen Elizabeth II, the end of the Korean War and the giving of citizenship rights to Australia's Northern Territory Aboriginals. Because every detail was meticulously planned, jumping ship happened smoothly.

Alex was another steward disgruntled with shipboard life who decided to come with me. Many merchant seamen who jumped ship in foreign ports were quickly caught by local authorities and returned to their vessel or sent home in disgrace. We devised an audacious plan to minimise that risk. Bob, a former *New Australia* steward, was in Sydney on another ship from England that was about to head North with migrant passengers bound for Brisbane. The crux of the plan was to get aboard that ship in Brisbane and the first move was to stuff our suitcases into laundry bags and pay a laundry van driver to take them to the Observer, a small hotel in the harbour side Rocks district. Leaving our uniforms in our cabins, we dressed smartly and strolled ashore.

New Australia sailed that night and we drank coffee in a small cafe on Circular Quay and watched her leaving Sydney Harbour, and I had similar feelings to that dark, scary night aboard the disabled *Coulgarve* in the Caribbean. Now it seemed as though we were adrift on land. The female publican at the Observer was a friendly soul, originally from Liverpool, and we all got drunk that night. Next day we bought train tickets to Brisbane and left that night from Central Station. As we sped North through the Australian night, Bob's vessel was sailing up the coast. Central Station reminded me of Lime Street Station, although there were not many 'Maggie Mays' around.

They were a short distance away in Sydney's red light district, Kings Cross. Like their sisters in Liverpool, the Kings Cross girls enjoyed good times with the World War II Yanks, and it was to be even better during the Vietnam War. Later, the action moved to sleepy old Fremantle, where most of the Pacific, Indian Ocean and Middle East zone warships take some of their R&R leave, and many enthusiastic amateurs compete with the prostitutes. My memories of prostitution while on *Coulgarve* are mostly carefree ones, with vibrant girls in happy surroundings; there was always a party atmosphere. Street prostitution today is more like a visit to the dentist, with the girls looking so serious – no carnival atmosphere, bright lights or music. Some even operate in used car lots on main thoroughfares.

*

It was December 1953 and hot, very hot in Brisbane. All the houses were on stilts. Somebody told me it was because of snakes, but they'd probably been on the Bundaberg rum. Brisbane residents built their houses on stilts to allow the air to circulate, and keep them relatively cool during long, hot summers. Another friendly laundry man meets us in town, puts our suitcases in a couple of laundry bags, and takes them aboard Bob's ship. We follow up the crew gangway, pick up our suitcases and head down the passenger gangway. We disembark as newly arrived migrants and at the foot of the gangway are greeted by another friendly soul, originally from Liverpool. An immigration official, he did not ask many questions and sent us to a migrant hostel, promising to find us work. He did arrange a job for both of us – not the sort that sends you into raptures in the middle of a hot Brisbane summer, but it was a start. We worked in Hardie's Fibrolite Factory while the regular employees were on annual leave. Fibrolite sheets containing asbestos were baked on steel plates in large ovens and our job was to clean the plates and the ovens with wire brushes. Hopefully, we were not there long enough to suffer any long-term effects from asbestos.

It was bloody hard work and bloody hot, so we drank gallons of bloody beer and bloody Bundaberg, in the good old bloody Queensland tradition. Enough, maybe, to wash away any bloody asbestos dust. Bloody Bundy with a bloody beer chaser, as we sweated and cursed and wondered why we were there.

Alec scored a job as a bartender in a club. He couldn't get away from hospitality. With the distant Barbara still in mind, I answered an advertisement for a young man to travel with a stage show around Australia.

When I got the job I could hardly believe it. How many people want to be a stooge for a hypnotist? Thousands, I was to discover later. First I had to get to Mount Gambier, which meant little to me at the time. The host of the show, a former radio announcer named Des Tochini, made the mistake of giving me money instead of tickets for the 2500-kilometre journey to Mount Gambier, a small town in South Australia. I travelled by train from Brisbane to Sydney then on to Melbourne, and that's as far as I got before the money ran out.

The Great Van Leowe, in his hey day

Des had given me the address of a hotel where he would stay in Mount Gambier, so I went to a post office and sent a telegram asking for money, post haste. That night I slept on a station bench. I was up early the next day, with just enough money for breakfast, then off to the post office for the expected funds. There was no money, no response. Not looking forward to another night at the station, I went to a nearby police station and said to the desk sergeant: "If I throw a brick through your window, will you put me in a cell for the night?" He was an understanding policeman, and he took me to a Salvation Army hostel. My father had always spoken enthusiastically of 'the Salvos' and the comfort and support they gave the troops in wartime. "They're not your typical bible-bashers; they're really there to give you a hand when you're having a bad time. Whenever the going's rough, you'll always find the Salvos there." That was the way of it with the Salvos in Melbourne. No bible-bashing, no recriminations, no lectures, just a helping hand. They gave me a good feed and accommodation for the night; next morning they took me to the station and gave me a ticket to Mount Gambier and some money. All they asked of me was to leave my suitcase and on my return to Melbourne to give them back the money and collect the suitcase. It was a fair deal; I thanked my generous hosts and boarded a train for Mount Gambier.

An extinct volcano, Mount Gambier is distinguished by the famous Blue Lake in its deep, dormant crater. My journey there was my first trip to 'the bush'. Country Australia really gets into your blood, like going to sea or your favourite holiday destination, it's refreshing and invigorating. Away from the big smoke and into the vast, quiet openness that is 'the bush'.

Australians had said to me "All you'll find out there is bloody gum trees, millions of bloody great gum trees," and it was true, literally millions of gums, the most prolific trees in Australia. In reality, the bush is as diverse as Australia's population. From ancient wild rainforests in the south of Tasmania, through rolling sandy deserts, densely wooded mountain ranges, wide, open plains, to brilliant green tropical jungles in the North, it's a land of many contrasts.

At a Mount Gambier hotel, shortly before opening night, I met the hypnotist Van Loewe, and he and Des gave a brief outline of what they expected of me. Years later as a journalist in Melbourne in a magazine feature titled 'All the World's a Stooge', I wrote that it's the audience that makes the stage hypnotist entertaining. He is merely the catalyst devising the basic structure for the performance, allowing the volunteers to bring it to fruition. In country towns, where everybody knows the volunteers, it can be hilarious and the volunteers are the unpaid stooges.

In a small theatre in Mount Gambier I was about to become a paid stooge. Van Loewe, bearded, with heavy eyebrows, was a sinister looking man in his early forties, who held his audience spellbound.

"Born in South Africa, educated in England, Van Loewe is a master of the supernatural," announced Des, looking resplendent in white tuxedo, black trousers, white dress shirt and black bow tie. The first part of the show featured tricks of magic and the mind.

Van had a laconic sense of humour, essential for an act like that. Sometimes it became too much for him and he had to turn away to restrain himself from giggling at the silliness of people playing the fool and paying for the privilege. It was a show admirably suited to the Australian bush, providing comic relief from the harshness and isolation. Today television game shows and reality programmes provide people with some escape from the sameness of daily life. In the bush, stage hypnosis was an opportunity to let your hair down in a generally uneventful environment.

It was not easy to be uninhibited in an Australian country town in the 1950s; everyone knew what everybody else was up to. A stage hypnotist provided a rare opportunity: if you were hypnotised, it was not the real you. Someone else was doing all those strange things and you could never recall what had happened. Ninety per cent of the volunteers were never hypnotised; some were; some thought they were; most did not give it a second thought. It was a chance to let go and not be responsible for your actions. The first half of the show built up the 'mystical powers' of Van Loewe. He made watches, wallets and other items disappear and reappear from a black velvet bag into which audience volunteers happily deposited personal items.

Having collected all the items in the bag, he turned it inside out and, seemingly empty, it was put aside. Later, when he turned the bag upside down on a table all the missing items fell out. It's a simple trick that you can find in any magic shop.

The blindfold trick was just as simple. A member of the audience placed two pennies, one on each eye of Van, covered the pennies with adhesive tape, then applied a blindfold over the tape and tied it tightly. When Van moved his eyelids the pennies came away on the adhesive tape, and he was able to see in a straight line down his cheeks. As he moved along the row of people seated on stage, holding various items in their hands, he dramatically moved his hands over theirs, suggesting vibrations. He was actually staring straight down at what they were holding. To the surprise of everyone, he named every item.

Next was the memory act. A blackboard bearing the numbers one to twenty sat in a prominent position towards the back of the stage. Blindfolded, Van stood at the microphone, centre stage, while Des recorded in chalk various items called out by people in the audience. Van then read out all twenty items with apparent ease, read them backwards, invited the audience to call out numbers and stated the item against each number or vice versa. With such an incredible memory, he was truly a man with an amazing mind. By now he had convinced any sceptics that he had extraordinary powers, the ability to hypnotise being just one of them.

In Mount Gambier that first night I was as impressed as the rest of them. When he strode confidently back on stage in the second half, I had to restrain myself from joining the rush to the stage. Even as a stranger I thoroughly enjoyed the antics of the locals. He assembled all the volunteers in a semi-circle, some seated on chairs arranged around the stage, others standing behind them.

Then he took them through some preliminaries, with soothing background music.

"Look into my eyes and listen to my voice, and as you listen you will find you are getting drowsy, you are getting drowsier and you are feeling good, getting sleepier and shortly you will be sleeping, you will only listen to my voice, only my voice and you will do only as I tell you."

Gesturing for silence, he stared intently at his assembled subjects, and slowly intoned: "As you listen to my voice you're getting sleepier and sleepier and you will do only as I tell you, and you will only listen to my voice."

He would walk along the group, lift their arms and let them fall limply, dramatically highlighting their trance like state and then he would weed out the obvious actors with remarks like: "Errol Flynn would be proud of you; you could win an Academy Award." Sheepishly, they would return to their seats. It confirmed his credibility with the audience. He would not tolerate anyone not under his influence, not completely controlled by him. Not everyone wanted to be hypnotised, not everyone could be hypnotised. He would send off those who were genuinely hypnotised, but obviously not going to perform animatedly.

Watching people sleep soundly on stage is not exactly entertaining. The audience wanted action and they got plenty. When he had relaxed his twenty or so chosen subjects, he would seek some basic responses. A carpet covered the stage in front of the semi-circle of subjects. First, he told them "You are now in a tropical climate, and it is hot, incredibly hot, and the humidity is unbearable" and they would start stripping off their clothes. Before they got too far he reversed the situation, saying: "You have now travelled to a very cold climate, you're in the Antarctic, and it's snowing, and freezing cold." Immediately, as if rehearsed, all of them headed for the carpet, wriggled underneath and wrapped themselves in it shivering, shaking and exhibiting obvious symptoms of cold. Later, I found that what went on under the carpet was best left under the carpet.

In the fantasy heat, throwing off their clothes quickly loosened inhibitions. Even before they dived under the carpet, sexual repression among young people on stage and sexual frustrations in older ones found release. When shivering and shaking and generally appearing freezing cold, they were quick to clutch each other, sometimes with obvious lust, which brought uninhibited audience response. Hidden from the audience, under the carpet things sometimes got out of hand, or into hand, depending on how you look at it.

Before it went too far, he would divert them to some new situation. "There's a snake under the carpet, the only way you'll get away from it is to get back on your chairs, back on your chairs" and they would all dutifully return. Des would round up any who went to rush off stage. "You are sleeping soundly, sleeping soundly and listening only to my voice, and you will do only what I tell you to do, sleeping, soundly, soundly, listening only to my voice," and again they were back to a drowsy state. He transported them to race meetings, football matches and a multitude of other situations, then convinced them they were movie stars and had them acting, singing and dancing. The audience found it hilarious, and many relished telling their subject friends about their antics when the show was over. Those who were genuinely hypnotised could not remember, those who thought they were, would think they didn't remember, and those who hadn't been hypnotised didn't want to remember.

The next night I raced up with the rest of them to become a stooge for the first time. During the first few performances I didn't do anything unusual, just pretended to be one of the crowd; learning what went on, how to react, not to overplay, and during the day learning to be Australian. How could I turn up in all those country towns with an English accent, pretending to be one of the locals just in it for fun? In the early 50s there were plenty of English migrants who had settled in country towns, so a new arrival with an accent was not unusual.

But I was to be a star turn in the show, so it would not be easy. Van and Des explained they could not always rely on the audience to produce entertaining people, I was their insurance policy. I just hoped they wouldn't lose their no-claim bonus. Having watched Van perform the memory act I was baffled, but once he taught me the technique I realised how simple it was.

Memorise twenty items from one to twenty, so I could say them forwards, backwards, number and item, item and number, exactly as he had done. Armed with my personal code, a simple association of ideas, and the more ludicrous the idea, the easier it became to recall. The first word in my personal code was 'bottle' and when someone in the audience yelled out 'camel', for example, I would picture the silliest combination of a bottle and camel. A camel in a bottle, a camel downing a bottle of beer or, for real effect, a camel with a bottle up its backside.

I was to perform the memory act, allegedly under hypnosis, during the second part of the show after Van had transmitted his 'extraordinary powers' to me.

One thing I had not seen was Van turning people into superhuman beings under hypnosis, or I may not have gone on with it. Fortunately I was young and fit.

"Ladies and gentlemen, with this subject, I am going to demonstrate extraordinary powers over the mind. I am going to take this young man, turn him into a rod of steel, an unbending rod of steel, and subject him to enormous pressures."

He would stand me side on to the audience in front of the microphone and intone: "Your body is now becoming a solid steel rod." Running his hands up and down my body, he would convince the audience I was going 'as rigid as steel', put a hand on my chest and tip me backwards. Clenching my fists at my side, stretching my stomach muscles taut, I would fall stiffly backwards to where Des caught my shoulders.

Then they would lay me between two wooden trestles. There I lay, stretched some two to three feet off the ground, stiff as a board, as Van invited members of the audience up on stage to stand on me. It's amazing what you can do if you have to. I just kept telling myself over and over; lie straight, stiff as a rod of steel. People standing on me would not affect me that much, and it was all right, as long as he didn't leave them up there too long. So long as he was not in a bad mood. So long as he was not stacking more and more people on me. I couldn't control that, and couldn't complain. Some nights I was close to buckling. Audiences were suitably impressed as I managed to convey the impression of not being aware of what had happened. To add variety to my growing stage repertoire, I did impressions of the singer Nat King Cole, who was in vogue then. I had a reasonable voice and could do passable impressions of Cole.

Looking back, I wonder how we never got bailed up, travelling many thousands of kilometres East from South Australia through the red dust bowl of western Victoria, the parched brown outback of New South Wales, the green tropical North of Queensland and far out to Mount Isa, the booming mining town. "Some bloody Pom Scarlet Pimpernel who thinks he's Nat King Cole, Einstein and Houdini rolled into one. Here one day, vanished the next." The Vindi boy had come a long way.

Only now, looking at detailed maps of the great wide land, do I realise how much of it I have been privileged to see. We travelled in a Tempo Matador van, with an air-cooled Volkswagen engine, which proved itself many times in harsh conditions. The only time we could not drive it was in Queensland when, playing the outback towns of Cunnamulla, Charleville and Longreach, heavy flooding forced us to transport it by train to Roma.

Thousands of people accepted me as one of the locals, someone who just happened to wander on stage and get caught up in the whole affair. Fortunately, through mixing with various nationalities aboard ship and travelling around, my accent was not strictly Liverpool, but more a rounded international one.

It quickly became Australianised as I worked at it consciously, a bit like an actor does with a character. Over time audiences seemed to accept me as one of them, although it was amazing that people who went to the show in more than one town failed to recognise me. I was apprehensive at times, but figured the best thing was to be seen as much as possible and make a big impact wherever I could. They would drop me a few miles out of town and leave me to walk in, or hitch a ride when I had to be careful not so say too much.

As soon as I got into town I would check into a cheap hotel, have a feed in a main street cafe, make myself conspicuous by what I ordered, talk to as many people as possible, go into local stores, knock things off counters, and, generally, try to be seen by as many people as possible so they might recall me being around. I talked to as many girls as I could, and not just for the show. They were attractive girls in country towns. It was in the small Victorian town of Horsham that I regained more of my lost adolescence, with Pamela, daughter of George, a local shopkeeper.

*

There were, in my honest opinion, two greats of stage hypnotism in Australia at that time, Van Leowe and Franquin (Frank Quinn). Franquin played major city theatres where he seemed to have accomplished stooges at every performance. Even when Van played big cities, he still only had the one stooge, his insurance policy, while Franquin's show seemed to be a series of well-rehearsed acts. Touring with Van was a unique opportunity to get to know intimately the country I had seen only as a visiting seaman, mostly from waterfront bars.

Occasionally, some of the *New Australia* crew went sightseeing. Danny and I once made a record in Sydney. We went to a small studio in downtown Sydney, sang two songs to piano accompaniment then received a freshly pressed record, with our own label affixed. In the rush to develop Sydney, the recording studio disappeared, along with some great old bars and shops; downtown Sydney lost most of its character and in many parts became just another concrete jungle.

Fortunately, historic parts of Sydney have been preserved. The harbour front Rocks area retains much of its early settlement character. Circular Quay, Macquarie Street and the approaches to the Opera House have been enhanced, but gone are the grand old bars of Sydney, and with them the grand old theatres. Along with them, much of the spirit of theatre died in Sydney.

The show was of dubious artistic merit, but it was big on laughs and a marvellous way to see the country and meet the people. Walking those last few miles into town or, if I was lucky, getting a ride with a knowledgeable local, was an excellent way to get to know Australia and its people. Walking gave me a good insight into the town, its buildings and services. Most of the time I walked, helping me get a foretaste of what was to come years later, when I would traverse much of the continent on foot. As a stranger to outback Australia, the first things to strike me were the heat and the flies.

At times the heat did get overpowering, but fortunately I had spent time in the tropics. The flies are a different proposition. It takes a while to learn the 'Aussie salute', waving your hand in front of your face at regular intervals to keep the flies away. It doesn't matter where they land, as long as you keep them off your face, out of your nose and mouth. No matter how accomplished you become at the Aussie salute, you have not really made it until you have swallowed an Aussie bush fly. You know it's happening, but you can't do a thing about it, like swallowing an orange pip; fortunately it's over quickly, both for you and the fly.

Charlie Henderson couldn't stand the Aussie fly. That's why he brought the dung beetle to the Northern Territory. The dung beetle breeds in cow dung, preventing the bush fly from proliferating in the same environment.

It is said that there is enough cow dung in Australia to cover the Australian Capital Territory, and there are many who would applaud the physical proof of such a claim. Charlie, a former US Navy flier would have approved. He had had enough of salutes during the Pacific War and he was no more into saluting a bloody fly than he would a bloody politician. I would like to have met Charlie before the Aussie bush fly, but he was still in the Philippines then, making a fortune, and I was walking around the Australian bush. The fly got to me first, but there were times when Charlie was a lot harder to swallow, although after my *Athelknight* experience I was happy to finally meet a US carrier pilot. My life was like a long surfboard ride, arriving on a different beach every other day, meeting people and covering great distances, but always at a leisurely pace. In the early morning hours, after a one or two night stand, I would be out on the road, two or three miles out of town, when along would come the rest of the show.

Incredibly, nobody ever sighted me getting in or out of that van. I travelled in the back with the props, real cloak and dagger stuff, always knowing at which hotel Van and the others were staying, so as to avoid staying there myself.

In some small towns it was impossible to avoid eating in the same café. In the 1950s almost every cafe in every country town was owned and operated by a Greek family. The meals were basic, mostly steak, eggs and chips, as much as you could eat, and reasonably priced. At times we could not avoid sitting at adjacent tables. If we were in town for more than one night I had to acknowledge their presence, without overt familiarity.

Before a show I could look, but not acknowledge them. On stage the same thing applied, no familiarity and no back chat with Des. It was a constant subterfuge. A few locals had their suspicions – sometimes, drinking in a bar after a show, a group of locals would gather round and buy me beers to try to get me to talk. Somehow I managed to get away with it. When you're young, you have that nonchalant attitude. In the same situation today I probably couldn't carry it off, I'd give off vibes, signals, and people would spring me.

I was delighted when told I was to take over as compere of the show. The stooge had come in from the cold.

I could be open, honest, indulge myself, strut my stuff. Des had become ill and was no longer able to travel. For me, it meant on with the tuxedo, into the glare of the footlights, and into the arms of the 'groupies'. 'Groupie' was a word that was not to become fashionable for some time. There's a common belief that 'groupies' started with the coming of rock and roll, but they have been around as long as travelling shows.

"I can't do it with the local boys because it will get around."

"I only do it with people passing through."

How often has that been said in a country town, somewhere in the world, where someone's in a spotlight, entertaining and commanding attention? There was also the reverse. "I want to, but I can't – I might like it so much, I'd be doing it with the locals and then I'd get a bad name."

I had my share of both, a reasonable result, so no complaints. While I enjoyed sex like anybody else, we had a responsibility to girls in those days. We might be frustrated, but they were worse off, with pressures over being talked about, getting pregnant or 'getting the pox'. As with the early days of AIDS, there was a terrible dearth of education on venereal diseases, and the same 'It won't happen to me' philosophy. Having come unscathed through a veritable VD battle zone, I was not into condoms, literally. I'd seen thousands of them scattered in parks and back lanes around Liverpool during the war.

While the Germans tried to flatten Liverpool with bombs, the Americans almost buried it with condoms. Kids sometimes picked up used condoms and blew them up like balloons. There's always been that high-risk streak in Liverpool. In my travels with Van Loewe, it was a long time before I sighted a condom, either new or used. If I had gone looking for one, the local chemists may not have known what I was talking about. In England we knew them as Durex, which is the brand name for a popular adhesive tape in Australia. I didn't relish using that, although lunch wrap would be used by US students a few years later.

Travelling with Van was not all fun and games. Hypnosis was not widely recognised as a science then. It has since been used extensively throughout the world for the treatment of various disorders. Despite a strong negative attitude towards hypnosis among medical practitioners, word somehow got around.

Most nights after the show we had a queue of people waiting at the stage door, hoping for treatment for themselves or their children. It was not an easy task for Van, but he did his best in the time available and in the confined spaces. Later he was to establish his dream, a hypnotherapy clinic in the Northern New South Wales city of Newcastle, and there he was able to take a more serious approach and treat many patients with various disorders. The clinic was funded with proceeds from the stage shows.

An early convert to the merits of hypnotherapy in the health field, I was present and astounded when a patient had several teeth removed under hypnosis in a dental surgery, without the use of anaesthetic and incredibly without bleeding. On the lighter side, Van once hypnotised members of the Australian Davis Cup tennis squad in New York by telephone from Australia in an attempt to improve their performance. Unfortunately, they lost the round.

Eventually we arrived in Mt Isa; I was apprehensive about our mind-reading act in a tough, cynical mining town. We were offering £1000 to anyone who could prove it wasn't genuine, and it was a dodgy business. Being the compere of a travelling hypnotist's show reminded me of a movie I had seen starring Donald O'Connor. He was a song and dance man, doing everything, pasting up posters, taking money at the front of the theatre, acting as usher and performing on stage. He seemed to be everywhere at once, and it was a bit like that being a compere with Van.

The mind-reading act was in the first half of the show. I would be out the front of the theatre before the show, rush backstage, sort out props, draw the curtain, play the recorded music, make the announcements, change the props and generally rush around non-stop till the show finished. For the mind-reading act I stood in the foyer holding an innocent-looking black slate with a sheet of perforated paper clipped to it.

"Would you like to take part in the mind-reading act?" I would ask, handing the slate and a ballpoint pen to a responsive patron. "Just take that away, so I can't see it, and write down a question, you'd like to ask. Once you've written it down, tear off the paper and put it away in your pocket, so nobody else can see it."

When enough people had obliged, I would hurry backstage, prise the slate apart and there, written clearly through carbon paper on to a second sheet of plain paper, was the list of questions. We used two thin pieces of material that, when clipped together, looked for all the world like one piece of slate. Some of the questions were easy, some required a quick flick through Encyclopaedia Britannica or one of the other reference books that we had backstage. I would write the questions and answers on a piece of paper and stick it to the table behind the large crystal ball, into which Van gazed intently during the mind reading act.

He would 'pick up vibrations' from somebody in the theatre who was interested in a particular subject. Although he had the question and answer clearly written down in front of him, he would go through the most extraordinary gyrations and gestures and drawn out identification of the question. Then with a suitable pause he would 'pick up' the full question and correctly answer it, followed by loud applause and further acknowledgement of his mysterious powers.

Like most entertainers, Van could be temperamental. In Mount Isa, only five minutes before the curtain was due to be drawn, he said he did not feel well enough to perform.

"You'll get tarred and feathered if you don't perform for this lot," I said.

"It's a mining town and there's some mean-looking characters out there." This to no avail; he would not go on, so I said I'd drawn the curtain.

"So what, I'm still not going on." was his reply.

"The mind-reading table's on stage, with all the questions and answers pinned to it," I told him. "If they storm the stage, it's going to cost you £1000".

He promptly replied: "It doesn't matter how I feel, the show must go on".

The show always did go on, and once we performed for three people. It was mid-winter and snowing on the Northern Tablelands of New South Wales. Only three brave souls had appeared out of the sleet and snow. We gave them a performance of sorts and their money back. It was a memorable tour for me, an unusual way for someone to see a new country for the first time. Van was heading back to the South Australian capital Adelaide to take a break, but he was planning another tour: did I want to come along? I was not sure; first I wanted to return to Horsham and Pamela.

*

When I arrived in Horsham by train from Melbourne early one Saturday morning, she was there to meet me. Thus began my first real love affair, an affair that brought out emotions I had never known. I was 20 and Pamela was 17, truly the girl next door, everything that had gone before had been fleeting. This was to last for the best part of a year and to remain with me forever, as first love does with everybody. It was my first real love in an idyllic and carefree country Australia. We caught tadpoles and frogs in Liverpool. In country Australia it was yabbies, a miniature inland version of the lobster. It was an ageless Australian custom, tying a lump of meat on a piece of string, tossing it into a small pond or dam and pulling in a struggling, seemingly inedible creature. However, when broiled it was a succulent morsel. There were other simple pleasures, like necking on a sofa with an eager 17-year-old ballet dancer with a lithe, supple body. We had a pact that penetration had to wait till we got married; it was mostly like that then.

In the 1950s in many relationships we never went all the way, so the desire never left us, and that's when many became heavy smokers. Now politicians tell kids not to smoke cigarettes, but say it's okay to whip your partner violently, pee all over them, or stick your penis up their bum.

The same adults who are involved in that sort of bullshit claim to be concerned about the future of the family. In the 1950s foreplay and newspapers turned me into a chain smoker. While Pamela was stretching her seductive body at ballet class, I was stretching my vocabulary in an after-hours job as a casual proof-reader, and the words, the ink and more nicotine got into my veins.

Pamela's father George had helped me get my daytime job in customer relations in a General Motors car dealership. I kept records of customer servicing, a fairly mundane clerical job, and a dramatic change from the type of life that I had led. I was in love, and all I wanted to do was stay in Horsham, get married and have kids. Getting married and having kids was something everybody did. Divorce was a rarity, certainly in Horsham. That's why George had his song. Whenever I went fishing with George, we would hardly be out of the drive and he would wind down the window in his old Customline Ford and at the top of his voice sing 'I'm as free as the breeze'.

I'm as free as the breeze,
What's to stop me and why?
I'm as free as the breeze,
Open road, open sky.

"Why do you want to get married and stay in Horsham? he would ask.

"Just look at her mother." I replied.

A Lift for Rupert Murdoch

In 1955 I got my first job as a journalist. It was the year that Australia's millionth post-war migrant arrived, a pilot less plane over Sydney created panic before being shot down just off the coast and, after 40 years of closing at 6pm, hotels in New South Wales won the right to remain open till 10pm. Sydney's *Daily Telegraph* Melbourne representative John Brennan told me I got the job as a second year cadet journalist because I was prepared to work for half of my current wage and walk to work. Twenty-one was a bit long in the tooth for a second year cadetship, but it was my chance to get into newspapers.

My time at the *Vindicatrix* Sea Training School and my subsequent Merchant Navy service had taught me to accept that the ladder of experience must be climbed slowly in a disciplined way. We were fortunate in the 1950s; now, if you don't have a university degree, getting into journalism is almost impossible. Potato peeling and scrubbing decks are not the sort of things you put in your curriculum vitae when you're going for a newspaper job.

The *Daily Telegraph* office was in the newsroom of a great Australian newspaper, *The Argus*. Staff names were a problem in the small office, John, John, Jack and John. John Brennan was approaching the end of his newspaper days, and would become a public relations consultant, one of the most successful in the country. John England was nearing the end of his many sexual conquests and about to get married, subsequently going on to a distinguished international career in radio journalism in Europe.

Jack was a racing journalist; if he wasn't racing for the track, he was racing for the pub. My first job for Jack was to race to the pub to pick up a carton of cold beers. Now, that's one thing that journalists and merchant seamen certainly have in common – doing what the senior crew tells you to do.

Unable to afford the tram fare, I walked to *The Argus* and back most days.

Second-year cadet wages just covered my rent, a few packets of cigarettes, a couple of beers and the odd feed. It was my big chance to get into a career.

Besides, you get to know a city better when you have to slog around on foot. Walking backwards and forwards, you think a lot about cities, distances, and town planners. Some town planners seem to have designed cities during fits of madness, and the social consequences have been immense.

In the 1950s Elwood seemed a long way out, especially on foot. The *Daily Telegraph* bureau was largely a way-station, a sifter of Melbourne news for Sydney consumption. I was keen to be out on the road chasing news. An opportunity came along, one that I would have been happy to miss.

"Sir Frank wants a precis of a judgement in the High Court, and you're it," said John Brennan. "It's not for publication, just the owner, Sir Frank." "What a relief, it's just for Sir Frank," I said. "I don't do shorthand and it's just a precis of a High Court judgement. What a breeze." "Get this one wrong and your career in journalism is stuffed before you get off the ground," Brennan warned.

God knows how, but I scribbled longhand notes of the judgement so eloquently given by those learned judges in their splendid wigs and robes. Somehow, I was able to make sense of it; I wrote a precis, telexed it to Sir Frank in Sydney and held my breath for a week. Said never to have altered an opinion for the sake of popularity, Sir Douglas Frank Hewson Packer was a hard case, and if my precis had not been right we would have heard him bellow from Sydney. I sometimes wonder if it wasn't just a Brennan test for the new boy.

When Brennan's successor, Keith Willey, fell foul of Sir Frank, I took the publisher's curt telex from the machine.

"Willey you're fired. Packer." was all it said. I took it to a nearby hotel where I knew Willey was having a couple of quiet drinks, and handed it to him. Willey didn't say a word, just quietly stared at the telex, then calmly said: "Have you ever drunk slivovitz?" "Never," I replied. I woke up in a toilet back at *The Argus*; I couldn't remember much, but I suspect we gave that slivovitz a pasting. I wondered if anyone kept slivovitz in 'the morgue'.

That was the term for the room where back issues of *The Argus* were kept in bound, year-by-year files. It was where the heavy drinkers had their 'cupboard drinks' filed – Scotch under 1933, gin under 1942, brandy under 1950, slivovitz...? It was the last I saw of Willey. Over the ensuing years he became a highly respected journalist in the Northern Territory. Life was about to change dramatically for many of Willey's mates on *The Argus* when they found themselves out of work and out of booze with the abrupt closure of the publication.

Only 38,331 people were living around Port Phillip Bay when *The Argus* was first published 111 years earlier. When the last edition hit the streets on January 19, 1957, Melbourne had a population of two and a half million people. Sadly, not enough of them were reading *The Argus*. Ironically, television station GTV9 had its gala opening the same night and journalists around the country began to feel insecure. About *The Argus* journalists, columnist Hal Richardson said: 'When they write of your joy and sadness a little of it rubs off on to them too. And a little of it stays inside them always.' True for many who finished up pumping petrol or selling shirts at department stores and who would have given their right arm for my job. Through good fortune, I had gained a journalism grading and a major salary increase with a country newspaper in the north-east corner of Victoria. A country newspaper is the best place to cut your journalistic teeth, with every conceivable assignment from births, deaths, marriages and funerals to social news, council meetings, courts, sport, bushfires, traffic accidents, murders, robberies and suicides, you name it, we covered it.

The *Wangaratta Chronicle* was only published three times a week, but always under pressure, and I learned a lot in a short time. The name Wangaratta derived from an Aboriginal term, possibly meaning 'resting place of cormorants'.

It would have been easy to lose my head scribbling copy while helping to fight a bushfire, wading through floods to help rescue victims and relaying stories directly from court via a copyboy. The courts were close by, so sometimes it was a single paragraph on each sheet of paper with the copy boy run off his feet. It was more urgent to render assistance than report on such events. We sped out to bushfires on fire trucks, jumping on as they slowed momentarily outside the newspaper office.

More sobering was helping ambulance officers carry the mangled bodies of the dead from an endless sequence of car smashes on the Melbourne to Sydney highway. At one of many railway level crossing accidents, an interstate express had hit the stationary car with such force that it had scattered the wreckage over half a kilometre. At the head of one victim's stretcher, I had to scoop up part of his brain as it started to dribble over the edge of the stretcher. Dead and crippled bodies became routine as fast cars and poor roads created a traffic war zone.

Being a country journalist was about involvement. If we were writing about a Red Cross appeal for blood donors, we gave blood first. Appealing for public support for the ambulance service, we went out in the ambulance on subscription drives, into the back blocks, to small towns where most folks could not afford a subscription. Gratefully accepting their offerings of cabbages, pumpkins, carrots, potatoes or fruit as payment, we drove back in town, set up produce stalls in the main street and raised the money that way. On the sporting scene, I had to cover Australian Rules football, even though I didn't know much about the code.

North-east Victoria is an Aussie Rules football stronghold, producing many talented recruits for the big Melbourne clubs. At the first game I had to cover, I sat next to an old hand. *The Albury Border Mail* football writer helped me to submit a reasonably intelligent account of the match. Soccer was easier; I had grown up on that in Liverpool. Managing editor Milton Lewis liked my soccer reports because they were so realistic, but I wasn't able to tell him why. While reporting on club matches, I was also goalkeeper for Wangaratta – that is until I was bitten by a dog.

Diving to my left to stop a solid drive from an opposition player, I felt a sharp pain in my left leg, flinched and let in a goal. Looking to my right, I saw that a stray dog had attached itself to my leg to the cheers of opposition supporters.

"Those bastards will stop at nothing to win a game," I thought as I wrestled with the canine intruder. My gashed leg required several stitches. Journalistic instincts told me it was too good a story to miss. I had to name the victim, and my game was up with Milton.

I met my first wife, Penny, in Wangaratta. A nursing sister at the local hospital, she returned to her home in Melbourne the same year. When I found a job with a Melbourne television and radio publication, I followed her. It was around that time I did a launch television commercial for a new cigarette called *Albany Trim Size*.

The night before the shoot, I went to dinner with the producer John Hearman and we consumed a few bottles of fine red wine. It was an early morning shoot and Hearman and I were suffering. The setting was a log cabin in the mountains, where I was to spend a weekend with a beautiful girl. There were two action sequences for me. One where I spun the cigarette pack along a log table, ensuring it came to rest with the brand name square on to the camera. The other was an intimate moment lighting my partner's cigarette with a candle which I lit from a log fire. We had problems with both.

We needed thirty takes to get the cigarette pack to finish facing the right way and every time I went to light the candle my hand shook. After several aborted takes, Hearman called a halt and wandered off clutching one of the props, a silver coffee pot. He came back several minutes later and said: "What you need is a coffee to fix your shakes." I felt I needed something stronger, but there was something about the way he said it that led me to try the coffee. It was heavily laced with Scotch and the next take with the candle was spot-on. While the crew packed up, Hearman and I retired to a quiet corner to finish our "coffee" and sample a few more Albany cigarettes.

In January 1957 the New South Wales Government selected Danish architect Joern Utzon's "split orange" design for Australia's new centre of culture the Sydney Opera House. The controversial design earned the 38-year-old a prize of £5000, while in the same year 'The Pub With No Beer' earned Australia's first gold record for Slim Dusty.

Adelaide's 36-year-old Rupert Murdoch had established a beachhead in Melbourne with Southdown Press, publishers of the women's magazine New Idea and the newly launched *TV Week*. After the death of his father, Sir Keith, in 1952, Murdoch returned from

England to discover his newspaper inheritance beset with many problems, including heavy debts and death duties. By 1957 he had consolidated and regrouped with the Adelaide News, the Perth Sunday Times, Southdown Press and his newly acquired electronic interest radio station 5DN. Southdown made an offer I could not resist – editing the Sydney edition of *TV Week*.

We worked out of a small office opposite the *Menzies Hotel* in Sydney's central business district. Keith Cornelius, Dallas Atkins, three secretarial staff and me were pioneers in a far flung outpost of the burgeoning Murdoch empire. Frank Packer said Murdoch was a young upstart who would not get far. At 65, Murdoch controlled Twentieth Century Fox, Fox Television, Asia's Star TV, Foxtel and more than a hundred newspapers in six countries.

I saw Murdoch frequently in Sydney and got to know him well. Sometimes I picked him up at the airport in my rusting 1955 FJ Holden car, drove him to his hotel and occasionally had dinner with him. At one such dinner I met Ewan Waterman, a wealthy grazier from South Australia who financially supported Murdoch in those early days.

We dined at the fashionable *Glen Ascham* private hotel in Darling Point, a ten-bedroom Florentine mansion built the year I was born and demolished in 1992. Murdoch was like a kid with a new toy, having gained his first television licence for Channel 9 in Adelaide on October 13, 1958. The station was scheduled to open the following year. While we were discussing programming, Murdoch rattled off a few of his favourite shows, mostly Westerns, and asked me to make a note of them.

"Get a cable off to McCadden in New York tomorrow and make sure he gets those programmes. Just add whatever others you think I should buy." As Sydney editor of his television magazine, he expected me to know what would rate well.

The following day I drew up a list of good-rating programmes from existing Australian channels and cabled McCadden. Through Murdoch's personal choice and my knowledge of viewing habits, his new station opened with a well-balanced programme format. On another occasion we were discussing circulation of *TV Week* and *TV Preview*, a rival magazine that was giving us problems. *TV Preview* had a circulation of six or seven thousand and we were not making any headway against it. I told Murdoch two young salesmen were running *TV Preview* on a part-time basis. "They've got regular jobs with H G Palmer, a television retailer. I'm sure they would accept an offer from you." "How much do you think?" Murdoch asked. "£10,000 would get it for you," I replied. "Right, fix it," said Murdoch.

The next day I did the deal with two very happy guys. "He'll give you £10,000, I've got it right here with me," I said, opening my briefcase with a flourish.

"We'll take it," they said. It was Murdoch's first takeover in Sydney, the tiny tip of a surfacing iceberg. His next move created a tidal wave as he emerged with Cumberland Newspapers, a company that every week produced 400,000 newspapers around Sydney's northern and western suburbs.

Another John named Glass did the deal. The Sydney businessman needed more than a briefcase for the £1 million it took to persuade former Fairfax journalist Earl White to part with his family company. It was not until a few days after the deal was done that White discovered that his unexpectedly large windfall had come from Rupert Murdoch. While it gave White a warm glow, the takeover sent a chill through the bones of Warwick Fairfax and Frank Packer, the incumbent Press barons of the harbour city.

The pair controlled the daily newspaper market and they were determined to keep out any intruders, particularly the Melbourne Herald and Weekly Times group. They had not bargained on Murdoch getting under their guard. Rupert Henderson, managing director of John Fairfax & Sons, dropped his guard completely when Murdoch offered close to £2 million for the ailing *Mirror* Newspapers. When the deal was concluded on May 21, 1960, Murdoch had joined the big league, and he's been on a global takeover binge ever since.

I liked Rupert Murdoch because you knew exactly where you stood with him. At Southdown Press in Melbourne, I often saw him with his jacket off, sleeves rolled up, working with the sub-editors and compositors at the final stages of production. In most things he led by example and worked long, hard hours. If you did the right thing by him, he did the right thing by you, no matter how unusual the circumstances, even over bent teaspoons. While strolling around Channel 7 one day I checked the staff notice board and found a terse warning to employees about bending teaspoons in the station canteen. Not realising what a great drama I would stir up, I wrote a humorous column piece about 'The Case of the Bent Teaspoons." Warwick Fairfax phoned Murdoch in the early hours of the morning to complain.

Murdoch rang me and said: "I wish you wouldn't stir Fairfax up. Tell me, is the column piece true?" "It was written jokingly, but it's true," I said. Murdoch rang Fairfax back and said he supported his editor's right to run the piece, which he added was 'just a storm in a teacup'. Channel 7 still banned me from the station premises for several weeks.

At head office there were some who thought I was getting too close to Murdoch. I was about to confront business politics for the first time in my life. The world of private enterprise gets far more credit than its due. It is no different to the bureaucracy, politics or sports administration, with more than its share of fools, cheats, liars, the insecure and the inadequate.

I have met businessmen who are frightened by their own shadow. Much of the business world discourages change and progress, and creativity is stifled by play-safe executives with their eyes on their pension funds. There are so many frustrating bastards just marking time.

With the success of *Yes Minister* and *Yes Prime Minister*, I'm surprised nobody has followed up with Yes Managing Director. It would be equally farcical.

Southdown management gave me some bullshit story about wanting me back in Melbourne, because they were 'missing your good feature stories'.

"You can do more for the magazine in Melbourne than Sydney," said national editor Rod Lever. This really meant he was getting bloody nervous about me being so close to Murdoch. It was back to Melbourne or quit, so I quit.

Quitting was a costly experience for Murdoch had allocated shares to me in Channel 9 and I lost them along with my job. I went to the journalists' union, the Australian Journalists' Association, and they said I had a 50-50 chance of getting the shares back in a court action.

They would assist me with part of the fees for a solicitor and a barrister, but there were no guarantees. I was broke and I needed another job, so I let it go.

Married two years and with my first child, Christopher, it was not a smart thing to just walk out of a good job, but I couldn't stand the bullshit. Maybe that's why I never wanted to be an executive. Murdoch can't stand bullshit either and that's why he's so successful.

*

I quit the fledgling Murdoch organisation up to my neck in debt. I had to send Penny and Christopher back to her parents in Melbourne and walk the streets for a while. Several weeks later I found a job with *The Sun*, a Sydney afternoon daily, and they came back.

At *The Sun* I almost qualified for the *Guinness Book of Records* with the shortest daily newspaper job in history. My mind flashed back to Sir Frank and the High Court and I thought 'This can't be happening again.' In a few short years I had worked for Packer, Fairfax, Murdoch and the *Melbourne Herald* there weren't many others out there.

On my first day with *The Sun* I was in a radio car despatched to a train derailment at an inner suburban station. After a fast drive the car pulled up at the station; I leaped out and rushed down to the platform, expecting a scene of mayhem and maybe a front page on my first day. The scene was calm and orderly; no one was seriously injured – there were just a few people with minor cuts and bruises; no horrified bystanders, no front page. I sauntered back to the car, sat in the front seat, picked up the radio microphone and sent through six or seven paragraphs describing the scene exactly as it was. When I returned to the editorial floor, the editor and the news editor tore strips off me.

"Did you go to the same train smash as *The Mirror*?" Both papers were already on the streets. *The Mirror* had a poster – 'Rail Horror' – and a suitably 'horrific' story on the front page. Reading my few succinct paragraphs in the stop press, I thought I must have been at the wrong station. I told them that I had written what I had seen.

"You don't just write what you see," they said. "You're here to help sell newspapers. Never let the facts get in the way of a good story.

You'd better learn quick or you won't last in this game." I got the message and tried hard, but I never quite measured up to the beat-up merchants of the day. Some of them could write a story in the lift going down to the radio car. Some could do it without even catching the lift. When I look at much of what passes for news today, particularly on television and radio, I cringe.

After I bombed out with the train story, the chief of staff relegated me to court reporting. It had to be a top court story to make the paper, so most of the time we played cards. Then we struck a bonanza with divorce and soon I was getting more front pages than the beat-up merchants, especially when a case involved a high-profile couple. And the editorial line changed to 'Don't let anything get in the way of the facts.' Somehow, the linen is dirtier when it belongs to the rich and famous.

Juicy stories were coming out of the Divorce Court and we could use any of the evidence presented there. Divorce lawyers loved publicity, so they produced some really juicy stuff for us. Judges were not averse to headlines either, especially His Honour Mr Justice Dovey, Chief Judge in Divorce.

When the rules changed and newspapers were barred from publishing evidence in divorce cases, we didn't have to worry – his Honour had the solution.

Over a drink during a recess he said: "I know you can't use the evidence, but you can use my summing up. I'll include any juicy bits you want in the summing up. Just let me know if there's anything you particularly want included." Funny, he always sounded so moralistic in court.

Divorce was becoming commonplace and the stories no longer rated, so the card games got longer. Then along came the Callan Park Royal Commission. A flood of stories came out of Australia's most infamous mental institution. The Royal Commission was a heavy piece of courtroom drama, but it did have some lighter moments. I was sitting at the Press table one day quietly listening to an England-Australia Test cricket match on a transistor radio tucked into an inside pocket, with the earpiece plugged in. His Honour, who was droning on about legalities, paused, looked directly at me and asked me to approach the bench. I thought 'Now I'm in trouble; he's noticed the earpiece – he's going to give me a real dressing-down.'

Beckoning me to come closer, he leaned across the bench and whispered "What's the score?" I told him, and in a loud voice he said: "Make sure you don't do that again Mr Williams. Now return to the Press table."

It was good to get out of the courtroom and back to sea for my next assignment, which involved the Australian Navy's new high-tech frigate *HMAS Parramatta III*. To test the advanced sonar and anti-submarine weapons system aboard the sleek new frigate, a World War II Royal Navy T-Class submarine would engage with it in a cat-and-mouse mission off the New South Wales coast.

The Navy had invited media aboard the two vessels and I scored the submarine. 'They'll make short work of this old rust bucket,' I thought as I stepped onto the deck of the former Royal Navy 'sardine can'.

The crew quarters were cramped on the vessels I served on; below deck on the submarine, sardines would have found it cramped. It reminded me of foraging in the cargo hold of *Coulgarve*. Ungainly on the surface, the vessel lurched and rolled heavily as we slowly exited Sydney Harbour into the rolling swells of a choppy Pacific.

When the conning tower cover clamped down, it became dank and claustrophobic. We heard that familiar siren and the slender steel canister began to descend silently into the bowels of the ocean. Once under the surface, the submarine became silent and almost motionless as we glided down into the ocean.

HMAS Parramatta III – Circa 1970s

Out of the harbour swept the imposing battle-grey *Parramatta* on its search and destroy mission. As we closed in for a totally unexpected 'kill' the Commanding Officer gave me a rare and privileged sight of the dramatic last seconds of a classic naval engagement – a sight enjoyed by the commander of the German U-boat as he despatched the lethal torpedo that helped to sink the first *Athelknight*. Starkly framed in the lens of the periscope was the port beam of the newly commissioned pride and joy of the Royal Australian Navy. *Parramatta* had entered the mock fray too soon, its acclaimed sonar technology already on the blink, its weapons neutered, its fate decreed.

As we surfaced off the Heads and rocked and rolled back down the harbour a photographer threw his guts up. "I'd be doing the same if we'd fired real torpedoes," I exclaimed. An officer said: "We'd all be feeling sick if we'd opened those tubes. Come and have a look and you'll understand." Like the old newspaper files at *The Argus*, the tubes served a fine peacetime purpose, holding a good deal more cold cans than an average fridge.

"It's the coolest place to keep them and we thought you newspaper boys would be expecting a can or two." My story in *The Sun* caused considerable embarrassment to the Navy and I did not expect any more such invitations.

I don't think anyone aboard the sub was aware that in World War Two the escort sloop *Parramatta* was sunk in the Mediterranean by torpedo attack from the German submarine *U559* on November 27, 1941 with tragically only 24 survivors from a total of 160 on board.

In a one-income family with one child, money was important, so I jumped at the chance to work the night shift at Australian United Press. It was September 1960 and I was sub-editing cable stories from the Rome Olympic Games. Dawn Fraser became the toast of Sydney, repeating her Melbourne 1956 performance by winning the 100 metres freestyle swimming gold medal and setting a new record of one minute 12 seconds. Herb Elliott broke the world record in winning the 1,500 metres and some heady copy poured in from Rome. Sub-editing it for Australian country newspapers was stimulating.

I had been fortunate in gaining some experience on the subs' desk at *The Sun*. The subs' room, 'God's waiting room for journalists', where ageing scribes sat out their newspaper autumns. One old sub caused a sensation the day a young copyboy walked around the subs' table distributing the ballpoint pens. In an uncharacteristic display of agility, he threw down his pencil, leapt to his feet and yelled: "That's the end of journalism as we know it," then stormed out of the room. The startled copyboy, who fled from the room with his boxful of pens, has long since replaced it with a PC and journalism has survived, despite American grammar and spelling checks.

It was a heavy load, doing the early morning to afternoon shift at *The Sun*, then starting at AUP about 7pm and working through the night to 3am. By the time I drove home to the northern beach suburb of Dee Why, there wasn't much time for sleep before heading back to start another shift. Fine for a couple of weeks, but I couldn't resist the offer from AUP chief of staff Norm Hurley, and continued for about six months. I kept thinking about the money and popping No-Doz tablets.

There were some embarrassing moments, especially when covering police rounds for both organisations. Many a copper shook his head and looked on in disbelief when I signed in twice a day for different media and I often encountered *Sun* colleagues covering stories on later shifts. I had told Hurley that if anyone badly needed the job then I would be happy to step aside, but as far as I know, nobody applied for work at AUP while I was there.

My embarrassing moments with police and colleagues paled into insignificance compared to Hurley's faux pas at a viceregal gathering in a leading city hotel. The Governor of New South Wales was addressing an attentive audience when I noticed Norm arrive and quietly sidle up to the banquet table in the middle of the room. 'Oh God, no – he's seen the oyster sculpture,' I thought.

Norm backed up to the expertly arranged mountain of Sydney rock oysters and reached behind him to sample one. 'If you can't get the people to the mountain, take the mountain to the people', I thought, as hundreds of oysters cascaded onto the floor and slid in all directions. The crowd turned and stared at Norm standing oyster in hand, poised to slide the juicy flesh down his throat. He was surrounded by hundreds of the bloody things.

Norm calmly swallowed the offending mollusc, crunched his way across the room, bowed and exited. I'm sure I even saw the Governor smile.

Australia spawned many great newspaper larrikins, but they are thin on the ground today. Robert Gordon Menzies was not smiling when another wild man of Sydney, of all things Scottish born, took the piss out of the Prime Minister during his famous waltz with the Queen in Canberra in early 1954. To record the historic event, Menzies invited three photographers, one of them our Scottish friend. As the PM, resplendent in white tie and tails, danced sedately with his charming Monarch, the cheeky photographer was in close attendance. Following their every movement, he took hold of Menzies' coat tails and momentarily mimicked Her Majesty's most loyal subject. Steadfastly, the PM ignored this dastardly affront and remained cool and dignified. Not so in his subsequent angry phone call to the photographer's boss, Sir Frank Packer, when Menzies decreed that the photographer would never be allowed to set foot in Canberra again as long as he lived. And, in typical Menzies' style, he added: "What's more, he will not even be allowed to fly over it."

The Sydney Opera House lottery, a fund-raising project for the revolutionary new building with a first prize of £100,000, was taking over the front pages. Both afternoon newspapers assigned at least four radio cars to each morning lottery draw. The first information on the radio was the suburb where the winner lived and as three cars returned to base, the remaining one raced off to the appropriate suburb. Then came the street name, number and winner's name. It was a mad race between *the Mirror* and *the Sun* to get to the winner first, and then it became a game. If you got there first, you could grab the winner and take them away somewhere and the other paper could not interview or photograph them. It was everybody's dream to win £100,000. For Mr and Mrs Basil Thorne of Sydney's south-eastern beach suburb of Bondi the lottery became a nightmare, and for their only child, eight years old Graeme, it proved fatal – he was kidnapped and his body found a month later. Eventually a Stephen Leslie Bradley was extradited from Sri Lanka and convicted of the murder.

Thirty years earlier we had experienced another form of media madness with the Simmonds and Newcombe affair. The pair had allegedly beaten a warder to death with a baseball bat and the media turned them into bloody heroes. Stories portrayed them as being clever for eluding the law. Decent, law-abiding citizens left food and drink out overnight for them while they were on the run and some kids even launched a fan club for them. The media wields a powerful influence over the public. It's not a case of giving them what they want, but what the media thinks they want. There's a hell of a difference. I've often heard media executives say: "They're not too bright out there; you have to get down to their level you know." In truth, it's the level at which the executives themselves feel comfortable. There were other compelling reasons for leaving *the Sun,* like being asked to dress up as Father Christmas in the middle of the year, and walk around asking people for their impressions.

*

Many intelligent Australian journalists had joined public relations consultancies, a new world with better salaries and expense accounts. I got a job with the biggest and best in Australia – Eric White and Associates in Melbourne – and I was with them for 12 months. I was based with a major client, *Trans Australia Airlines,* and I rarely visited the Eric White office. The salary wasn't as big as I'd expected and the battles over expenses reminded me of the Sydney newspaper editor who decided taxis were no longer a claimable item and that everyone should travel by bus. Then some wag came into the office one day with a sack full of bus tickets, poured them all over his desk and demanded he be reimbursed on the spot.

We hadn't had much to do with the business world, but we'd knocked around a lot, worked in all sorts of situations – and we had flexible minds.

Meaning we could listen to a whole lot of crap in the boardroom, while wondering how soon it would be before we got to the pub for a beer. We had the perfect excuse: having to spend time with journalists to get publicity for clients. Sometimes they got bad publicity. Then we put on our damage minimisation hats and went back to the pub for a few more beers to see if we could turn things around.

Working for an airline was the other side of the fence for me. In 1961 the Department of Civil Aviation had taken me to task over a front page story I wrote for *The Sun* about a tragic aviation disaster. Shortly after take-off from Sydney airport on the night of November 30, an *Ansett Airlines* Viscount aircraft had disappeared off the radar screen in a violent storm. The aircraft just vanished without trace. The next morning, a huge media team was out in the search area immediately surrounding the airport.

At the time of its disappearance the plane was in the first minutes of a flight to Canberra. There were some compelling human interest stories: the hostess who had done a trip swap hours before the flight; another hostess who had a dream about a crash landing a few days earlier; the Canberra newspaper proprietor who turned up too late for the flight. The next morning we were out in boats on Botany Bay, combing the area with official search teams while aerial searches by Airlines of NSW and *TAA* DC3s were concentrating on the open seas to the East.

We were in the right spot. At 6.30 am a search helicopter sighted an oil slick and what was later identified as a torn Viscount cockpit seat cushion.

Scattered human remains were later found on a nearby beach. Later in the morning Navy divers found the main wreckage in five metres of water. We were on the spot when the divers came up. Some of the 15 passengers and crew were still strapped in their seats, heads and limbs torn off by the force of the impact with the water.

In a follow-up story I said the crash resulted from metal fatigue; part of the wing had fallen off, throwing the Viscount into an uncontrollable dive.

As a precaution the Department of Civil Aviation might ground all Viscount aircraft in Australia. The story got a big run and a departmental heavy telephoned to ask where the information came from. How come we were experts, when they had not concluded the investigation into the cause of the crash? I was not being a beat-up merchant because I had found that air safety authorities had discovered metal fatigue in a Viscount in South Africa and had grounded the aircraft there for inspection only days before the Australian crash.

Before joining *TAA* I had made only one flight, in a DC3 from the central Queensland town of Charters Towers to the coastal city of Townsville, one of the roughest areas in the world for turbulence, particularly on a "milk run". Although it was an early morning flight, everyone else was drunk when they came aboard at the many stops en route. When the DC3 started bouncing all over the sky, I realised they had all done the trip before. That was in 1954 and I had not flown since.

In the early 1960s *Ansett* and *TAA* operated Viscounts and Electras. They were reliable aircraft until the Botany Bay crash tarnished the image. Electras from Australia were still flying in Brazil in the 1980s, commuting from Rio to Sao Paulo, every hour on the hour. They were just as comfortable as ever with big windows, and a spacious lounge down the back; there was plenty of room to stretch your legs. It may have been premature to pension them off when Australia entered the jet age.

At *TAA* we created havoc with the announcement of the choice of Australia's first domestic jet aircraft. Like everything under the old Australian two-airline system, the announcement had to be made simultaneously by *Ansett* and *TAA*. The government had accepted *Ansett*'s choice of the American MacDonnell-Douglas DC9, and the decision did not go down well with *TAA*, especially the technical people who had opted for the British Trident.

The politicians had their say in Canberra and the rival airline PR people had the opportunity to have their say in the capital cities. Both airlines had ordered the same equipment and both PR consultancies had the same timeframe for the announcement. How do you score an edge over your rival if you are announcing the same thing at the same time, and all you can put out is a story and a photograph? We planned our coup well.

Several days before the announcement, we photographed models of the DC9 painted in *TAA* colours against a neutral background and superimposed them to scale over aerial photographs of Australian cities. Shortly before the appointed time for the official announcement we rushed them to the main newspapers in each capital city and they were the only photographs published. When the photographs appeared, the *Ansett* PR consultants Michael Fitzgerald and Howard Bull were contemplating suicide. I got suitable credit for the idea and a new job to boot, cleverly arranged by Fitzgerald and Bull.

Another of their clients was management consultant John P Young. Intercontinental Hotels had asked Young to find a PR manager for Melbourne's new Southern Cross Hotel. When Fitzgerald and Bull asked if I wanted the job they were honest about their motives. "That gets rid of you from *TAA* and makes our job a lot easier," they said.

In due course, I returned to the Airline Industry and worked to get a third viable airline into business. But that was later. Little did I know that my move into PR in the Hotel sector was going to lead to one of the biggest events in Australia's history. It was 1964 and we were about to experience the one and only visit to Australia by the Beatles.

The Southern Cross Hotel

The salary paid by the hotel was nearly double what I was getting at Eric White's and the Southern Cross Hotel was the newest hotel in Australia. Business executives, socialites, used car and real estate salesmen got themselves paged there just for kicks. Fitzgerald said he could guarantee me the job because they had done a deal with the management consultant. I didn't ask any questions. A formal interview was arranged with the hotel manager and that went smoothly. Pete Sutherland was an American war hero. He had led a squadron of fighter bombers over the Yalu River in General Macarthur's controversial Chinese border raid during the Korean War, so we shared a common background and I passed the test.

Sutherland was a strong leader. He told me that to get on in business one should pull off the biggest success or make the worst possible mistake; never fall in the grey area in the middle. I suspect he picked that up from Macarthur. I have enjoyed my share of successes, had some monumental failures, but I've managed to stay well clear of the grey area. Sutherland was one of those rare, intelligent managers, who would let you have your head to do the things you believed were right, as long as you kept him informed and were aware of the consequences of failure. Years later I would work with another achiever from the aviation world who had the same approach to management. It only works with a team that is able to respond effectively. Pete Sutherland and Bryan Grey (*Compass Airlines*) had another attitude in common: with a plan that needs many people to make it work, don't canvass opinions – set it up, then advise them. It was a top down approach and it worked if you had good leadership and could mobilise people toward your vision.

The Hotel's venture into late-night shopping was a classic example. Promoting the Hotel's shopping centre complex was not without its problems. It was on a hill at the wrong end of town, there was little passing traffic and the shopkeepers enjoyed very few brisk trading days. For months after it opened, it was not uncommon to arrive in the morning and find shops completely stripped, with the tenant gone and the rent overdue. Some had even taken the light globes. We tried jazz concerts, brass bands, fashion parades and other promotions. A young singer named Judith Durham (of *Seekers* fame) sang there with a jazz band featuring that great trumpeter Paddy Fitzallen and Radio 3UZ's John McMahon said: "One day she'll be famous." We revived big brass bands with a series of lunchtime concerts and when the American Sixth Fleet visited we staged a night show featuring its rock, jazz and conventional military bands. At Christmas we raffled a giant Christmas stocking with a Volkswagen stuffed in the toe, and in the hotel ballroom we staged a black tie dinner to raise money for the Hotel's entrant in the Women's Hospital Miss Teenage Quest.

The dinner was an all-male affair, mainly bank managers and bookmakers. A sumptuous meal was accompanied by fine wines while stunning girls in skimpy French maid outfits served vintage ports, cognacs and Cuban cigars. Thanks to generous sponsors, one lucky guest won a luxury sports car for his wife, another took home a black poodle adorned with a diamond necklace and everyone took home a bottle of expensive French perfume. At midnight, newsboys distributed a special edition of *The Sun* with photographs taken that night.

The official photographer had a field day with French maids sitting on the rickety knees of aging guests. The next day I received dozens of phone calls about the asking price for the negatives, but I resisted the temptation.

We attracted extensive publicity and many people, but not enough to keep the shopkeepers happy.

One day I said to Pete "I want to break the law". People had been pushing for late night shopping for years. If the shopping centre remained open late one night we would get widespread publicity. The only hitch was that shopkeepers who traded after hours faced heavy fines and even gaol.

"Sounds okay to me, but *Intercontinental* can't be seen to be in any way involved because it's not legal," said Pete. "Put the shopkeepers up front. Let them set it up."

So that's how we played it. I met with some of the more progressive shopkeepers and put the question: "Who's prepared to go to gaol?" Nobody would go that far, but some were happy to risk a fine. "With illegal trading, first offenders get a heavy fine so if you haven't done it before you're okay," I told them. "The hotel will pay the fines, but no one's ever to know that." They all agreed and appointed a media spokesman.

I selected the night, prepared a news release in the name of the spokesman and arranged a band and other entertainment. We were careful not to telegraph our intentions. The government officials who policed trading hours always went home at about the same time as the shopkeepers. How could they ever find anyone trading after hours?

Just before 5.30 pm, I dropped the shopkeepers' news release into a number of radio stations. 'It's time Melbourne came out of the dark ages and had decent shopping hours,' said the release. 'We're staying open till midnight tonight. We know we're breaking the law, but the public deserves a better deal.' When the news broke hundreds of people flocked to the shopping centre and bought everything in sight.

The media turned up in droves and when the government officials arrived, it was all over. The story was on late television news and radio all night and the morning papers had front-page stories and photographs. It was a success; politicians were fuming and shopkeepers had dared do something progressive.

Phone calls and telegrams of support came from around Australia and overseas congratulating the shopkeepers on their initiative. Nobody suspected any hotel involvement, so Pete was delighted.

Under pressure from the media and the public, the State Government decided not to take action against the offending shopkeepers, apart from warning them not to do it again. That was like waving red rag to a bull. To maintain credibility, the move could not be seen as an isolated publicity stunt. All the shopkeepers were fired up. It took little urging from me. "We don't mind if we do go to gaol," they said and they did it again with trumpets blaring. They ran advertising inviting all of Melbourne to enjoy late night shopping with free food, drinks and entertainment. For the first time ever a Melbourne television station crossed to a live camera on location during the evening news. People queued to get into the shops and spent money as if it was their last chance. Some of them had flown in from interstate.

Two government officials inflamed the crowd by taking the names of shopkeepers. I had to lock them in a vacant shop because the crowd was in an angry mood. Eventually the shoppers dispersed and the officials hurried off into the night. The media coverage was astounding. Across the front page of *The Sun* was the headline 'Jeers As Night Shops Banned.' -

'More than a thousand angry shoppers booed and shouted as Department of Labour inspectors closed shops in the Southern Cross Hotel plaza last night. Police stood by as the crowd jostled inspectors, chanting leave them open and go home. The shops had opened in defiance of the law for the second successive Friday night.'

The Government was having hysterics so Pete said, "Let's call it a day."

"I don't know if we can – the shopkeepers want to stay open every night," I said.

"Well, if they do, they will have to pay their own fines."

Pete was right. He had given me my head, so I pulled it in at the right time. Most overseas entertainers who visited Melbourne stayed at the Southern Cross; Sammy Davis Jnr., the Beatles, Judy Garland, to name a few.

In 1964, Judy Garland's career was on a downward trajectory and she had just been released from a CBS TV series, which hadn't rated well. Seeing opportunities was Harry M Miller's competitive advantage and he had signed Judy for three Australian concerts, two in Sydney and one in Melbourne. Now the first Sydney concert was held in a boxing arena, the only one big enough to hold 10,000 fans, and it was very well reviewed as she gave a great performance over two hours.

Judy Garland – leaving the Southern Cross Hotel (Getty Images)

The second concert was also successful, but there had been reports that Judy was 'drugged up' and performing like an automaton. She had not been happy with the venues, but Miller placated her until it became clear that she was quite unsettled. A number of plane trips, a simple hour between Sydney and Melbourne in those days, had been booked, and cancelled. In the end, they sent her on the slow train between the two capitals and she arrived exhausted from the journey. Still, Melbourne fans were ecstatic and 8,000 of them had paid good money to see her.

As I look back now, if Judy Garland had sued for invasion of privacy she could have sent the hotel broke. It was the night she finally came apart on stage at the old West Melbourne Stadium (Festival Hall). Judy was as drunk as a lord. The saying has not changed to 'as drunk as a person,' so maybe I should say 'as drunk as a lady.' I had been a fan of Judy from the days of Saturday matinees in Liverpool and now she was in Melbourne, in my hotel. Yet, once inside her suite, she didn't emerge and we now know that's what she was doing in there, preparing those famous tonsils with some good vodka.

The lady was no tramp; it was the company she kept. The media had applauded her all those years, glowingly reporting all her triumphs, but suddenly her long-running list of hits ground to a dead stop. She went from a hit to a has-been in a few tragic minutes on a makeshift stage in a building that had seen many a boxer crash to the canvas. After keeping her fans waiting for more than an hour, the megastar appeared briefly and sung several songs, in-between times, mumbling to herself and to the fans, and some of them leave. Most people can see that she is drunk and then suddenly she was no longer there. Her minders rushed her back to the Southern Cross and up to the Presidential Suite with the media in hot pursuit.

They were like a pack of hounds after a fox – but Judy was a rabbit, a frightened, exhausted rabbit trapped in a hotel warren. Judy would leave and life would go on, the hotel and the media would still be around. I had an idea and turned to Pete: "We've got to give the media a suite on the top floor, make it easy for them. She has to face them somewhere, so let's make it as easy as possible for everyone." We opened a suite on the top floor near the lifts – the only lifts that Judy could use to get out of the hotel. It was what she desperately wanted to do.

The media were happy; they had a good location, and Judy would have to accept the consequences of her failure. In the media room the fridge was well stocked and there was plenty of food. Catching a journalist putting a bottle of Scotch inside his jacket, I blew my top and his colleagues backed me up. That's one of the reasons why I wouldn't let the media into the Presidential suite when Judy finally left. Keeping them out was a wise decision. Judy left as she arrived, head held high, a star and a lady despite the scars from her aborted performance. While everyone was chasing Judy towards the lift, I let myself into the Presidential suite and locked the door behind me.

The huge presentation basket of Australian wines and liqueurs remained untouched in a sea of flowers from fans, bunches and bunches, everywhere.

I walked into a bedroom and accidentally kicked the first empty vodka bottle, then found others strewn around her bed. One week after she collapsed on stage in Melbourne, Judy Garland was in a coma in a Hong Kong hospital. Asked sometime later about just what had ailed her in Hong Kong, she replied, wryly, "Australia."

The Beatles

Shortly after Garland left, five Liverpool boys flew into town and many Australians never recovered. It was June 1964, when Beatlemania struck and the airwaves were awash with 'Love me Do', 'All My Loving' and 'She Loves You.' Since then, journalists, sociologists and others have advanced all manner of explanations for why Australians reacted the way they did. I was there and the Beatles visit was one of the biggest events Australia had ever seen.

The Beatles arrive, Jimmy Nicol filling in for an ill Ringo Starr (Pinterest)

There are journalists who are loath to admit it was media hype that led to the mass hysteria. A few would admit that Australia has long been a media driven society, with television now the prime mover. Nobody doubts that newspapers and radio have long influenced people's behaviour. However, some in media are selective, claiming credit when things go right, but raising a variety of other factors when things go wrong. Here's a classic quote in a Beatles souvenir insert in *The Australian* thirty years on:

"The tour liberated young Australians who had not previously dreamed of openly disobeying their parents, police, civil authorities or indeed any adult."

That's strange. Adults organised the tour. Adults used wild scenes from other Beatles tours in publicity. Adult police and adult civil authorities set the parameters for the Australian tour. Adults took advantage of teenage girls at the Southern Cross Hotel and elsewhere. The hotel was awash with schoolgirls. Adults herded selected girls into holding rooms, then tossed them under sweating adults.

But according to a writer in The Australian 30 years later:

"The Beatles became the catalyst for the suppressed frustrations of kids who had begun to realise that unquestioning obedience to anyone older than themselves was no longer a sacred law."

The kids enticed into Melbourne's Exhibition Street by someone older The Beatles dodge hysterical crowds at the Southern Cross than themselves, then herded into bed by someone older than themselves, went along with unquestioning obedience. Their main consolation is that they lived to tell or not to tell the tale, for media hype almost created a tragedy. Before the Beatles became an international success, an astute Melbourne promoter, Kenn Brodziak, had lined up the group for an Australian tour. In July 1963 he had booked the relatively unknown group for £1000 a show, although later Beatles manager Brian Epstein had negotiated an extra £500 a show.

With American promoters offering $50,000 a show by 1964, Brodziak was laughing all the way to the bank and schoolgirls were giggling all the way to the Southern Cross Hotel where the Beatles would stay for four days.

A rare picture of the five boys

The fact that the boys were going to stay in our Hotel said a lot for just how prestigious the place was back then. As the date for their arrival approached, Pete Sutherland was in his element with a 'war cabinet' and a battle plan that included a 'field hospital'. The 'Merseyside Marines' were landing and Pete and his hotel troops would give them the best covering fire possible.

Security was tight, but it didn't stop girls from smuggling themselves into the hotel in laundry bags and it reminded me of jumping ship. Were all laundry van drivers corruptible? Several desperate girls scaled the roofs of adjacent buildings to get to the mezzanine floor of the hotel and at times it was frightening. For Ringo Starr, who would arrive after the others to take over from stand-in drummer Jimmy Nicol, it was a nightmare.

Although not as much as nightmare as it was for Jimmy, whose career went into a nosedive and he left the music business in 1967. Still, Jimmy must have thought his luck was in as, on June 3 1964, the day before they were flying out, Ringo had collapsed and was rushed to hospital with tonsillitis. Jimmy Nicol was hired as a temporary drummer so that their world wide tour could continue. Australia was the fourth country they were visiting and Jimmy had played in several concerts in Denmark, the Netherlands and Hong Kong. Nicol played with the group in Adelaide, but that was to be his last performance when Ringo was temporarily cured and reunited with the group in Melbourne on June 14, with three concerts to be played on the following three nights, then Sydney and beyond.

Perhaps Jimmy should have realised that, London born, he was never going to be more than a stand-in for the Liverpool Lads.

On June 14, the street in front of the hotel was awash with frenzied girls and the visiting contingent of US Air Force cadets, who were staying at the hotel, must have thought it was Christmas. Some of them were unwrapping their pubescent presents before the main party started. And, adding fuel to the crazy situation, radio stations were whipping the fans into a frenzy in front of the hotel.

The Beatles on the balcony of Southern Cross Hotel (Herald Sun)

Mindful of the mayhem that was possible, we had arranged for the Beatles' car convoy to drive the wrong way up the one-way Little Collins Street and into the exit of the car park – a simple but effective part of Sutherland's battle plan. As the Beatles, minus Ringo, came up a deserted side street and in through the car park exit they must have thought nobody had heard of them in Melbourne.

However, when they stepped out on to the balcony at the front of the hotel they must have thought the whole city was there to greet them. If they had delayed their appearance on the balcony a minute longer there could have been a terrible tragedy. Thousands of young fans were pressed against those plate glass windows, a dense crowd pushing behind them; faces were distorted against the straining glass. Mounted police pushed into the crowd, throwing girls across their saddles and forcing their way to the front doors of the hotel where a chain gang led to the 'field hospital' where doctors and nurses tended the casualties.

Bodies were swiftly slid along the floor, dozens of them, some feigning distress, others genuinely ill. It looked for all the world like an episode from M*A*S*H as crushed, distressed, shocked or play-acting, all were treated compassionately and either taken to Royal Melbourne or St Vincent's hospitals, kept under observation or politely ejected. More than 350 fans were treated for fainting, hysteria and minor injuries while ambulances took 40 serious cases to hospital.

It was so bad that TV Reporter, Tony Charlton, stated: 'Mothers, if your child is out there, you should be ashamed'.

Ashamed or not, many of the girls wandered off into the arms of American cadets while minders rounded up other eager girls who stood patiently in long queues outside the Beatles' rooms, waiting to be served. I was on the right track when I took up singing and tap-dancing in Liverpool. Travelling hypnotist shows paled into insignificance.

In the spirit of the 'field hospital', bodies were slid into place for attention then politely ejected after compassionate treatment. The lads from Liverpool had an insatiable appetite, and the Liver Birds must have been crowing from their lofty perch. For many celebrating the joys of sex for the first time, the day could have been their last celebration of life for those plate glass windows could have shattered at any time.

Apprehensive, I was retreating slowly backwards up the foyer stairs as hundreds of bodies pressed against the plate glass. Then I had a sudden flash.

"The Beatles are to go out on the balcony soon. We need some notices saying they're on the balcony now. We can hold them against the windows." I rushed down the stairs to reception and got everyone in sight furiously writing 'Beatles on Balcony' on large sheets of paper. For a moment I thought it was too late, but as we held the notices against the windows, magically the crowd pulled away and the air of panic began to subside.

It had been too late for Ringo when he arrived earlier in the day with Brian Epstein, the band's manager. PR consultant Eleanor

Knox had brought him through the front entrance to the hotel and when the crowd recognised him they pounced like a flock of starving locusts, causing Ringo to stumble. We rushed to the door and police helped us drag him and Epstein inside. Ringo was shaking like a leaf, and when asked how he was, he replied "Give us a drink, that was the roughest ride of my life!"

So I took him up to Pete's office and poured him a large Scotch. He drank it straight down and asked for another, and it was then I noticed that fans had pulled out clumps of his hair.

'That's why they grow their hair long,' I thought. 'Girls keep tearing it out. If they didn't have long hair, they'd all be bald by now.' Ringo was still shaking, but another large Scotch calmed him down.

"Rough town you've got here, mate," he said.

"Tell me about it, mate – I'm from Liverpool.

He grinned and said: "Well, you'd feel right at home here then."

The media wanted to know everything the Beatles did. We couldn't tell them everything. There were simple questions like "What did they have for breakfast?" I felt a bloody fool when I rang up to ask them. "Tell them anything," said one of the minders. So I just made it up. Chip butties. Jam sandwiches. Eggs and beans.

I should have said Guinness and oysters. With all those young girls lined up, waiting their turn, *It's Been a Hard Day's Night* had taken on a whole new meaning. George Harrison drove off in a sports car late at night, headed to a bayside beach, and a journalist asked if he had a secret girlfriend. "No," I said, "he just went out for a rest."

Those four days flashed by with the group working very hard to deliver six sold out performances. And, then they were gone and we all had the same feeling as when the Sydney Olympics finished.

Moving into Television

After the Beatles had gone, some said Melbourne would never be the same again, but it was a city that kept its double standards a little longer. It was less than twelve months after The Beatles 'liberated young Australians' that the Vice Squad seized copies of *The Trial of Lady Chatterley's Lover*. Melbourne didn't lift its skirts in public again till Melbourne Cup time in November 1965 when London model Jean Shrimpton arrived on the scene.

Jean Shrimpton at the Melbourne Cup, 1965

Then it became a case of "throw another barbie for the Shrimp," with Toorak socialites flashing their knickers all over town as they caught up with the miniskirt revolution. Shortly after that, Victoria got rid of the 'six o'clock swill' (where the pubs closed at six o'clock so the men could get home to their families) and Melbourne has been on a boozing and bonking binge ever since. I enjoyed the Southern Cross; it was like a shore bound ocean liner. The main difference was that the passengers changed more often.

While the Beatles were at the Southern Cross, a job with Channel O came up, and it was the 'singing scouses' who landed it for me. Station manager Len Mauger was keen to get their autographs for his young daughter. Every day we would send bundles of autograph books up to the Beatles' rooms, but somehow the only one that got lost was the one belonging to the daughter of my prospective new employer. Worse, it already held a number of valuable autographs. 'That's the end of that job,' I thought, but fortunately we tracked down the book and it had been duly signed by the Beatles. Reginald Miles *Ansett*, founder and chairman of *Ansett Airlines*, had gained the new licence for Channel O, later to become Channel 10.

Construction of the new station was about to begin, so it really was a job that started from the ground up. Michael Fitzgerald was the advertising and publicity manager and I was responsible for station promotion. When Fitzy died of throat cancer, Melbourne lost a legend. A respected journalist and PR consultant, he was mentor to scores of young hopefuls in both professions and was never short of a laugh.

There are innumerable tales, tall and true, about Fitzgerald. The two I like the most involve a lawn mower and a chainsaw. The lawn mower was the one he used to leave running at the back of his lengthy back garden in the outer suburb of Croydon, so his wife Barbara would think he was mowing the lawn.

"It used to work all the time. I just skipped over the back fence and down to the local golf club for a beer with the boys. One day I forgot to check the fuel tank and the bloody thing stopped. After a while Barbara walked out to see if there was anything wrong and caught me climbing back over the fence half pissed."

The chainsaw figured in an argument he had with Diana, his partner, after he and Barbara parted company. Diana threw a wobbly one night and said their relationship was over. She was leaving and wanted half of everything, the house, the furniture, the bank account, the lot, so early the next morning Fitzgerald went to a hardware shop in South Yarra and bought a chainsaw.

Diana awoke with a start as Fitzgerald started to saw the timber house in half and she couldn't leave for laughing. Diana was with him throughout the long, debilitating illness that finally claimed the irascible Fitzy.

Getting Channel O off the ground was a daunting task. Not only did we have to advertise and promote the new station against the existing ones, we had to persuade people to pay to have their sets converted to pick up the new channel. We decided our task would be easier if we could somehow influence the ratings, those magical percentage figures that can lead a TV or radio executive to an early grave. When you rely on viewers and listeners recording their own watching and listening routines in a diary the margin for error is high. On occasions people would claim to be watching a particular television show when they were in another room doing the ironing.

'People meters' have replaced the diaries, but they are not totally reliable. The meter might be on, but is anybody home?

I decided to do some research of my own and find someone who was at the ratings coalface. I struck it rich in more than one way. She was a diary collector and we got a large bundle of them before the ratings company did, and on the sixth floor of the *Ansett* building, the base for the embryonic Channel O management and production team, I photocopied the diaries then returned them to the collector. She then took them on to the ratings company. Many of the diaries taken to the sixth floor of *Ansett* Transport Industries had been filled in by the collector and she had influenced others who had not completed their diaries.

"It's a common thing for people to come to the door with their diaries and say 'Oh, do you mind finishing it for me I haven't had time'," she told me. "Other people will invite you in and finish their diaries at the kitchen table. Some will ask you what you've watched at particular times and write that in. A number of people just never record anything. Few of them can really remember what they have watched."

Was that what advertising agencies relied upon to spend client millions? We set up a bank of telephones on the sixth floor and every night phoned hundreds of people and asked what they were watching, and we got our own ratings, which were probably more accurate than others. It enabled us to analyse viewing habits and tailor our programming and advertising accordingly. Channel O attracted a massive 60 per cent audience on opening night, but it was to be a long time before the station got that sort of rating again. The opening live variety show was a disaster, audiences quickly plummeted and it was a long struggle to get back to a reasonable level again.

Ansett Airlines executives rarely had a kind word for Channel O because the airline carried the television station financially in the early days. Fortunately, for *Ansett*, the Australian Two Airline Agreement guaranteed that the airlines would make money. The agreement gave a blatantly unfair advantage to three men in particular: *Ansett*, Sir Peter Abeles and Rupert Murdoch, as dollars poured out of the skies to two airlines protected from competition by the government. I was to have a long association with the *Ansett* group but eventually play a major role in the demise of the two-headed bureaucratic monster.

When created by government, such cartels are extremely difficult to break. Placed in such advantageous situations, the recipients of the favoured treatment can wield considerable influence over successive governments and that was the case with the Two Airline Agreement. Fitzgerald and Bull were the *Ansett* PR consultants who got me the job with Intercontinental Hotels.

Fitzgerald gave up consulting and joined the new television station, taking me with him. Howard Bull took over the consulting role with the airline and I left the television station to join him. Wings within wings.

Howard Bull: there's a great name for a public relations man. We spread plenty of it around during the eight years I was with him. It was the swinging sixties and every year there was something new. The main reason I stayed in the job for so long was the diversity of our client base. While *Ansett* was the flagship, we had clients in almost every field of commerce, health, government, local government, tourism, entertainment, engineering and construction, including the London based Freeman Fox and Partners, designers of the Westgate Bridge.

Melbourne has had a tragic history with bridges over the Yarra River, which flows along the southern edge of the city business district. When the King Street Bridge developed giant cracks overnight it caused a major scare, but over time the problem was corrected.

When a 2000-ton span of the Westgate Bridge crashed to the ground on October 15, 1970, killing 35 construction workers, the shock waves rocked the nation. When I phoned him in his distantly comfortable London office, Sir Edward Freeman said: "You can test aircraft – that's why test pilots get killed; but you can't test bridges – you just build them." It may have been a valid comment, but of no comfort to grieving families. We urged him to fly to Australia and accept the consequences, meet the media and display some genuine concern. No shrinking violet, he flew to Melbourne and, while it did not silence the critics, Freeman Fox and Partners seemed a little more credible and Sir Edward a little more human.

It was the best we could do in the face of the tragedy. The subsequent Royal Commission into the collapse of the bridge found that Freeman Fox and Partners had to bear a large part of the blame for the disaster.

We had grim assignments and we had joyful ones. One involved a group of blind kids during a visit to Melbourne by the aviation wonder of the age, the Anglo-French Concorde.

Security and seating was tight while the supersonic jet was at Melbourne airport and we could only watch as VIP passengers took to the skies. Taking a group of blind kids out on the tarmac to touch the sleek, silver bird was an uplifting proposition. "What the hell, it's lunchtime and all the heavies are filling their faces; why not give these kids a real thrill?" The security guards knew me and didn't see anything unusual in our taking a group of kids on board. When I realised that they were painting their own picture by touch, smell and sound, I decided the only way for the kids to get the full picture was for them to sit in the cockpit and feel some of the controls, then walk out on the incredible swept-back wings. We got by without a problem and were just leaving when a British Aerospace executive spotted us.

"You've had these kids in the aircraft and they're blind! You must be mad! They could have touched all the wrong things!" he exploded. Lucky he didn't see them crawling over the wings!

We organised Melbourne's most talked about penthouse party in Nathan Beller's first high-rise apartment block on the beach front at Middle Park and it attracted many of Melbourne's socialites. The party went for 24 hours and got extensive publicity. We had flown

Aboriginals from Melville Island in Northern Australia to stage a corroboree for the social set. For television cameras, fashionably dressed, heavily jewelled women about town danced to didgeridoo music with near-naked, heavily ochre'd tribal dancers. Beller, President of the Jewish Board of Deputies, wanted to publicise his real estate business and we did it in style. It did not endear him to the more conservative of his flock, but Beller was too taken with our consultant Meegan to care. He pursued her with intensity, but soon after she departed for India where she married a man who became a military hero.

In shipping, we handled *Flotta Lauro* and for the first time I got to spend more time on the passenger gangway than the crew one. One of the many incidents I had to deal with involved a passenger who unfortunately dropped dead of a heart attack halfway up the passenger gangway. Not in itself an unusual event, with so many elderly passengers going on ocean cruises, but it degenerated into a demarcation dispute between the Achille Lauro crew and the local Port Melbourne wharfies. Knowing that news media would be about as anxious as I was that the unfortunate passenger's body be removed from sight as quickly as possible. Sadly, ship's crew and wharf crew began a heated argument about whether the body should be moved onto the vessel or into a wharf shed. For several minutes the argument and the body raged up and down the gangway until local police arrived on the scene and accepted responsibility for the dearly departed. Luckily no photographers or cameramen had appeared during the unseemly ruckus.

Dudley does his Balls

There were underlying motives for males when the sexual floodgates parted in the sixties. The women's movement had just begun to mobilise its forces for the big assault. Males were being forced to take their first tentative steps on the long march to female emancipation. Bonking as many of them as possible was comparable to the Dutch boy putting his finger in the dyke. The tide was too strong, but we probably postponed events for a few years before becoming engulfed.

I had always put the women in my life on a pedestal, and was respectful, caring and attentive. Suddenly, all men were bastards, and all women were angels. While most of my female friends and acquaintances were happy and successful in their careers, the pendulum had swung wildly and the propaganda began to bite. Equal rights for women were long overdue and for many the situation has not improved at all, but like all revolutions it went too far. I could handle most of the diatribe, but not the ridiculous person speak: chairperson, spokesperson, barperson, personiser and so on, where would it all end? Would mankind become person kind, human become huperson, woman become woperson, womaniser become personiser, manhole become person hole? Would someone named Chapman become Personperson? Although I went to a female dentist and doctor, hired female staff on equal terms and preferred female company, I eventually became one of the first victims of International Women's Year. It was my second time riding the marriage-go-round, my turn to feel the heat. From an early age I believed that women were in control, emotionally if not financially. Take Dudley Moore. Channel Nine's weather girl, Lindy Hobbs, sent Dudley's temperature soaring and turned him to jelly. After promoting two of their Australian tours, I was a great fan of Moore and Peter Cook.

Their revue *Behind the Fridge* was a knockout and we had fun with the publicity. We had a giant mock-up fridge waiting on the tarmac when Moore and Cook arrived at Melbourne airport. Instead of coming down the passenger steps they got inside the fridge and arrived at a media reception as cargo. "Don't give us a chilly reception," quipped Moore.

When the Dudley Moore Trio toured a dispute was raging over the development of the Melbourne city square, which at the time was a demolition site. From a nervous music shop manager, we borrowed a piano, and Moore, in white tie and tails, played the classic Steinway on a heap of rubble in the middle of the demolition site. Later, we ran a PR campaign SOS Save Our Square, but it was not the city square we were trying to save. The campaign was funded by a client the Theosophical Society, whose adjacent building was in danger of demolition. The slogan should have read SOS Save Our Society.

A man who spent most of his life trying to save Melbourne society from itself was the Victorian Chief Secretary, Sir Arthur Rylah, regarded by many as the state's greatest wowser. Sir Arthur, like many self-proclaimed moralists, had a hidden side; he was most affable when pissed.

I arranged for him to open the *Top Hat* nightclub, the first licensed premises in Victoria to operate under a 3am licence. Getting him to do it was a major challenge, so we arranged a Secretary's Quest through one of our clients, Riddell, a secretarial employment agency. Riddell sponsored the quest for Melbourne's best secretary for the publicity, while our primary motive was to engage the Chief Secretary's secretary as the award presenter so that I could get close to her and Sir Arthur for the nightclub's opening night.

Once he had accepted, I needed his hat size, so I took his secretary to dinner and we finished up back at her flat, which was closer than I had anticipated. Why did I need the hat size? So a stunner in French maid's outfit and fishnet stockings could sit on his knee and put a top hat on him.

Why? Because it got us a front-page pic in *The Sun* to publicise the Top Hat.

The comedy duo in their hey day, in front of the camera

Unexpectedly, Dudley Moore called me late one night. "I didn't know you were back in Australia," I said. "Nobody does," said Moore. "I'm in a grotty little flat in Prahran." I hurried over there. It was grotty and it was little – not the sort of place you would expect to find Dudley Moore. Over a carafe of cheap red wine that seemed to go with the flat, it all came out.

While touring, Moore had met Lindy the weather girl and done his balls.

"I've come back because I couldn't stop thinking about her. I want to take her away for a few days, maybe to Sydney. Will you help me set it up?" Lindy was very attractive, and very young, and that was why Dudley asked me to ring her mother.

"Mrs Hobbs, I'm ringing on behalf of Dudley Moore. It's John Williams, publicity man for the Dudley Moore show. Dudley wants to know if he can take your daughter to Sydney with him. I can assure you that it is all above board, she will be well looked after, and they'll have separate rooms." Not only Peter Cook but also Dudley Moore

Mrs Hobbs was quite taken with Moore, and said it was fine with her.

I wanted to say "Well, to tell you the truth, he really wants to screw the arse off her," but I didn't know how broad-minded she was.

I really don't know if he did, but Moore was smitten, and he hung around for some time. He never seemed the same again. Moore reminded me of that species of spider with that weird ritual where the female devours the male after sex. Have you ever known a woman who gives you that feeling? Moore would not have made a big meal, but he was done to a turn.

It was no surprise when, in 1964, Moore went into group therapy in the US. Group therapy, of course, attracted more and more women to him.

That was of considerable interest to the producer of the movie Ten, who was in the same therapy group.

"In Ten I became famous by osmosis," said Moore in a TV interview. He spoke for many men when he made the frank admission: "I'm a dud husband." Moore could be hilarious on stage and film, but often deeply depressed in real life, like many of his fellow comedians including Marty Feldman, Spike Milligan and Tony Hancock.

When in May 1997 I saw the headline 'Dudley home for one more chance', two things crossed my mind. First, the sub-editors were still holding out against the capitalisation epidemic, and Dudley was still out of control. He had astonished friends by flying home from New York to California to be reunited with fourth wife Nicole Rothschild. It was described as Hollywood's most dangerous relationship. Moore was stepping back into a triangle with her HIV-infected drug addict former husband, Charles Cleveland, and her two hyperactive children. Sixty-two and still depressed, Moore wanted to "give it one more chance." He had married Nicole in 1994, a month after being arrested for attempting to strangle her.

Dudley Moore made a lot of people laugh, but inside was a lot of sadness. He passed away in New Jersey in 2002 after a long illness.

Celebrities and a Tragedy

As you can see, my life as a PR consultant was varied and I got to meet some very famous people along the way, as well as having to manage tragic events. Shortly after the events with Dudley Moore, I found myself having lunch with Marty Feldman and discovered him to be a most serious person. Quite different from the high antics of the comedian we all knew at the time. Part of it was the eyes and he seemed just as conscious as I was about them. I enjoy eye contact, but found it extremely difficult and our conversation became somewhat stilted, and I felt this made him anxious.

The son of a Jewish dressmaker, Marty Feldman, who was born in London's East End in 1933, left school at the age of 15 for a career as a jazz trumpeter but ended up in comedy instead. In 1961, Marty discovered that he had severe hyperthyroidism which led to the appearance that Marty is remembered for today. The disease affects the tissue around the eyes and is called thyroid-related orbitopathy We always got requests in advance about what visiting entertainers wanted to see or do while in Australia. Feldman wanted to play a game of soccer and to meet Bob Hawke, then the charismatic leader of the Australian Council of Trade Unions.

He and some of his touring entourage played with the famous London soccer team, the Show Business Eleven, so they were talented competitors.

We arranged a match with the suburban Box Hill team, and a few of my friends helped make up the numbers with the Feldman team. It was my first game as goalkeeper since being bitten by the dog in Wangaratta.

Several hundred spectators turned up, everybody took the first half of the game quite seriously and it was fairly close; then, in the second half, Feldman picked up the ball, scored a rugby touchdown and pulled down the referee's shorts.

When I rang future Australian Prime Minister Hawke at the ACTU he gladly accepted the invitation to meet with Feldman, but said he wouldn't be wearing shorts.

"Marty asked if he could meet me? We've been fans of Marty for a long time and Hazel and the girls will be delighted to come to the show," he said.

Hawke, Hazel and their daughters Susan and Roslyn enjoyed the show. During interval, I took them backstage and after the show we all went to Feldman's hotel. Most of us sat around on the floor in Feldman's room in the Old Melbourne Hotel. My second wife Bronwyn and I talked with Feldman's wife and Hazel and her daughters while Feldman and Hawke engaged in a long and sometimes heated discussion over Israel. Hawke was quite passionate about Israel and the rights of the Jewish state. Although Jewish, Feldman had a radical viewpoint on Israel, arguing that it had created more problems than it had solved.

They debated the issue for some time and the drinks flowed freely. When Hawke and his family eventually left, Feldman accompanied them to the door and, as the family were walking along the hotel corridor, said in a loud voice: "You Commie bastard, Hawke." Hawke laughed loudly and kept walking. He gave up drinking, drifted a long way right of centre, but still has the same passionate viewpoint on Israel; even a liberal Jew could not shake it.

Having worked with many entertainers and politicians as a journalist and public relations consultant, I got to know some of them well. Humility, the ability to laugh at themselves, and to remember those who helped them on the way up are rare characteristics among people who achieve fame.

Australian rock star Johnny O'Keefe was one entertainer who did have those qualities. We became friends, and he often called into the *TV Week* office in Sydney, singing all the time. "O'Keefe, you've got the worst voice I've heard," I would say, and he would laugh, but he'd keep on singing, always bubbling over, never still for a moment.

We did some weird things to get a story in those days, like interviewing O'Keefe under Sydney Harbour. O'Keefe regularly went scuba diving near the beach front house of his friend and promoter Lee Gordon. On a fine day I donned some scuba gear and followed him in. I hadn't tried it before, and kept thinking 'You're crazy to swim in the harbour – what about the sharks?' But O'Keefe just kept going, so I followed. We didn't venture out too far, just enough to get some underwater photographs to prove to readers that we had done it.

O'Keefe told me that his family, who had a furniture business, had given him a hard time for being a rock singer.

"My brother Barry once paid for me not to sing at a law function he was attending," O'Keefe said. "So you're not the only one who says I can't sing – most of my family do."

Barry O'Keefe went on to become a Queens Counsel in 1974, President of the NSW Bar Council from 1989 to 1991, then Senior NSW Supreme Court Judge, and later Head of the Independent Commission against Corruption.

In the late 50s, having a brother who was a rock singer would not have been regarded as a positive factor at the start of such an illustrious career.

"I think my family wanted me to follow them into the furniture business," O'Keefe told me.

"With a voice like that you should have taken their advice, O'Keefe." Then I showed him the *TV Week* cover picture that for some time he had been hoping would appear, having already featured on the cover of rival magazine TV Times.

"Whatever it is, you can certainly sell magazines." He kept coming back long after the cover picture appeared, there were others who didn't. O'Keefe died as fast as he lived, struck down by a heart attack in 1978, aged 43.

Robert Gordon Menzies also died of a heart attack that same year, but he was 83; both had seemed immortal. A decade earlier the gravel-voiced O'Keefe had survived severe head and facial injuries suffered in a collision with a gravel truck in the northern NSW coastal town of Kempsey.

But helping celebrities achieve fame was the only part of the job. There were sad times too and the Viscount 700 aircraft crash on New Year's Eve 1968 was one event that Howard Bull and his staff didn't want in our scrapbook. It happened 27 miles south of Port Hedland, in the North of Western Australia, at 11.35 am. The aircraft caught fire on final approach, the captain keeping it in the air for several agonising minutes before it plunged to ground and disintegrated in a fireball. All twenty-one passengers and the crew of five died in the inferno.

On the other side of Australia in Melbourne, we were blissfully unaware of the tragedy. It was lunchtime on New Year's Eve and we were at the pub getting an early start to festivities. I got the phone call and felt sick. It was too far to go home and pack a bag, so I went straight from the pub to the airport.

On the four-hour flight to Perth I sat next to a grieving father whose son had been on the fateful flight. Like everyone aboard the Viscount, the young man's life had ended violently, abruptly. We were on a normal, regular flight from Melbourne to Perth, it was New Year's Eve and the air hostesses still had to be bright and cheerful. I plied my fellow passenger with abundant drink and eventually he slept. It had been a moving experience, listening to his proud words about a young son, whose life had suddenly been taken away. We had arranged transport and accommodation for him in Perth, so we relaxed and tried to enjoy an event that few people experience – two New Year's Eves in the same year. We left Melbourne in 1968 welcomed in the New Year of 1969 in mid-air somewhere above the desolate heartland of Australia.

Arriving in Perth, we wound our watches back to 1968, and waited for 1969 to arrive. You have to fly west to another time zone for such an experience. The crashed flight was an *Ansett* aircraft on loan to MacRobertson Miller, a small Western Australian airline. My brief was simple – just keep the *Ansett* name out of it. The PR people for 'Mickey Mouse Airlines', as MMA was popularly known, looked after everything else. I never did get to the crash site. After reading some graphic descriptions in official reports, I'm glad I didn't. Flying is one of the safest forms of travel, but when a crash occurs it involves so many lives.

The fire that led to the tragedy was caused by a tiny faulty part in the cabin pressurisation system. Shortly after take-off from Detroit in a DC10, just such a tiny part caused the huge aircraft to shudder and shake violently. My first reaction was to look at the cabin crew seated opposite me and they had all gone white. For several agonising minutes it seemed as though our number was definitely up as the DC10 bucked and bounced like a rodeo horse. Then, as suddenly as it had started, it stopped. Only an American could handle a grave situation in such a light-hearted way.

"Gosh, I guess that had you all worried for a time," said the boyish sounding Captain on the PA. "Well, it had all of us worried too, till we found out what was causing all that shuddering and shaking. It was just a little old tiny ball joint air intake got stuck just up above you. For such a tiny part it sure gave us all a big scare. Fortunately, there's two of them so we've just switched to the other one. Hope you enjoy the rest of the flight." I never did find out what the next move would have been if we had done both balls at the same time. You sure as hell need them when you're flying out of Chicago.

On another DC10, on another take-off, and suddenly we levelled, dived, levelled again and then continued to climb. Different cabin crew, same white faces. "Sorry about that folks – we had to duck under another aircraft that's landing on the runway we've just left. I can't figure out why. Well, enjoy the rest of the flight." There were no aircraft going up to the Viscount crash site till the next day. "We're not going to Hedland until tomorrow, so let's go to a party," the MMA guys said. "We'd already been invited when we heard about the crash.

It's no good sitting around being maudlin, so let's go and party." They know how to throw a party in Perth. We drove out to a home in an up-market Perth suburb and our hostess greeted us at the front door, looking particularly sexy and Roman. She was delightfully draped in a white bed sheet, toga style. She handed a bed sheet to each of us, together with a handful of safety pins. "You have to take your clothes off before you come in," she said. Standing on the front doorstep, we pinned the bed sheets around us as best we could, dropped our clothes in a nearby bedroom and headed for the champagne that was flowing freely. It was a wild party; we got very drunk and turned our heads off aircraft. When they dumped me at the front of my hotel I was still wearing only the bed sheet. The metal grille door of the hotel was padlocked. It was 3am and the night porter was sick of New Year's Eve. I kept pressing the bell. "Piss off, I've had you bastards," he said.

"But I'm a guest," I explained.

"I've heard that one too," he said.

"I'm here with *Ansett Airlines*, because of the Viscount crash at Port Hedland."

"That's a likely bloody story."

"No, no, check the hotel register, you'll find I have a booking, my name's John Williams."

"Piss off." "What if I'm right? You're going to be in big trouble then."

That made him think. He checked the register and sure enough my name was there, so he opened the door and let me in.

"That's a crazy bloody way to walk around." he said, "Don't you wear clothes in Melbourne?"

Imagine waking in a strange room in another city and discovering you have no clothes. It took me a while to work out where I was and what I was doing. Fortunately, one of the airline PR staff phoned. It had been a great lark in the early hours of the New Year, but now they were sober. I couldn't buy any clothes because it was a holiday and all the shops were closed. I had work to do, serious work. Eventually they turned up with my clothes, I got dressed and, looking a little the worse for wear, headed for the office. We had a manual covering every detail of public relations activities in the event of a crash. One section dealt with co-operation with the media.

"Don't appear for one minute to be covering up, go out of your way to give them the facts. In doing this, it gives you the opportunity to get across the safety record, the flying hours of the experienced flight crew, the safety record of the airline," it said – don't dwell too much on the poor bastards who got killed.

I had had a number of pleasant trips to Perth. One involved a group of media, together with regular fare-paying passengers on the first air-conditioned bus service from Adelaide to Perth, 2724 kilometres across the Nullarbor. Across the Nullarbor is a misnomer; the highway only skirts the edges of the vast, desolate plain. It is flat, extremely flat. I know, I've traversed it on foot, by bus, aircraft and car. I haven't crossed it by train, but one day I'll get around to it.

Taking an air-conditioned bus from Adelaide to Perth with a mixed group of media and passengers is fraught with danger. We had no choice as it was an inaugural service. As it was, they got on famously after they had broken the ice, and there was plenty of that broken in the back of the bus. We had a temporary bar for the media, and the passengers got into the spirit of it. Everybody started to fraternise as the trip progressed.

The air-conditioning broke down not long after we left Adelaide. It was impossible to fix, so we had to continue without it. A tyre blew out at about the same time. The travel writers we had enticed on the trip were used to travelling first class with international airlines or on ocean liners to exotic destinations around the world. Travelling on a bus with no air-conditioning across some of the most inhospitable territory in the world was a challenge.

The food was basic – roadside cafes, steak, eggs and chips, meat pies with sauce. We took along large quantities of brandy, port, and various liqueurs so the media could at least indulge in after-dinner drinks. With three overnight stops on the four-day trip, relationships between media and passengers began to develop. Sex is a great leveller.

For most of us, it was our first chance to see Kalgoorlie, the legendary gold mining town in Western Australia. Apart from gold there were two other lucrative businesses in Kalgoorlie: the local two-up school and the famous Hay Street brothels, absolute necessities in an outback mining town. The populace was protective of its ladies of the night, but for some strange reason they wouldn't let them swim in the town swimming pool or shop in the main stores. The old media hands stayed well away from Hay Street, but not young Harry Landman, an enthusiastic Melbourne radio reporter with tape recorder always at hand. Harry decided he would do an exposé on the brothels. That was his first mistake; the second was to talk about it in a loud voice in a crowded hotel bar. A police sergeant was there within minutes, asking who was in charge of the media group.

"I am, Sergeant," I said.

"I want to have a word with you."

The sergeant politely informed me that if I didn't lock Harry in his room for the night and confiscate his tape recorder, he would lock him in the cells and "break his bloody tape recorder over his head." Harry took the first of the options. In a rough and tough mining town, the girls depend a lot on the police and too much media coverage could close them down.

The local police would then have much bigger problems – if there were no prostitutes in Kalgoorlie, the rise in sexual assaults could be astronomical.

Air hostesses have played many roles in my life and *Ansett Airlines* ran an advertising campaign featuring a real airline hostess, Susan Jones. She was attractive, intelligent, well spoken, caring, loved Shakespeare and other things intellectual; she was an airborne role model for all Australian girls.

We ran a publicity campaign in conjunction with the television commercials and newspaper advertisements. It was rare then – a happy marriage between advertising and public relations. Eventually for Susan there came a happy wedding day with the commercial cameraman. *Ansett*, still crapping on about hostesses being single, went for a sequel and the agency pushed it strongly; it was a second bite at the money cherry.

We said it wouldn't work, but gladly took the money and gave it a go. As it turned out, we were wrong. Jan Elliott was a winner; it was the pitch that was wrong. The campaign was copycat, when it should have been a new ball game, featuring a girl who just wanted to have fun.

The airline establishment watched her like a hawk. They got their knickers in a knot when we went to Perth on a publicity junket with a 'chaperone' hostess. The hotel got the bookings mixed up and Jan and I finished up with adjoining rooms, while the chaperone was dispatched to another floor. The hotel clerk had only surnames and assumed it was just another airline crew. We dodged the chaperone, went out on the town and worried the hell out of the airline.

That paled into insignificance compared with the publicity launch for the first 'token' indigenous Papua New Guinea hostess. "Watch the native waiters, they'll be worse than the whites" she said when we broke a racial taboo by going to dinner in one of the PNG 'white' club dining rooms. She was a strikingly attractive, intelligent university graduate who had lived in Canada before being recruited by *Ansett*. From the minute we walked into the dining room every eye was upon us, and I could sense the hostility. The native waiters looked daggers at her, while the white diners eyed me with that superior look. She was the first of a group of PNG females to crew *Ansett* flights between the mainland and the territory, which had not yet gained independence.

While many people got a laugh out of the pill episode, it has happened with many girls, irrespective of their origins. The company watchdogs issued the PNG hostesses with the pill as part of their indoctrination, and the instructions included the line 'make sure to take all of them.' Some of the new girls took that literally and took all the pills at the same time. When they found out they fell about laughing and fortunately suffered no after effects, literally or figuratively.

It was not my first trip to our neighbours in the near north. Papua New Guinea is a fantastic place for flying. My first trip there from Sydney in a DC3 took three days via Brisbane and Cairns. We had taken off from Sydney in a thunderstorm and the ever reliable DC3, returning from a major overhaul, was bouncing all over the sky. It was one of the roughest night's flying I had experienced. We were flying at night to enable the crew to build up their night flying hours, the one thing you avoid in Papua New Guinea. Flying in daylight is dangerous enough, as I was about to discover.

We took off for Lae shortly before dawn the next day and as *the sun* rose we could clearly see a myriad of reefs and shipwrecks in the clear waters of the Coral Sea. It was as calm as a millpond and the water had an unusual yellow tinge. I went up front and sat in the jump seat behind the crew. Looking ahead, I was shocked to see we were heading directly towards a sheer mountain range. Aircraft seem do that whenever and wherever you fly in Papua New Guinea. Why in God's, or the Emperor's, name would the Japanese ever contemplate fighting a war in such hostile and precipitous terrain? It made no sense at all.

The sandstone caves carved out by the Japanese in Rabaul still hold the answer to what was once one of the great maritime mysteries of the Pacific War. Rabaul was the staging and supply base for Japanese on the Kokoda Trail and in Milne Bay, Lae, Guadalcanal, Bougainville and battle of Coral Sea.

Coast watchers had filed numerous reports of major shipping movements on Rabaul Harbour, but every time the RAAF flew bombing missions there the harbour was deserted. The next day, Coast watchers would report more movements. Again the RAAF would fly a sortie only to discover the waterway deserted. In a daring mission Coast watchers infiltrated the port and found the answer.

The Japanese had cleverly excavated huge sandstone caves into which landing craft and other small vessels on bogies were transported along a railway track. During the day Rabaul harbour was deserted while Japanese vessels sat on bogies in the sandstone caves. At night they were returned to the water to transport men and supplies.

Approaching over the water, we were running out of fuel as we made a left-hand turn and lined up the wreck of the Japanese vessel that marks the end of the runaway at Lae. As we stepped out on the tarmac it was like walking into a giant oven. Not since those steamy days in the jungles of Venezuela had I felt as debilitated as I did in Lae. In both places cold beer in an air-conditioned club was the only answer. My host, Bryan Grey, then Manager of *Ansett* MAL Airlines, had other ideas.

"We've got a Caribou going up to Mendi in the Southern Highlands – it will be a good experience for you," he said, and next thing we were sitting on a cargo pallet immediately behind the Caribou flight deck. As we taxied out to the runway I noticed that the large rear ramp door was still down, and above the noise of the engines Bryan yelled "They always leave it to the last minute so the air can flow through and cool the plane." As the crew revved up the engines for take-off I thought 'They're certainly waiting till the last minute.'

Then off we lurched and quickly gathered speed. Bryan and I had headphones on, so we could hear what the crew and ground control were saying. As we looked in disbelief at the still open door, we both locked an arm and a leg around the ladders leading to the flight deck. Bryan was going pale and my heart was pounding as we lifted off and stared down through the gaping hole at the end of the cargo pallets sitting on their rollers. A Caribou on take-off stands on its tail as it reaches for the sky. "Christ, you haven't closed the rear door!" screamed the voice from the control tower. 'If we've got Him on board we might stand a chance,' I thought as I clung to the ladder.

"Roger, we read you," came the calm voice of the captain. "We'll attend to it when we level out." That's what years of flying in Papua New Guinea teach the good pilots.

Anything can happen at any time, so just stay cool.

Meanwhile all we could do was hope that the chocks holding the rear pallet on the rollers didn't give way. Looking back over the pallets, with the blue waters off Lae framed in that gaping hole, we were seconds away from the fastest roller coaster ride in history. Gradually we began to level off and as we reached the horizontal the door slowly started to come up. When we flew straight towards the cliff face at Mendi I hardly noticed, and the sharp right turn to land was child's play. Nothing could faze me now. Then I saw the broken chocks; only one remained intact, and I nearly threw up.

After the cargo was unloaded, Bryan and I supervised the closing of the door before we taxied to the end of the strip. At least this time we would breathe easier, despite the heat, as the Caribou thundered down the short runway, made a sharp left and flew away from the cliff face. That first cold beer later in the pilots' bar in Lae was nectar from the gods. The indigenous people of Papua New Guinea have many gods and countless superstitions and rituals and on four eventful trips there I ignored some powerful superstitions and rituals and incurred the wrath of various gods.

Between numerous flights in many types of light and heavy aircraft with varying degrees of exhilaration and sheer terror, I experienced Anzac Day two-up in Madang, spent two days and nights with a patrol officer moving an entire village from one hilltop to a more fertile one, and felt my first earthquake in Rabaul while making love. I swear to God the flight hostess actually said "Did you feel the bed move?"

The Australian patrol officer and I knew we had incurred the wrath of native gods when the landslide moved the road from in front of our eyes as we were driving back to Lae. When we slid down the mountainside in a sea of mud, hit the bottom road and our vehicle kept moving we said a prayer to all of them. Earlier, we had helped the villagers move themselves, their pigs, dogs and whatever was worth carrying to their new home. Rogue pilot Bobby Gibbes, retired Wing Commander DSO DFC and bar, got me into trouble with a native tribe. Gibbes has done many things in his long and colourful life.

He was a jackeroo, World War II fighter ace, hotelier and coffee planter. After retiring he sailed his catamaran *Billabong* solo from Egypt to Singapore, and also built and flew his own light aircraft. On a PR assignment for *Ansett*, I had taken a group of Australian journalists and photographers to Madang for the celebration of the recapture of the town from the Japanese. We flew with Gibbes in a Beechcraft Bonanza to a small strip near a native village and discovered that all the men were out hunting for food.

Although it was forbidden by tribal custom, he took us into a House Tambourin where everyone picked up and examined skulls and various artefacts. When the village women started yelling and screaming at us we all ran back to the Bonanza for a fast take-off.

While there have been many dedicated pilots who have achieved many aviation milestones in Papua New Guinea, others have given the hill tribes hell. It was a favourite trick of some to fly low over hillside villages and blow the thatched roofs off the huts. Others have bombed villages with all sorts of rubbish. When you see natives reverently tending the graves of the thousands of Australians buried in war cemeteries around the country, it makes you wonder. Many pilots have gone troppo there. Gibbes frequently ignored the regular radio schedules and refused to give his position.

I was with him one day when he overflew Lae by many kilometres and was preparing for final approach to the airstrip while way out at sea.

His instruments clearly showed the miscalculation. Sadly, Gibbes' distinguished flying career ended when his plane crashed in a PNG village. For a man who survived being shot down twice once in a desert in North Africa and once in a PNG jungle it was a tragic ending.

Running with Rafferty

I remember the local who told me "The missionaries came to our country to do good, and they did bloody good." Like many a good missionary, Tony Rafferty left his native Ireland to do good, and he did bloody good – nobody had run the 900 kilometres from Sydney to Melbourne. The run was a major triumph for the ebullient Irish distance runner.

In his native land Rafferty, through feats of strength and achievements in body-building, had become known as the 'Iron Boy of Belfast'. In Australia he has spent many years in the health and fitness business, mainly as an instructor in gymnasiums and has written a number of books on fitness and running. When he first arrived in Australia he worked for some time at the BHP steelworks in Wollongong, an industrial coastal city south of Sydney.

I met Rafferty when he asked one of my PR clients, the Pharmacy, Guild to sponsor a 24-hour non-stop endurance run around Melbourne's Albert Park Lake. I joined him on a few early morning training runs and we talked about doing something really spectacular that would get international publicity.

Tackling Australia's tough, hilly and winding Princes Highway coastal route certainly would. In 1971 the world running boom was a long way off; Rafferty was a pioneer of fitness, not interested in creating records but in being the first to tackle the most challenging runs. 'Run for your life' was his catchphrase.

In the time we were together, he inspired many heart attack victims to take up running; now it is standard advice from doctors. The

Guild agreed on the sponsorship fees and we flew to Sydney. It was January and I was to get married on the 10th in the middle of the run, having already set the date. We had added a charity cause to the run and had a team of volunteer fundraisers who would travel with us.

We had six support vehicles, several caravans and several hundred collection tins. Rafferty armed himself with seven pairs of running shoes. Before the long and arduous run was over, he would need a lot more. Rafferty was a stocky man, with a big barrel chest, which obviously contained a much bigger than normal cardiovascular system, vital for the punishing sport of endurance running.

We started from the Martin Place Post Office in the heart of Sydney. I was running along with Rafferty, but I didn't last for more than a mile before jumping aboard one of the support vehicles. Rafferty's wife, Elaine, our masseur Murray, his girlfriend Heather and several other friends were there to give support to Rafferty, taking turns running with him. They were all reasonably fit. I was a drinker and a smoker. I had switched from cigarettes to cigars, or I may not have done so well. Cigars didn't carry health warnings back then, so I presumed they were okay, and maybe it's all in the mind. Rafferty had been a smoker, and still had an occasional cigarette, but not during an endurance run, although there were times when he confessed he would have loved to have one. He also enjoyed his beer, wine with meals and an occasional port or two at night during a run.

His love of a beer had the media totally confused on the final stage of the run into Melbourne. While they were out in their radio cars, scouring the highway for Rafferty, he was in a pub at nearby Dandenong, having a few quiet beers before running into the big city; he deserved it.

His target on the first day of the run was his former home city of Wollongong, 45 rugged miles down the coast. Not only had he worked at the steelworks, but he'd fought a number of professional wrestling bouts there and had many keen fans. That first run was a harrowing experience for all of us, with traffic especially dense, particularly the seemingly endless streams of huge trucks. Rafferty ran against the traffic for safety; the support vehicles would go about a mile ahead, stop for him to catch up, and then repeat the process.

It was dark when Rafferty started down the final, arduous downhill stretch, an incredibly steep and winding mountain range, into Wollongong, running from memory, close to collapse, blinded by the continual glare of powerful headlights on trucks, tourist buses, and cars and motorcycles. I had struggled through a few more miles at intervals throughout the day and was starting to learn about endurance running, and a lot more about drivers and driving – a terrifying awakening.

Many drivers don't seem to have the mental and physical capability to react to different situations quickly enough. I had a frightening experience with motorists in Victoria, while driving home one night from Channel O.

A car struck a police motorcyclist and catapulted him across the road just ahead of me. Instinct told me not to stop immediately. I drove a short distance beyond where the accident had happened and parked a good way off the road before running back to see if the policeman was okay.

He was on his feet, and going to a nearby house to phone for assistance, cut and bruised, but seemed to be in control. The bike was lying on the side of the road, and the car that had hit him was just a few yards further down the road. "I can't move the bike or the car till I get help," he said. "Can you help direct the traffic around them?" I raced up the hill with a flashlight to signal on-coming traffic to slow down, but to no avail. Within minutes, fifteen cars had crashed end to end, because of the drivers' failure to take precautions. When the convoy of police cars arrived at the scene in response to the call for help, it looked like a battleground.

Signs and special lighting on the support vehicles ahead of Rafferty made it obvious there was a runner on the road. He leapt off the road many times to avoid cars, buses and trucks that were travelling too close to him. Running on the gravelled edge of the road, not in the traffic lane, Rafferty allowed plenty of clearance. Maybe some drivers did it deliberately, maybe some didn't care, and maybe some hated runners as much as cyclists. If he had given up that night, nobody would have blamed him. Why get yourself killed for health and fitness? We had known it was going to be rough on that stretch, and that was the worst day for Rafferty – or so he thought.

Early next morning we headed out of smoky, grimy Wollongong, down towards the clean, clear air of the south coast resort areas. There was still considerable traffic, but not as many trucks, and the scenery was becoming far more pleasant. The best monitor of pollution in big cities is endurance running. On a 50-hour non-stop endurance run around the city of Sydney for the David Frost Guinness Book of Records TV programme we discovered what pollution was really about.

The surrounding scenery is important for endurance running, helping to take your mind off what you're really doing. I was building my own stamina, running up to three and four miles in a stretch, and learning not to think about what I was doing. "Think about things that are totally remote from where you are and what you are doing," Rafferty said.

"It's great to think about things like politics, religion, take in the countryside, really concentrate, try to get all of your senses concentrated on anything but running." I am not into religion and I would run miles to get away from a politician.

As we headed down the coast towards the Victorian border, the scenery was becoming greener and it was easy to keep your mind concentrated.

Through the vivid green rolling hills of the dairy country down to the tall forests along the mountainous border regions, the world of public relations seemed a long way distant. Everyone should go bush at least once a year; go for a long distance run, take a month; it does wonders for the mind as well as the body.

Rafferty was running free and enjoying the challenge, while the charity volunteers were collecting heaps of money and having fun too. Thousands of people turned out in the towns along the route and their reception was warm and enthusiastic. It was a gutsy effort by Rafferty. The equivalent of two marathons a day, not at the same pace as a marathon runner, but nevertheless a gruelling task for any athlete. He was losing weight rapidly and showing the strain of the run. His spirits lifted when we cracked a bottle of champagne as he crossed the Victorian border.

Rafferty kept Murray busy throughout the day and at the end of each daily run. He was suffering shin soreness and having problems with his feet, but generally he was in good shape. One hundred and fifty kilometres from Melbourne he tore a leg muscle and we rushed him to the nearest doctor's surgery. The pain was so intense, Rafferty bit clean through a heavy towel.

The doctor advised him against continuing, but Rafferty desperately wanted to make it to Melbourne. He kept going, absorbing tremendous pain at times, slowed to a walk. Fortunately, the last stages of the run were relatively flat and he finally reached Melbourne.

A long, long way home for Rafferty

A huge, enthusiastic crowd waited in the city square to greet Rafferty, as he ran up Swanston Street he got a magnificent reception. It was the first time in Australia that anyone had run such a great distance. In the middle of the run, I had driven on to Melbourne and got married, returning to the run with my new bride, Bronwyn (an *Ansett* hostie at the time). She travelled with us for two days before having to go back to work. Both the run and the wedding on the run were worthy of the Guinness Book of Records.

I had acquired a taste for running, visited the great Australian outback again, and was ready to opt out of the stressful world of public relations. We started organising a run across Australia, but we kept it quiet because other people were trying to jump on the highly-publicised Rafferty bandwagon.

He had clocked up a number of firsts over shorter distances and other runners were envious. They did not seem to have any ambitions of their own; they just waited for Rafferty to make a move, then tagged along.

Despite our efforts to keep it quiet, news of the run did get out. We became involved in a race across Australia, which put incredible pressure on Rafferty and the other runner, George Purden. The publicity for the cross-Australia run was incredible, and we managed to obtain financial support from Kellogg's vehicles from General Motors and a large caravan through a friend. The distance, 6000 kilometres from Perth to the east coast, was a staggering challenge and to be forced into a race with another runner made it really tough.

Authorities had banned endurance races across America many years earlier because of people getting lifts in cars when they were allegedly running and playing dirty tricks on each other to grab the big cash prizes offered for such events. Rafferty wanted to establish new endurance runs and be the first to do them, while Purden had an obsession to beat Rafferty.

Although Purden had been running for a long time, he was unknown and he hated all the publicity going to Rafferty. In fairness, Purden was a tremendous runner, which he proved by starting days after Rafferty and reaching Sydney one day ahead of him.

When we learned that Purden was going to make a race of it, we decided two things. First, Rafferty would attempt to beat him to Adelaide, which meant he would be the first man to run across the Nullarbor. This was regarded as the hardest part of the run. Second, he would not stop in Sydney, whether he was in front or behind. He would run an additional 1000 kilometres to the Queensland Gold Coast, setting a new world distance record for endurance running.

Inevitably, there were claims of cheating by both Rafferty and Purden, some media reports being libellous. I had to appear in the Adelaide Supreme Court to gain an injunction preventing one such report from being published. We had an independent film cameraman and a sound recordist who monitored every aspect of the run. They testified that at no point had Rafferty even contemplated cheating.

At the start of the run Rafferty got a rousing farewell from a race day crowd at Perth's Ascot Racecourse. Thousands of punters lined the rails as he ran down the straight, out of the course and off on the longest run in Australian history.

Before dawn that morning Rafferty had gone with the camera crew to Fremantle to begin running from the beach. He wanted his run to start from the Indian Ocean and finish at the Pacific. Purden and his team obviously picked up this information because they went scurrying down to Fremantle and filled a bottle with water to pour into the Pacific in Sydney.

Flooding on the normally dry, dusty Nullarbor astounded us. In parts the dirt road was like a small river, quite treacherous for Rafferty, the Holden cars and particularly the caravan. We got badly bogged many times in that unexpected Nullarbor mud. Caked in mud from head to foot, Rafferty at times resembled Britain's famous Peat Bog man. He could rightly claim to be the first person to swim the Nullarbor.

After leaving Perth, Rafferty had run to Kalgoorlie and on to its sister mining town of Norseman. Thousands of schoolchildren turned out in both towns to cheer the gutsy Irish runner on. While we hadn't bargained on floods when we left Perth, we were prepared for other emergencies. Police had told us that a number of people had disappeared while crossing the desolate Nullarbor by car. Because of its remoteness, local and international criminals were holed up there. Only one police car patrolled the 700-kilometre Eyre Highway from Norseman to Eucla and muggings and armed robberies were common.

The favourite ploy was to have a vehicle parked on the side of the roadway with the bonnet up and flag down a passing motorist. Some travellers had been assaulted and robbed, others had disappeared without trace. We stocked up with shotguns and marine flares and took along my Doberman, Kelly, so we could cope with any eventuality.

One morning before dawn near the vast Fraser Range Station our fears were confirmed. The previous night we had been at the property and the owner had told us that the families in the district made regular day and night radio checks with each other. If there was no answer from anyone on the circuit all the others would head there, suspecting the worst. Showing us a frightening array of weapons, he was quite emphatic that he would shoot first and ask questions later.

It was 5am when we came off Fraser Range and on to the highway. Rafferty was running alone just ahead of the support vehicle that I was driving. Murray and Kelly were in the back seat. Spotting another vehicle ahead, bonnet up, flashlight waving, we accelerated up to Rafferty, bundled him in the car, made a U-turn and raced back to Fraser Range. There was no time for marine flares or shotguns as the other vehicle chased us to the property, and then gave up. We waited for daybreak before starting out again with shotguns loaded. Fortunately, there was no further sign of trouble.

The largest hardwood forest in the world surrounds Fraser Range and all of it is crown land. No wonder criminals on the run hang out there.

Rafferty had gradually built up the distance he covered each day from 50 kilometres in the early stages to around 85 kilometres by starting before dawn and running into the night.

Kelly was enjoying the vast Australian bush – it was a huge change from being confined to a suburban home to having the run of the world's biggest backyard. Dogs are not endurance runners, so like the support crew Kelly was putting in short bursts of running, then jumping back into the car. The run ruined the dog for city dwelling. When she started to dig up our backyard swimming pool we had to find a home in the country for her.

Lucky I spotted her, for she had reached the inner plastic liner of the large above ground pool. A few more minutes' digging and 5000 gallons of water would have come cascading in through the back door.

We had a set routine each day for lunch and dinner. The caravan would go ahead and we would take it in turns to set up camp, light a fire and have food ready when Rafferty reached that point. There's nothing like campfire cooking, even though most of the ingredients came out of tins. After leaving Norseman we found great difficulty obtaining fresh food. Australia's original inhabitants would laugh at that.

Many people living in cities have never really seen the stars. At sea, with Rafferty across Australia, and on other runs, I have been fortunate to see many clear night skies – skies that were ablaze with stars, dense masses of them stretching forever. Exposed mostly to traffic, radio and television, city people also miss the sounds of the night. Myriad sounds penetrate an Australian outback night. Just before dawn, the sound of silence itself can be heard.

Across Australia thousands ran with Rafferty. Many had suffered strokes or heart attacks and had been told to get outdoors and do some running.

Rafferty inspired them and me. By the time we reached Adelaide, even I was running 30 to 40 kilometres a day, unthinkable just a year earlier.

We knew that Purden was hot on our heels when one of his escort vehicles came to check our position. Our film crew waited for him one day and found he was within a day of running us down. To achieve his goal to be the first to run the Nullarbor, Rafferty decided to run the final 120 kilometres into Adelaide without a break. I clocked up my personal best by sticking with him for the last 60 kilometres.

We ran into a deserted city in the early hours of the morning. No welcoming crowds or media – just the satisfaction of being the first. The next day, as Purden was on his final leg into Adelaide, we went to the races to relax for a few hours. As we backtracked on our way out of Adelaide late in the afternoon we passed Purden running in. Rafferty waved, but Purden just kept running. We knew then he would go to any lengths to be the first to Melbourne and Sydney.

The running boom was taking off in Australia. In America it came much later, but not before we ran the outback Birdsville Track, the Blue Mountains from Bathurst to Bondi and 50 hours non-stop around Sydney for a David Frost television show, when Rafferty used a line that Frost couldn't handle. "I could be the first person to go to sleep while being interviewed by David Frost."

50 Degrees in the Shade

I first me David Waddington when Rafferty was running the Birdsville Track – a torturous six-day endurance test with daily temperatures that hovered between 40 and 50 degrees Celsius and at night plummeted to freezing point. The run took us across towering sand dunes and endless stretches of flat rocky country in four deserts – the Tirari, Sturt Stony, Strzelecki and Simpson – from Marree in South Australia to Birdsville in Queensland along the original rustlers' route that once filtered stolen cattle from the North to the markets of Adelaide. It was gut-wrenching, soul-destroying; it was run in a combination of modern running gear and Arab headdress to keep out the blistering heat of the sun.

We found our way by means of rock mounds – the beacons that guided the Afghan camel trains of the 1800s. The Afghans left not only the rock mounds to posterity, but also the camels of which some 10,000 survive today. Other introduced species including donkeys, foxes and rabbits abound, as do wedge-tailed eagles, hawks and falcons.

Waddington, a young producer-director, was seeking finance for his first feature film, and we sometimes mused about a camel for Spike Milligan, who was cast in the role of a hawker. Milligan settled for a horse and cart. It was a role Milligan was so comfortable with that he just played himself. It would have come as no surprise to me if one day he had simply disappeared out of shot into the bush. It would not have been out of character at all, for Milligan often talked about 'going bush.' His affinity with the environment was clear, for he was himself an endangered species needing protection and preservation for the future good of mankind. One of our most precious commodities, laughter has survived the ravages of war and the excesses of the consumer society.

Rafferty is another rare species although, sadly, Waddington's documentary film of his epic desert run never reached a screen.

Kellogg sponsored the Birdsville run, but in a fit of executive madness, the cereal giant could not, or would not, find the extra few thousand dollars needed to cover the post-production costs. Extraordinary scenes languish still on a cutting-room shelf, like Rafferty swimming across a turbulent Coopers Creek with fish and birds in rare abundance, the normally dry, lifeless landscape carpeted with swathes of yellow and white wildflowers.

Most times Coopers Creek is dry and dusty, but when Rafferty ran to Birdsville unusually heavy rains and floodwaters from the north had created a raging river five miles wide in places. The man from Adelaide would testify to that; we came across him and his Aboriginal stockman, a horse and a few head of cattle on a section of the track sometimes used by road trains hauling live cattle to market.

"Everything we had was washed away by the floodwaters," he told us. "I finished up on this tiny little island a few feet in diameter. My fellow inhabitants were spiders, lizards and some bush mice. Fortunately for the mice and me, survival was the common denominator. An RAAF helicopter winched me to safety just as the floodwaters engulfed our tiny refuge, washing everything else away."

When the flood hit his isolated property it swept away his home, his outbuildings, machinery and stock, creating a new river where once his property had stood, and he had returned to Adelaide to buy the horse float, a horse and a car to tow them back up the track to start again.

"It seemed better than going back to an accountancy practice in Adelaide," he said.

He produced some fine looking beef from his 'meat safe' – a hole in the ground – and under a glowing mantle of stars we enjoyed the tastiest barbecue steaks then slept on 'the track'. Rolling out our sleeping bags, we accepted his assurance that there would be no road trains through till midday the next day. You take a man like that at his word.

We had several vehicles including a military six-wheel drive Austrian Pinzgauer, two jeeps, a Puch racing motorbike and a trail bike, so we could have stayed and helped him carve out his new life, but we had our own challenge to complete.

One of our drivers was putting the Italian racing bike through its paces when he sighted us having a break at the edge of a large claypan. He gunned the Puch and headed straight for us, expecting that we'd leap aside. He was not to know the small patch of water in the centre of the claypan was in fact a deep waterhole. I will never forget the look on his face as he clung to the bike which slowly sank out of sight. Fortunately, we managed to restart it as soon as we dragged it out of the water, saving the rider the pain of having to sell his house to replace the expensive machine.

We got brilliant footage of the Pinzgauer tackling towering sand dunes at night under floodlights, with the vehicle ploughing crablike up the almost vertical walls of the dunes, clutching desperately at the upper lip, slipping, recovering and lurching precariously across the top, its tracks etched deep in the sand. I recall grotesque images of Rafferty, muscles straining, seeming ten feet tall in the heat mirage as he plodded through the oasis illusion that rippled above the searing desert track. As I peered through the lens of the camera, I wondered about those doomed ancient and modern travellers who perished in the region. How often that shimmering effect must have led them on, so real, so wet, so deceptive.

A crew member on a motorbike poured water over Rafferty's head while the runner drank hungrily from a water bottle. This was our survival routine, the one we had to follow religiously every 20 minutes to prevent dehydration. Running 500 kilometres from north to south, the Simpson Desert is one of the most unforgiving stretches of territory on the world's driest continent. Straddling the borders of Queensland, the Northern Territory and South Australia, the Simpson boasts more than 1100 sand dunes rising as high as 40 metres.

Running in waves, the dunes give it the appearance of a frozen ocean. It was not crossed until 1936, when farmer Ted Colson journeyed across it from West to East with Aboriginal Peter Ains and several camels. The desert has claimed many victims, including an English migrant family of five who died when they left their car about 45 miles from Birdsville in December 1963.

We filmed a thermometer in the shade of a tree with the mercury passing 50 degrees, exploding out of the top and flowing down the sides. Few creatures survive for long out there without water. It was our first night out from Marree when we encountered the mice, just a few hundred at first, but then a whole sea of them washing around inside our tent; we were sitting right in the middle of a bloody ocean of them. The next night we slept in the open, pulled the blankets over our heads and let the bastards run right over us. We had been smart enough to lock all of our stores in the Pinzgauer and by morning the sea of mice had swept on in search of food.

Pushing himself to the limit in the harsh conditions, Rafferty made Birdsville in six days and the whole town went wild in the local pub. Sitting on the Diamantina just above the South Australia and Queensland border, Birdsville is as outback as you can get.

Tony Rafferty kept running, boy did he redefine endurance, and I moved into the film business.

My Film Career

By this time, I was a free agent and, after talking extensively with David Waddington, the two of us moved into a small office in North Sydney where, alongside theatrical agents Jean Cinis and Martin Bedford, we started preproduction for the feature film *Barney*. The script, location surveys, casting and other pre-production work opened up a fascinating new world, with costs being of paramount importance. To get finance for *Barney*, we had to have our figures right for the Australian Film Commission, which had agreed to invest in the production subject to our getting a major US producer and distributor involved.

We started our negotiations with Columbia Pictures' chief executive in Sydney, Mike Tarrant. I set out for Hollywood carrying the script and budget for *Barney*. Plan B involved Rafferty running from London to Moscow and back, a run-for-peace project to bust through the Iron Curtain. Through Kellogg, I had set up meetings with its headquarters marketing people in Battle Creek, Michigan, and with the New York and London offices of its advertising agency, J Walter Thompson. If the London-Moscow run was too ambitious, we proposed to run across America. While in America, another plan evolved for Rafferty to organise an executive fitness programme for the Ford Motor Company. Executives at Kellogg in Battle Creek and J Walter Thompson in New York told me the Berlin Wall would be there forever, while in Detroit, Ford had decided its executives did not need fitness programmes.

It was no mean feat gaining floor space for Aussie Two-Up in the MGM Grand Casino in Las Vegas. John Fowler of the Grundy Organisation, prolific producers of Australian soaps like *Neighbours* and *Prisoner* and game shows like *Wheel of Fortune,* had asked us to come up with a special promotion to help launch some new shows in the US. A programme buyers' convention was being staged at the MGM Grand and Grundy had taken a suite there. I contacted the manager by phone and convinced him that Aussie Two-Up would be a novel attraction for the convention. To attract the programme buyers we proposed giving each of them a souvenir Two-Up kit.

For authenticity, we managed to locate several hundred 1930s pennies which expert players say are the best weighted coins to use – apparently it's something to do with the head of King George V1 being on them. Wooden kips for tossing and an instruction leaflet made up an ideal pack, but that's when everything went wrong. Because we packaged them that way, US Customs in Hawaii ruled them to be 'complete gaming devices'.

Much later, John Fowler found a home for them: one Anzac Day he gave the lot to the RSL and they've given a great deal of enjoyment to veterans ever since. I made amends for the Two-Up foul-up in 1981 when John Fowler asked me to design a corporate logo that would best project the multi-faceted Grundy Organisation. As designers often do, I turned to nature and discovered the icosahedron. With graphic artist Jenny Wiseman we took the natural crystal to finished artwork, with a surprising twist.

Around this time, I teamed up with Michael Berry and our first major PR client at Berry-Williams was the Government of Brazil. The assignment was to arrange for a team of Australian journalists to travel to Brazil to see the 'economic miracle' at first hand. A country known largely for its awful lot of coffee, Brazil was undergoing a revolution in development and growth.

Reflecting this, my sister's husband Miguel, the Brazilian Ambassador, had taken a whole floor of a building in the centre of Canberra to turn what had been a diplomatic-only post into a major trade centre for Brazil, and our brief was to make Australians aware of the potential for trade between the two countries.

Miguel and Maggie came to Australia because I had never had the chance to meet him. When he was offered a choice of postings, including Beijing, he chose Canberra. Years earlier, when Miguel went to Liverpool to ask my parents if he could marry Maggie, he invited them to the planned London wedding. At the time they had not counted on the London media. The headline 'The Diplomat and the Showgirl' attracted the media in droves and led them to decide on a quiet wedding in New York. For financial reasons my parents were unable to attend. Ultimately Canberra became the city where all of our family came together for the first time. My brother Joe and wife Madge and sons Chris and Neil and daughter Janet migrated from England. My mother and father lived with Miguel and Maggie and later took an apartment there and, sadly, both of them later died in Canberra.

Our second Brazilian client was the Bank of Brazil. We were asked to stage an official launch for the bank in Sydney, so we arranged for Premier Neville Wran and his wife Jill to perform the ceremony at a cocktail party in the Brazilian consulate. Because of his keen interest in Brazilian music, we booked Don Burrows and his group to play at the party and the night was a big success.

Shortly afterwards we started working as consultants to Facom, an Australian subsidiary of Japan's Fujitsu corporation. 'Computergate' was a political and public relations war zone and when it was over the South of France seemed like a good place to relax. Michael Berry and I submitted successfully for the Australian Film Commission campaign for the Cannes Film Festival and for associated activities at MIP TV in Italy. With my experience as co-producer on *Barney*, strong acceptance of our 'vintage year' theme and Len Evans as a publicity bonus we won the day. There are many in film and media who say nobody's yet come close to matching the 1979 campaign.

Apart from writing the back page for *The Australian*, Evans agreed to arrange and host an Australian lunch at the exclusive Port Canto Yacht Club. It was difficult enough then to get Australian wines into France, and the vociferous French farm lobby would have had apoplexy if they had known we planned to serve Australian cheeses, so we smuggled them in through the Australian Embassy in Paris. French Government officials must have thought the Ambassador was a wine and cheese freak. So what's unusual about that in France? Evans and I flew separately to Cannes and met up a few days before the festival opened. I caught a flight from Sydney to Cannes through Rome and Paris where I had arranged 24-hour stopovers, and found myself sitting next to a novice Catholic priest, also on his first trip to Rome.

As with most priests I had met, he was fond of a drink; we got quite drunk on the long journey and he was sound asleep when we started our final descent into the Italian capital. From the window seat I saw that we were coming in low over the Vatican and, quite excited, I started to shake the priest to wake him up.

"Wake up, we're right over the Vatican," I said.

"Bugger the Vatican and the Pope too, I need a pee," was his reply as he staggered off down the aisle. He may be the only novice priest to have urinated over the Vatican from a great height.

When we landed at 6.30am I caught a cab to my hotel, washed, brushed my teeth and wandered off into the holy city. With no sleep for 36 hours I was starting to hallucinate, seeing endless streams of Fiats as chariots wildly lurching through the city. Italian friends have told me since that it was no illusion; they get that feeling all the time, Nearing the Vatican, I was passing one of the many stalls selling religious artefacts when a stall holder stepped out in front of me and said "Hey, you from Balmain?" Now I knew I was hallucinating.

"I gotta brother Tony has a fruit shop in Balmain." At the time I was living in Balmain and I occasionally shopped at an Italian fruit and vegetable store.

"Yeah, Tony says to say hello," I said.

"You wanna' nice statue, a crucifix?"

"I'm not even Catholic, I'm Protestant," I replied.

"For you I have a special today, two for the price of one."

"No thanks, I'll say hello to Tony for you."

"Hey, you know Tony and you're Protestant, I'll make it three for the price of one."

I declined politely and instead bought three fine oil paintings from a street kid artist, and made a note to ask my greengrocer if he had a brother who sold religious items in Rome.

Still not sure about my mental state, I walked around the Colosseum in awe; stood transfixed in the odd sentry post along cobbled side roads; drank coffee on the Via Veneto, entranced by the girls in their Sunday best; threw coins in the Trevi Fountain; got drunk as a lord in a nightclub-disco and picked up my suitcase on the way to the airport the next morning. That was just a practice run for Paris. No sleep since leaving Sydney, but who knew when I would be back this way again? I wondered how my friend the novice priest was feeling. The magic of Paris gave me new energy and after dropping my suitcase off at my small hotel, I walked along the bank of the Seine, checked out Montmartre, the Champs Elysées and the Eiffel Tower, then hailed a taxi and asked to be taken to the liveliest bar in town.

"Champagne, champagne!" chorused the three bar girls who descended on me as I wandered into a dimly lit bar and strip show in a Paris back street. Six hours and buckets of champagne later in the early hours of the morning, I discovered I had run out of money. I had been buying champagne for the entire strip show and had been dragged on to the stage to join their act. One of the strippers, accompanied by a sinister looking guy, took me back to my hotel where I handed over $200 more in travellers' cheques to make up the balance of the bill, picked up my suitcase and headed for Orly Airport.

"Well, I've certainly done Rome and Paris over and I'm probably lucky to be alive," I thought as we headed south on the Air France flight to Nice.

I was off to Cannes and the coming of *Mad Max*, but first to the bank for some money. At least I had picked up some good column pieces for Len Evans, particularly the one about 'Tony from Balmain'.

Evans had moved from England, where he spent his childhood in Suffolk, to Australia as a young man in the mid-fifties. At Circular Quay he worked for some time in the Ship Inn, a 6am 'early opener'.

"Circular Quay was the seediest place in the world," he said. "Alcoholics going to work would pour into the pub. At 6 pm it was something to be believed. They fought for a drink. We had to stop a fight every five minutes." A connoisseur and 'bon vivant' of fearsome repute, Evans confesses to a strong liking for bread and butter in pan gravy. When I went with Len to a superb French restaurant just out of

Cannes one night he surprised me by blending a number of different wines at the table.

"I would have thought that was sacrilege to a wine connoisseur," I said.

"Don't be bloody silly," said Evans, "there's too much bullshit about wine.

It's individual taste – if you like it, drink it."

At the Port Canto yacht club lunch, Evans tore strips off the French waiters when they served some of the 'heavier' Australian reds in port glasses.

In the Australian waiters' champagne race along the beach, waiters from beach front restaurants turned in excellent performances in the soft sand, dashing 25 metres while carrying trays of champagne in glasses and it was a difficult race to judge – another piece of Aussie folklore in our 'vintage year' campaign.

Mad Max took Cannes by storm and the Mel Gibson classic quickly developed a cult following, with many journalists watching it night after night, then off to the Mad Max bar, the delightful Le Petit Carlton off the Rue d'Antibes. Thousands of journalists, stars and publicists turned Cannes into a dream factory but for a moment it nearly became a nightmare. While quietly strolling along the glorious two kilometre Boulevard de la Croisette in the late afternoon I was attacked by three muggers, but fortunately was able to fend them off and they ran away.

The incident was quickly erased the next day by the magic of lunch on a vine covered terrace at La Colombe d'Or Hotel. While starlets threw off threw off their clothes for the movie paparazzi in the Ritz Carlton beer garden, AFC publicist Rae Francis was trying to throw off Michael Petrovich who was acting out an intriguing role-a near death portrayal of himself.

"He says he's dying of cancer and he's going to commit suicide," said Rae with a wry grin. "It's getting very heavy; he says he can't live without me." Michael was one of those people who always seemed to be acting out a heavy role. A fine actor with superb presence and delivery, he was always cast in sinister roles in UK television and movies.

I had met him at Rae's sprawling timber home, with its spacious garden, on Sydney's trendy Balmain waterfront. The old house was a magnet to her wide business and social circle of actors, poets, writers, painters, sculptors, journalists, film makers, politicians, executives, advertising agency and public relations people and a clique of Leos. Francis had a male tabby cat that enjoyed a sexual relationship with her boxer dog that was years ahead of Sydney's burgeoning 'bonk it if it moves' set. The pair would have been a huge hit in Sydney's gay and lesbian Mardi Gras. After the initial shock, their David and Goliath act became just another part of the Wharf Road atmosphere.

Petrovich had worked with me on a new script for *The Hypnotist*, a feature film project based on an earlier outline submitted to the AFC.

"It's too much in the vein of *The Thirty-nine Steps*," said one of the AFC script development assessors when giving it the thumbs down.

'Damned with faint praise,' I thought when I read his assessment, which implied that I had been plagiarising. The script was original, largely based on my own experiences with Van Leowe, and I had never read Buchan's book, let alone the script for the Hollywood blockbuster.

Anyway and back on point, I've never seen my first feature film, *Barney*, which David Waddington and I co-produced for Columbia Pictures and the AFC in 1976. I even have a DVD, which I keep, without opening the box. Here's why.

Barney was the Australian film chosen for the launch of the major *Hoyts* cinema complex in Sydney, but someone stuffed up and forgot to invite me to the opening night. I did go to the cinema to soak up the first night atmosphere, with the cast arriving in horse-drawn vehicles, celebrities posing for the cameras, the glitter and the searchlights, but decided to see the film another time at a normal session; it didn't last long and I never made it.

In Hollywood the pundits say "Never make a movie with kids and animals, it's hell." As well as a child lead and a wombat, we threw in a shipwreck for good measure, but Waddington's casting of Spike Milligan as a hawker was a master-stroke that helped us maintain our sanity. If you're riding a motorbike down a country road and see the ghost of Milligan thumbing a lift, ignore him and ride on; whatever you do, don't stop, unless you have a sidecar, extremely large pillion bags or belong to Greenpeace. For Milligan had a fetish about aluminium cans that uncaring motorists have flung from their vehicles, further polluting our environment.

As dedicated to the environment as he was to brightening the lives of millions with his zany style of humour, Milligan was a zealous and active participant in stopping the rot. Each morning I picked Milligan up from his mum's place at Woy Woy, 60 kilometres North of Sydney on the central coast of New South Wales and our major film location in Glenworth Valley, 40 kilometres inland. I lost count of the times we stopped and of the empty cans we collected. I thought I had allowed ample time to transport our star so that we did not incur any costly delays in production, but we only just made it that first day. On meeting Milligan's mum Flo, it was obvious that his sense of humour had come from this warm, hospitable woman who was constantly laughing and joking with 'Terry', and it was easy to understand the close bond that existed between them.

Barney was a milestone production in the resurgence of Australian feature films in the 70s, before such international successes as *My Brilliant Career* and *Mad Max*. It tells of the adventures of a young boy in the early days of the remote British colony of New South Wales. Milligan played an amiable hawker who helps reunite young *Barney*, Brett Maxworthy, with his father, Lionel Long. *Barney* contributed significantly to the development of the industry in the 70s, bringing *Columbia Pictures* back to Australia as an investor for the first time since the 1930s boom. We completed it on time, for a modest budget of $230,000, brought the revolutionary *Panaflex* camera to Australia for the first time, and became the first production unit in the world to win an insurance claim against Panavision for lens flare.

After being cooped up in a tiny city office for months working on preproduction, it was invigorating to be back in the bush to film it. Waddington had chosen his locations well and we had spent several days going over and over outdoor scenes at various points throughout the valley, and we were ready for anything, bush-rangers, stagecoaches, hawker Milligan, mounted troopers, *Barney* and the wombat. As our convoy converged on the floor of the valley it looked like an early American wagon train with Indians on the warpath.

It was a memorable scene for me. Three weeks and four locations later, with a mountain of developed film in the can, it was over. Apart from one actor with a broken arm, suffered in a fall from a horse at full gallop, a confused and bedraggled wombat, a dispute with Panavision and a bankrupt production company, we and *Barney* were in good shape.

As well as chauffeuring Milligan, I had driven to Sydney at the end of each day with cans of film for developing, and then back with the daily 'rushes'. Up before dawn and in bed about midnight, I had held hoses for rain sequences, horses for riders, peered through lenses, helped set scenes, bellowed through megaphones, laid frequent chase to the wombat, pulled on ropes to help rock a full-sized square-rigger on a lake and a scale model in the surf, and appeared in a cameo part. It was Donald O'Connor all over, with a touch of Hitchcock. Columbia said the shipwreck scene was the best they had ever seen, and asked if we had shot it in a tank.

No sir; we shot it at night in a raging bloody surf with a borrowed priceless model ship delicately manoeuvred in and out of bloody great rocks by a bloody clever Royal Australian Navy diving team while a bloody smart cameraman and assistant kept the precious Panaflex dry as they floated through the bloody mayhem. That was another memorable scene for me.

On Long Reef beach, surfie volunteers had joined the rest of the *Barney* crew manning ropes and lights as the four-foot model, lovingly constructed to scale over several years, bobbed around in a ghostly light in the heavy surf, while Navy divers held her off the jagged rocks. Thank God I talked the two elderly model makers out of accompanying their precious craft to the film location.

At Old Sydney Town, off the Pacific Highway near Gosford, we had tied long ropes to the masts of a full size replica square-rigger and used muscle power to simulate the rocking motions achieved in the surf. Below decks we shot the internal sequences as the vessel was being rocked, and sequences from the two locations were joined to produce the final shipwreck scene.

We skilfully married the Tommy Tycho orchestra in Sydney with singer Julie Anthony in London in a unique telephone hook-up between two studios 13,000 miles apart, to produce the mix for the *Barney* theme song.

"Julie, we've invited the media for this unique occasion," I told the young Australian who was wowing them in the West End. "But nobody's turned up." "What's new? I'm an Australian," she replied. "If it was an American TV star they'd be there in droves."

Barney was just a good Australian family film, produced on a shoestring budget with a talented cast and crew. It got lost in the extremely complex and murky financial web spun by US studios and distributors. Many of the dreams of hopeful young film directors have finished entangled somewhere in that dubious world-wide network, in which all sorts of 'costs and expenses' are deducted as movies travel around the marketing and distribution networks. When the paperwork arrives back in Hollywood, many films are lucky to break even.

Stars like Sean Connery and Michael Caine have sued major studios over dubious returns from box office successes. In response to an inquiry from me, *Columbia Pictures* in a letter on December 18, 1978, advised that "as at September 30, 1978, only $13,500 of the Australian Film Commission's $100,000 advance had been recovered." My sister Maggie has seen *Barney*; with the appropriate US title *Lost in the Wild*, on Brazilian television more times than she can remember, so someone is making a dollar from it.

Rockcruise

From the first time I first boarded *New Australia* in Southampton I had been fascinated by ocean liners. Take the ill-fated Rockcruise. With his distinctive eastern European bearing, Kasonowski was a portly and greying man with a deceptively young face. He had a condescending look and patronising voice, the cigarette held between his fingers like a quill pen. "So, you want to charter an ocean liner? Any ocean liner, or did you have a particular one in mind?" he asked us in his office at Chandris Lines in King Street, Sydney, in 1979.

Michael Berry and I looked at each other, shrugged and Michael said "No, we thought you might recommend something."

Kasonowski's eyes widened, and a half smile creased his smooth jowls. "You want a big one or a small one?"

"Well, it doesn't really matter, as long as it's an ocean liner," Michael said.

Kasonowksi looked as though he wasn't hearing right. 'They want to charter an ocean liner, they don't know what size, they won't tell me what for – they can't be serious,' he thought.

"We just want to get some idea of cost," I said, thinking 'This guy believes we're not the full quid.' By this stage Kasonowski had just about chewed the end off three or four cigarettes, and was looking decidedly bored with the whole conversation.

Raising himself in his chair, he asked: "With crew, without crew, do we cater or do you?"

"Can you give us a cost for both on a daily basis?" I ventured, wondering what his reaction would be if I told him I went to sea as a galley boy.

He picked up his pocket calculator and started to add up some figures, fingers flicking cigarette ash over the desk. "With the vessel *Australis* a dry charter will cost you $55,000 a day and a wet charter $66,000 a day." That was it, the discussion was over, and he would go no further.

"We'll get back to you, Mr Kasonowski, thanks for your help," I said.

"Call me Janus," he said, thinking 'I'll probably never see them again.'

From the look on his face, that prospect did not cause him any great concern. *Australis* was originally America which saw war service as West Point and then went back into service with US Lines in 1946 as America. Chandris bought her in 1964 for service from Europe to Australia from 1965 to 1977 and renamed her *Australis*. Venture Cruises bought her and renamed her *America* for cruises out of New York, but that didn't work and she returned to Chandris as *Italis*, only to be laid up again in 1979.

The vessel then had three further names, *Noga, Alferdoss* and *American Star* before she ran aground and was written off. So, long before I was to learn about *Vindicatrix* being the ship with three names, a former Vindi steward boy was negotiating to charter a ship that would have seven names! Built at a cost of $17.5 million, *SS America* sailed on her maiden voyage to the Caribbean on August 10th 1940 nine months after World War II began with her name and a large US flag painted on her hull to guard against submarine attacks. As a Philadelphia newspaper published in August 1940 said: "Above all else you are sailing American Seas, under the American flag on an American ship armed with nothing but the Stars and Stripes."

In May 1941 the US Navy requisitioned *America* and commissioned her as the troop carrier *USS West Point*. She was repainted Navy grey which earned the vessel her wartime nickname: 'The Grey Ghost.' Her early assignments included a voyage to Suez to embark 5,353 men of the Australian 7th Division for Adelaide via

Fremantle and taking 5,526 American troops from the US to Wellington New Zealand. She then was assigned to troop runs across the North Atlantic. From June 1944 to June 1945, *West Point* made 27 Atlantic crossings carrying 140,000 passengers to British ports, Casablanca, Le Havre, Marseilles and Oran and returning with US wounded and POWs. Crossing from Boston to Liverpool in August 1944, with US 95th Division troops, West Point carried 9,305 people, the most carried on any vessel during World War. On westbound crossings she carried wounded or POWs.

West Point sailed on 145 missions and carried 505,020 American, British, Australian and New Zealand troops, wounded troops, POWs, Red Cross workers, diplomats, entertainers and other civilians over 456,144 nautical miles. In November 1946, a converted and repainted *SS America* sailed from the naval yards at Newport to New York, arriving there on the same day as the *Queen Elizabeth* which had also returned from war duties.

Following a racial discrimination claim by some of her workers in September 1963, *America* was forced into a lay-up that lasted till February 1964.

After suffering substantial losses, the United States Lines sold *America* to Chandris Lines for $4,250,000 with an agreement that she would not compete with US liners from American ports for five years. It was also on condition that she would be made available for war emergency use under the US or Greece as part of NATO.

The liner sailed from New York to Piraeus where Chandris renamed her *Australis* and spent nine months converting her to a one-class, air-conditioned vessel. *Australis* carried many European migrants to Australia and made a number of round the world voyages with full fare passengers.

Chandris sold her to Venture Cruises of New York in 1978; she returned to New York and was again renamed *America* and repainted blue with white topsides.

After sailing in June 1978 the *America* was arrested for failing to pay debts.

Because she was incomplete and badly overbooked, angry passengers had forced the captain to turn *America* around and head back to New York where 960 passengers disembarked. The US District court ordered that *America* be auctioned on 28th August 1978.

Because of the forced sale, Chandris got the vessel back for $1,010,000, returning a $4 million profit. Chandris then renamed the vessel *Italis* and planned some Mediterranean cruises. But the cost of vital repairs and renovations was too high and in 1980 Chandris sold *Italis* to Inter Commerce Corporation which planned to use it as a floating hotel in Beirut, but the project never went ahead.

Laid up in Piraeus, she was renamed *Noga* and was sold for use as a prison ship in the US. In September 1984 *Noga* was sold to Silver Moon Ferries and renamed *Alferdoss*, meaning 'Paradise' in Arabic. *Alferdoss* was later towed to the centre of Piraeus harbour and anchored there for about ten years waiting for removal to the ship breakers.

At this time she was literally a ship with three names – *Alferdoss* on the bow, *Italis* on the forward funnel and *Noga* on the stern and bow. A syndicate from Australia advertised for financial partners to purchase the vessel to save her, but she was purchased by a Thai company to be used as a floating hotel off Phuket and again renamed, this time as *American Star*. The company put the vessel into dry dock, where her hull was found to be in remarkably good condition.

American Star was under tow by a Ukrainian tug when she ran into a savage storm near the Canary Islands and the towlines broke. *American Star* ran aground in January 1994, with a helicopter winching the four crewmen to safety. She broke in half and was declared a total loss. Only the bow section remains but this may eventually be destroyed by pounding waves.

We did see Janus again and gave him the $66,000 deposit, and he could scarcely believe it. His opinion of us changed quickly and we shared a bottle of Scotch as he warmed to the idea. Later we became good friends and he told us about those early thoughts.

As he sipped his Scotch Janus looked at us quizzically and said: "A Rockcruise – we've never thought about that. We've come up with all sorts of ideas, including a cruise for homosexuals out of Adelaide, but never a Rockcruise."

The wreck of American Star in the Canaries (back section salvaged)

Michael and I had thought about it often, and everyone we talked to said it was a winner. So we found the investors to put up the initial $250,000, booked the bands and solo performers including *AC/DC*, *Dragon*, *Skyhooks* and Renee Geyer, and Janus secured *Australis* for the cruise, which was to follow her last voyage to Australia.

We had an impressive line-up of acts and an exotic itinerary including Auckland, Suva and Noumea, and there would be concerts for the locals in each port of call. It caught the imagination of young rock fans and was outselling all previous cruises out of Sydney. Sadly, we ran out of time, had too few ticketing outlets, the payment terms were too harsh, and our investors were reluctant to commit another $50,000 to save it.

With the final up-front payment to make to Chandris only a few days away, we had not made our sales target. We could not use passenger monies because we had deposited all ticket revenue into a trust fund to protect them.

In Brisbane a radio station conducted a public appeal to rescue the cruise and listeners made cash donations, but to no avail. "Meet the final payment, or cancel the cruise, said Janus. "You have no option." Our accountants tried to raise additional loan funds, but it was too late. After returning all passenger monies, it was time to move on.

In the City of a God

In August 1984, a dingo took 10-week-old Azaria Chamberlain from a camp near Uluru in Central Australia; with the baby clutched in its mouth, the dingo disappeared into thick scrub and the body never recovered. The Mother, Lindy, was later jailed, and then acquitted when it became clearer that she had been telling the truth.

However another rock monolith was of more personal significance to me that 1984. Easter Island, with its magnificent grey statues, is mute testament to a mysterious earlier age. My first sight of the remote island on my way to Rio de Janeiro made me feel more comfortable on the flight from Tahiti to Chile.

When I boarded the LAN Chile 707 flight I was taken aback by the plywood interior of the aging aircraft; it had the ambience of a Hollywood set. With its huge domed ceiling lights, it could well have been one of those 707s used in any of a dozen air disaster movies. It was an uncanny feeling as we lumbered for what seemed like an eternity down the runway to lift off.

The aircraft shuddered and rattled violently, and most of my fellow passengers looked as apprehensive as I felt. Finally, with a shuddering lurch, we left the ground. Those who were Catholics made the sign of the cross, and the drunken ones became rowdy, yelling and whooping with delight. Some jumped up and embraced each other, the Catholics and the drunks and the drunken Catholics, and I thought 'Maybe it is a movie.' It was 1977 when I first proposed a yacht race from Sydney to Rio round the notorious Cape Horn and here I was seven years later finally putting the deal together.

I also thought that the race could help to promote better understanding, more trade and more social and other links between Australia and Brazil. Apart from social visits to the Embassy in Canberra and some meetings with the new Ambassador, Marcos Cortes, things had been relatively quiet on that front. My sister, Maggie, her husband, Miguel, and their three children (and two Great Danes) had departed for Brasilia two years earlier. Since then I had focussed most of my attention on Rockcruze and Computergate. When Marcos telephoned me from Canberra to let me know that the Brazilian Government had expressed new interest in the yacht race, I knew the time was right to make my move. I already had a commitment from the Cruising Yacht Club of Australia to handle the technical staging of the race.

Apart from running Australia's major yacht racing classic, the annual Sydney to Hobart Yacht Race, the club had considerable experience in staging other coastal events and races to nearby Pacific Islands. The Cruising Yacht Club suggested that Rear Commodore Peter Drysdale, a Dutchman in his sixties, who had made Australia his home and yacht racing his hobby, would make an excellent Sydney-Rio Race Director. A retired home-builder, he would be able to put in the many demanding hours needed for ocean races to be successful. Drysdale was super-fit and raced the yacht *Sonya* of Gosford in most of the club races. He was an expert in race communications and safety.

For the Rio race, Drysdale gained the support of the Wireless Institute of Australia and its sister organisation in Brazil, the Pacific ham radio network and the Australian and South American Antarctic bases. One of the enthusiasts in the ham network was a Pitcairn islander named Christian, a direct descendant of Fletcher of the Bounty. As the start of the race drew near, we also tapped into the radio and other communications systems of the Australian, New Zealand, Brazilian, Chilean and Argentine Navies, the British Antarctic Survey Relief ships *RRS John Briscoe* and *RRS Bransfield*, the British Navy patrol boat *HMS Endurance* under the command of Captain Barker and the Cable and Wireless station on the Falkland Islands. The onshore facilities on the Falklands were put at our disposal by the Governor, Rex Hunt.

The establishment of this complex safety net put Argentina in a bind that delayed its invasion of the Falklands. Ironically, I became one of the first commercial casualties of that idiotic conflict when *Aerolineas Argentinas*, after being conscripted for the war effort, reneged on a contract for free tickets for yacht crews, media and others. Despite several attempts to redress the situation with airline management in Buenos Aires, *Aerolineas* put me in a financial bind: just retribution for delaying the mindless war.

Like many Dutchmen, Rysdyk came across as an arrogant man, disdainful of others. As this was a character profile that fitted most of the people I knew who raced yachts it did not perturb me. I probed for the more understanding and charitable side of his nature and was rewarded. As a child Rysdyk had lived in a small town in Argentina. He was keen to return to South America, particularly Argentina, but Cape Horn was the major attraction. Sailing around that barren rock is every sailor's dream.

Rysdyk and I agreed on a $40,000 fee for the club to be responsible for the technical staging of the race. I was to find overall sponsorship and make the event as successful as possible. For it to work at all we needed a Brazilian yacht club and that was no easy proposition. A recent riot by crewmen in the exclusive yacht Clube do Rio de Janeiro had resulted in the Whitbread round the world race being barred from Rio. The club had more motor cruising and game fishing members than yachtsmen. The prospects of it hosting another overseas yacht race were slim following the Whitbread experience. The only way to find out was to go to Rio.

Armed with letters from Ambassador Cortes and the CYC, I went on my first exciting trip to Brazil. It was one of sixteen trips in less than two years and gave me some of the most memorable moments of my life. My wife and I were keen sailors, often crewing in races on Sydney Harbour on weekends, and she was to be an avid supporter in what would become at times a frustrating and harrowing experience. My one big regret is that my brother Joe, who spoke Portuguese almost as well as my sister, never got there with me. Both had always been good at languages. I had learnt a smattering of French and Spanish, but had never studied a second language.

The cheapest way to fly from Australia to Rio was to go to Tahiti with UTA, from there to Santiago with LAN Chile and on to Rio with the Brazilian airline Varig. Marcos had arranged for me to make a courtesy call on the Chilean Ambassador in Canberra and he and his staff were extremely kind and anxious about assisting me. However, they seemed quite puzzled about my choice of that particular date to travel to Santiago. South American friends in Sydney had expressed surprise about me visiting Chile at all, for the regime of General Augusto Pinochet was one of the most repressive in Latin America.

Few people in history have abused power as badly as Pinochet after he led the bloody military coup against the government of President Salvador Allende on September 11, 1973. Allende had led his country since 1970 with a liberal parliamentary form of government, implementing a socialist society. It was ironic that Allende had appointed Pinochet as Army commander-in-chief only days before he met his untimely death. With CIA collusion, Pinochet masterminded the coup and then crushed Chilean liberals, arresting no less than 130,000 over three years. In 1974 Pinochet scuttled plans to rotate the presidency among coup leaders, and he was still in power in 1980 when I set off for Rio by way of Santiago.

After a brief stopover in Tahiti, including a few hours' rest at a hotel near the airport, it was time to board that memorable LAN Chile flight to Santiago by way of Easter Island. The Pacific is a big ocean and finding Easter Island without modern navigational aids is harder than looking for a needle in a haystack. Despite its seeming antiquity, our 707 aircraft and our obviously experienced crew found it with ease, although from my first glimpse of the remotest place on earth as we emerged from thick cloud, it looked too tiny to land on. Up to the mid 1950s the island had no airport and was resupplied just once a year from Chile. The sub-tropical island is only 12km long and 24km wide, and yet a new four-kilometre airstrip is an emergency landing site for the Space Shuttle.

The native population is Polynesian, but politically Easter Island is part of Chile, which is 3600km away. A civil war in the 18th century, Peruvian slave traders and introduced diseases had ravaged the population by the time Europeans first arrived there and by 1910 only about 130 of the original 7000 Easter Islanders remained. There are about 3000 people living on the island today and most are involved in the tourist trade.

We were not on Easter Island long enough to visit the statues, but there was a brisk trade in replicas at the airport. We had a far more relaxed take-off for the next leg to the Chilean capital and my first breathtaking glimpse of the magnificent snow-capped Andes. The drive in from the airport reminded me of all those dingy shanty towns I had seen in Central America, only this was shanty city, with poverty and suffering on a gigantic scale.

Immeasurable indignities and despair for one of the happiest races on earth, row upon row of substandard concrete cells, festooned with loops of washing, not a fresh coat of paint to be seen. Squalid, overcrowded high-rise catacombs swarmed with ant-like columns of people under gaudy banners mockingly proclaiming another term of office for Augusto Pinochet. Hung with military precision from street poles and public buildings, the banners marked the route to the central business district with its colourfully decorated shops and cafes.

You would expect that a street with the name Avenida Bernardo O'Higgins would be in Dublin or Belfast, not Santiago. A hero of Chile's independence, South American-born O'Higgins who fought with great distinction for the Mayans against Cortes' Conquistadors was one of many Irishmen who achieved hero status in Latin America.

Irish soldiers of fortune were active again in Pinochet's Chile, as they would be in Nicaragua. The CIA was again in bed with the forces of darkness. There were no mercenaries or even tourists in sight that day, only neatly attired groups of soldiers and police on every corner. The city itself was on duty.

As I nervously checked into the *Carrera Hotel*, I was uncomfortably aware that, apart from one or two staff, everyone was in uniform – extravagantly colourful uniforms of blue, white and khaki, top brass everywhere, with voluminous, peacock-like displays of ribbons and medals dangling heavily from ageing torsos. The hotel lobby resembled a military tattoo without an audience. This was no ordinary day in Santiago. I was beginning to wish we had not got off the ground in Tahiti. "From Australia", said the desk clerk, and I felt the eyes of a hundred generals fall upon me. After checking in, I hurried to the lift and up to my expansive, high ceiling room with its traditional period furniture and huge marble bathroom. The large picture windows looked out on a square in front of the Presidential headquarters, surrounded by more soldiers.

Two things caught my eye, the bomb-shattered roof and, oblivious to the pomp and power, the teenage couple passionately kissing in the adjoining park, quietly softening the impact of the moment.

The happy, carefree spirit of Chile was shining through. It lulled me into taking some photographs. As I started to focus on the shattered roof, I saw the soldiers again and hastily drew the curtains. Exhausted after the flight from Tahiti, I slept for a while, then showered, dressed and headed for the nearest bar. As I left my room I saw him sitting there, not uniformed, but with 'official' written all over his face, which he was trying to bury in a newspaper as I walked by. He would be there until I left two days later. I often wrote journalist on entry forms, hotel registers and other official documents when travelling. Sometimes it was good, sometimes it was bad.

It was four in the afternoon in a rooftop pool bar, and I was the only customer.

"Buenos dais, Tenor," said the bartender.

"Buenos dais. Uno cervesa, por favor," I replied, thinking: 'I'm going great guns.' Glad I didn't know the Spanish for that.'

The bartender sensed my limitations. "English?" "No, I'm from Australia." "Some of my friends are in Australia, in Sydney." he said.

"That's where I live."

"Going to be a big night in Santiago, the presidential inauguration, a big celebration. Many fireworks," he confided.

I wondered what he meant by fireworks. Under a new Constitution, Pinochet had declared himself President for a further eight-year term. The electorate would eventually reject him in a 1988 plebiscite, but he clung to power until March 1990. Chileans kicked him out when free elections were finally held.

A band was rehearsing in the adjacent restaurant. It sounded good and the restaurant looked inviting, so I booked a table for one for dinner. It was the only table for one that night, and I was the only male in the place who didn't have a chest full of ribbons or a uniform.

There were starched white dress uniforms, shiny medals and row upon dazzling row of coloured ribbons, as far as the eye could see, but the beautiful Chilean women outshone them all. I sat at my table for one, isolated in a giant Gilbert and Sullivan setting, ringing with exciting, incessant Latin American music.

There was a loud explosion outside the hotel, but it was only the start of the fireworks for Pinochet. Santiago was letting off steam as its overlord Augusto dug a deeper bunker in his dung heap of power. I dug into a sumptuous steak and settled back to enjoy the splendour of the night. You have to do that in South America: either turn off, relax and enjoy yourself or be constantly depressed.

I had been buying drinks for the band after they had asked me what Sydney was like for musicians. I told them they would do well if they could get there, and they made a special tape for me, in case someone might like to invite them over. They invited me to go with them to some less salubrious bars around town, and I thought about it, but I'm glad I didn't.

I've been back to Santiago three times since and never felt comfortable there. Maybe it's different now that Pinochet's gone. Nobody could tire of flying over the Andes, precipitous, snowy mountain peaks as far as the eye can see – a stark grandeur that only nature could sculpt. You get a similar feeling flying into Rio, the city of God, with its sacred granite monolith Corcovado, the lofty Christ, arms outstretched, giving his blessing to rich and poor alike; Sugarloaf, and the long, curving, off-white beaches of the rolling blue Atlantic, hills strewn with a multitude of chalk white villas and red and brown high-rise apartment blocks, interspersed with the ground zero 'favelas' of the poor. Christ by night, floodlit, emerging out of the swirling cloud, floating majestically across his multicultural flock, a million twinkling candles at his feet. Cariocas – Rio locals – take their cars up to the base of Corcovado and wash them in the spring water that pours off the mountainside. Christ washing the modern feet of the poor. Where would South America be without religion? "At the football," Cariocas would say.

"There's a crazy Australian outside who wants to run a yacht race," they said at the exclusive Clube do Rio de Janeiro.

I didn't dare say: "Former Scouse galley boy, now Australian."

Fortunately, the club commodore's memory of the Whitbread was fading. They deliberated for days, and did not give me an answer until the day before I was due to fly out. It was late afternoon when I got to the club, but it was midnight before I got the final answer: "Commodore Helio Barrosso and the Clube do Rio de Janeiro would be extremely pleased to join with the Cruising Yacht Club of Australia in staging the first Sydney to Rio Yacht Race." The Clube do Rio de Janeiro is the playground of many of the super rich of Rio and at no time was this more evident than the opening of the game fishing season.

It was gourmet butchery on a grand scale. A fleet of 30 or more big game boats had returned from the hunt and were landing their magnificent, silvery catch of giant marlin, sailfish, bonito and shark, glistening in *the sun* against the deep blue Atlantic backdrop. The exultant, gladiatorial barons of Brazil were downing gulps of Chivas Regal from upturned bottles; sweating crews hauled the stream of bloodied corpses to the scales. Tales of the big one that got away mixed with the drinking and the dancing. A montage of skimpily clad, sun-bronzed women draped across the multi-million dollar fleet evoked the carnal air of hot afternoon at a Spanish bullfight. Shuffling black women paused in their endless polishing of the tiled clubhouse patios to stare impassively at the members.

The Chivas Regal spoke volumes – not a single malt in sight. They appeared pretentious, but they were charitable to a man, for there's an irony and morality in the annual slaughter of so many splendid creatures. Once weighed and recorded for trophies, the tons of dead fish are flung into refrigerated trucks and convoyed around the favelas to feed the poor. The final destination of the carcasses of the splendid fighting bulls of Spain is not known to me.

When Helio Barrosso and three of his equally rich friends made their pilgrimage to the legendary lair of the blue marlin on Australia's Great Barrier Reef, I felt it incumbent upon me to entertain them on their way through Sydney. A stretch limo at the airport, a stylish cruise boat of suitably large proportions and lunch on the harbour set me back $3000. On the Reef, a mother ship, two game boats, a plentiful supply of aged Australian beef and fine Barossa Valley reds, with ample stocks of Chivas Regal, would provide them with a day's fishing and full board and lodgings for about the same cost.

Corcovado watches over the fabled city of Rio

For me, travelling to Brazil was a necessary investment to keep in touch with the big league in Rio, for the salubrious yacht club had opened a window to a different world, a world far removed from the humble Churrascaria where the not-so-poor ate. When I first entered one of the vast cafeteria-style eateries, I noticed the fat man scoffing away just inside the doorway. Fat men are good for business, and he could always manage the short walk to the cab rank, so he was paid in food to eat there. The flashing knives were disconcerting as slices of meat, barbecued at the open fire, fell on to your plate from swords held perilously close to your ear. The set price of a few dollars is considered worth the risk by the population of a city that has more risks than most.

Women tourists are warned not to wear expensive jewellery, especially earrings, in Rio for fear of muggers, particularly when going out at night to eat. Churrascaria – is that your ear, my dear? My first week in Rio was exhausting: the steep train ride to Corcovado, the precipitous cable car up to Sugarloaf; the frenetic gyrations of the glisteningly black, overtly sexual samba dancers; the generously heaped mountains of fechada – pork and rice with lashings of black beans – piled on your plate like a model of Sugarloaf; the sensuous smorgasbord of nubile girls stretched along the beaches of Ipanema and Copacabana;

the daring young hang-gliders soaring like eagles over mountain peaks and apartment blocks.

I was not aware the Brazilians had been in World War II. They didn't stand a chance, cut off completely somewhere in France, overrun by crack German troops; of an entire division of fine young men, not one returned. Every name is there, finely etched in granite in the chill subterranean stillness of the Brazilian War Memorial.

Some say there are more Australian gum trees there than there are in Australia. Without Rio, Australia as we know it would not exist, for the voyage of the First Fleet almost ended in Rio. The vessels were stranded there for a month, while Captain Phillip, who fortunately had served as a captain in the Portuguese Navy and later with the Portuguese Viceroy, negotiated the fresh supplies so desperately needed to build up the strength of the ragged crew and its frail human cargo. It was enough meat, fruit and vegetables for an entire army. The British Government would have refused to pay the full price, leaving the fleet to founder, but Phillip talked his way out of paying the fees.

Although the poor wretches were below decks, anchored a mile offshore, miraculously, only one of the convicts died there. None of them were able to see the beautiful city.

The First Fleet ran out of fresh meat 500 miles out of Rio Some of those on board never made it; those who did survived by eating flying fish. Thanks to Phillip's Portuguese connections, much-needed repairs were made in Rio, enabling the fleet to complete its epic voyage to Botany Bay. A transpacific flora interchange began with the First Fleet, with sixteen Brazilian orange trees taken on board for planting in Australia, and it continued on hundreds of subsequent voyages, sometimes by design, at other times by accident.

Seeds of the jacaranda tree were carried in the clothing and on the footwear of the crews of the many ships that journeyed backwards and forwards via Rio. The first wheat to be grown in Australia was from seed transported from Brazil. Queensland gum trees abound in the north of Brazil, Tasmanian gums in the south, and an Australian continental mix in the middle.

Approaching the capital, Brasilia, is uncannily like driving into Canberra; located in the central highlands, 1194 kilometres from

Rio, it was founded on April 21, 1960, the third federal capital after Salvador in the colonial period and Rio from 1808 to 1960. Inserted in all Brazilian constitutions, the idea of an inland capital came as a direct result of continuing invasions and harassment by the Dutch, the British and the French from the 16th century. The construction of Brasilia was not just the building of a new capital. To integrate and bring together a country of 8.5 million square kilometres and more than 100 million people, work started on a huge road network at the same time. Set in the middle of dense jungle, Brasilia began from the air with parachute drops of materials to build the airstrip that became the gateway for equipment and building materials. Construction took a record three years, comparing favourably with nine years for Washington. Driving out to Maggie and Miguel's farm at Santa Antonio, 60 miles from Brasilia, I passed between rows of Australian gum trees of astounding growth. I have been to the farm several times and marvelled at the ingenuity of the family, making their own bricks and building it themselves. It was their opportunity to escape the vast concrete canyons of Brasilia, an architecturally stimulating but socially drab tropical version of Moscow – block after block of pre-cast concrete units.

Everyone says if you are money-hungry, get into gold, but I'd say get into concrete. There's infinitely more of it on the surface of Earth than there is gold under it. While the crown-like cathedral of Brasilia is a spectacular concrete salute to the Catholic faith, it's the kilometre-long university building that impresses, as roller skating students and academic staff mill around it.

We spent a Christmas on the farm. Miguel killed a pig and I dug a pit to roast it in. At the Embassy residence in Canberra, Maggie and Miguel had two Great Danes that were built like mountain lions, and my sister was breeding more of them at the farm. While the pig was slowly cooking, a small but deadly jararaca snake bit two of the dogs. We nursed them through the night in a real-life nativity scene, one of them giving birth as it fought for life.

One of the newborn litter died, while the others survived. Everyone trod warily for the next few days. It's only small, but the jararaca is the deadliest snake in the world. There were deadly people around, too. The Santa Antonio region looked a bit like the Nullarbor, and Miguel had nearly as many guns as we'd seen at Fraser Range. With its dirt road and wooden side walks the main street of the pocket-sized town was like a scene from the early American West. Roughly cut beef carcasses, swarming with flies as they hung outside butchers' shops in the dusty street, reinforced the frontier image.

It is reported that in 1385 a Portuguese heroine named Almeida killed a contingent of seven soldiers in Spain with a baker's shovel. If any of the bandit gangs roaming the region in Volkswagens had turned up during the night a shovel would not have been much use to the Ozorio de Almeida family, but Miguel had one gun that would have blown a Volkswagen apart. The former Portuguese colony is like that. Miguel could tell a good yarn. Irish jokes are not just Irish; they are international, because Brazilians tell the same stories about the Portuguese or the Argentinans.

True stories are the best, of course, like the time Miguel told his next door neighbour that Great Danes ate cats. His neighbour didn't believe him, so to prove Miguel wrong he brought his cat over, sat it in front of a Great Dane and the dog promptly ate it.

"Why did you let it do that?" the distraught neighbour whined.

"But it was you who brought the cat," replied Miguel.

When we went for long walks at night before retiring, Miguel always took a gun with him. I wondered if it was for the bandits, or was his neighbour still sore about the cat? There were other cats around, fleet-footed jaguars; we looked for them, but never found one. When my mother and father stayed there on two occasions they had been a bit nervous and I understood why. Brazil is a lot different to Liverpool – a lot different to most places.

The 8600-nautical mile Sydney to Rio yacht race went too far for many, an event too dangerous for most. To those who were brave enough to face the challenge we said: 'Each yacht sails with the sure knowledge that it has to be completely self-contained, self-reliant, that it is sailing into an area of potential maximum risk with no help available other than the skills and courage of its crew. If you fall overboard down there, you are dead. Life expectancy in the freezing waters is about five minutes – not enough time for a yacht to turn and rescue anyone.'

While we had no major drama in the race to Rio, the Whitbread, the BOC Challenge and other events around Cape Horn have all seen tragic loss of life.

When French yachtswoman Isabelle Autissier stared death in the face in the Southern Ocean in January 1995, prompt action by the Australian Navy and Air Force resulted in her rescue from mountainous seas. Plucked from her disabled yacht by a naval helicopter, Autissier praised the international conventions that commit all nations to rescue operations in such circumstances. The BOC single-handed race is one of the few remaining tests of character and courage in a world gone soft on televised armchair spectator sport.

Headline-seeking politicians who complained about the cost of Autissier's rescue, as well as friends and relatives of crew on the rescue vessel *HMAS Darwin* who complained about cancelled shore leave, did Australia no credit. The swift success of the rescue effort did, and for those involved it was an invaluable experience. No more, no less than Australians would have expected of New Zealand, Britain, Chile, Brazil and Argentina when a large number of their own, including a boatload of teenagers, faced the challenge of their lives in the race around the Horn in 1982. Since this we have had the miraculous rescues of Frenchman Thierry Dubois and Britain's Tony Bullimore.

Predictably, out from their seats in front of the telly once again came the whingers. 'Wasting taxpayers' money again' was the mournful cry. What a load of miserable people they are, and they never get it right. No amount of money could ever bring to Australia's defence forces the experience and expertise acquired from that one mission.

In worldwide goodwill, the dramatic rescues of Dubois and Bullimore were two of the best investments Australia has ever made. There were also the so-called yachting experts who said the race was too dangerous. With the base of Mt Everest now resembling a Butlin's holiday camp, mankind has few physical peaks left to challenge. We should salute the likes of Dubois and Bullimore for reminding the world that there are still some alternatives to boring yourself to death with television or the Internet. Oswaldo Bighi would testify to that. In a token gesture by the Brazilian Navy Minister, Rio naval cadet Bighi was given the opportunity to join the young Australian crew of Buccaneer. The Brazilian naval sail training vessel Cisne Branco, formerly the American racing yacht Ondine, was entered for the race, but the Minister withdrew it on safety grounds. I pleaded with him to keep the sole Brazilian entry in the race for the sake of national pride, but it was too big a risk politically.

To sail around Cape Horn was a challenge that Australian journalist Philip Cornford could not resist:

Down here at latitude 60 degrees south, as Anaconda II sails into iceberg country, it gets so cold it burns. Icebergs are all around us, some of them huge floating mountains which dwarf all preconceived ideas of the size and majesty.

The biggest we saw, as Anaconda sailed into flurries of snow and sleet, was more than 1km long, a flat-topped plateau which soared 150m in a sheer cliff face. It was all sharp edges, chiselled by a bitter wind. The waves breaking against it turned a brilliant translucent blue, backlit by the ice.

The big bergs filled us with awe at the forces which cast them adrift, but it is the smaller icebergs which cause us the most alarm. Some of them protrude only 2m above the sea, and we keep a sharp lookout 24 hours a day. Iron-hard ice would rip Anaconda open. But it is the wind pushing the monsters north which torments us the most: a chill, numbing breath from the great ice continent below. It blows all the way across the Southern Ocean to Cape Horn, and feeling its sting the Spanish explorers evocatively named the tip of South America Tierra del Fuego Land of Fire.

The same wind sears our exposed flesh, freeze-burning a chill through to the bone. With the temperature wind-chilled to minus 15C, it takes merely seconds for fingers to stiffen into claws as hands begin to sting. The pain becomes so intense that men curse, whimper and cry out without shame. Then, as the cold bites deep, the flesh begins to burn. It burns to haul down a frozen spinnaker and replace it with a genoa. It burns to haul on a sheet. It burns to hoist a staysail, work a winch or reef a mainsail glazed with ice. We worked furiously to do all this yesterday, producing a furnace of body heat beneath our protective clothing, until our chests steamed. And all the time, for the two hours it took, our hands.(At this point, radio contact with the yacht was lost).

Before the race Cornford had written:

For all the problems the yachts will face at sea, getting them there has been a great personal triumph for the man who conceived the race. Williams began on his lonesome in 1979.

A FORTUNATE LIFE

Reading the account of a day in the life of 19 year old crew member Dougal Kennedy made all the effort worthwhile:

We set sail from Sydney Harbour at lunchtime on a lovely sunny January day. I remember the feeling: the excitement, the tenseness, the butterflies in the stomach, the crowds waving us off.

I was no novice to sailing I'd been doing it since I was eight years old, and had my own boat at 10 which I'd saved up for out of paper-round money (although having saved up the money, my uncle bought it for me an eight-and-a-half foot trainee sail boat). How I got into the race was a bit of a fluke. I was a cadet builder for a man who owned a yacht, had bought all the gear and was entered for the race when he had to withdraw. So he recommended me to the skipper of Anaconda II, Josko Grubic, as his replacement. Not all of the 15-man crew had had sailing experience. A couple were beginners, although we all had to prove ourselves regardless. The important qualifying factors were: the ability to get on with other people, self-motivation and a quick wit. We would need all of them! "There were certainly times when I got lonely, when I thought: 'Oh God! I want to go home'.

We all had those moments. One of them sticks out vividly in my mind. We were six days away from rounding Cape Horn, and becalmed. It was freezing and we were all irritable and wondering what on earth we were doing there. Those were the times when the odd argument broke out. It was inevitable, really, living as we were in close proximity to each other 24 hours a day; the odd frustration would break through. But that didn't happen too often. And the trip did so much for me much more than I ever would have thought. It was much harder, both physically and mentally, than anything I'd anticipated, and there were moments of real loneliness. But I learned to cope. And I learned to appreciate the simple things in life, like warm beds and clothes, and chocolate, which was worth its weight in gold! And which I had not thought to take, so that I had to sell, or barter other items for some when I got desperate. We all had our little superstitions. At one time, when we cast our fishing lures behind the boat, we were worried an albatross would get caught in them and die they were flying around at the time. It's an old sailors' superstition that if you kill an albatross, then bad luck will follow. I also took along my two little toy koalas that I'd been given when I was a kid, to bring me luck. I was lucky enough, though, just to be on the boat and see the things I saw.

Like the Southern Lights which I never expected to see and which were so spectacular, like white flashes of fire in the night sky. And seeing my first iceberg in the Southern Ocean. That was so eerie. Just this huge silent block of ice floating about 150 metres high in the ocean, with these amazing colours in it, ranging from pure white to deep, deep blue, with light blue and grey shades streaked through it. And rounding Cape Horn, which is every sailor's dream, and which was one of the main reasons I wanted to enter the race. The fact that we rounded it in a gale force 12 wind with 12-metre high waves just made it more exciting. We even saw the lighthouse on the Horn, which is unusual as it's normally shrouded in fog. Then there was the sheer elation of arriving at last in Rio.

We pulled in at mid-day to welcoming crowds, brilliant sunshine and an enormous lunch right on the mooring followed by a fantastic samba show at night in which we all took part, including the crew from the winning yacht. But in all this, I haven't really talked about my day, have I? I'd start at 1 am, because we didn't really have a working day as such. We had a continuous 24-hour rota, three hours on watch, three hours off throughout the race. For example, I would be on watch from 1am to 4 am.

A normal watch activity would be trimming the sails, changing them according to the wind, and general boat maintenance, cleaning it up, looking after it as you would a home. Then at 4 am it was back down to bed. It took about twenty minutes to get undressed and twenty minutes to get dressed again at each watch. We had so many layers of clothes to take off, hang up to dry, then put back on when we got up. There was the thermal underwear first, followed by the polar suit a sort of synthetic wool, non-moisture absorbing one-piece; followed by a woollen shirt, jeans, woollen jumper, two layers of wet-weather gear lined with insulation to keep cold out; sea boots, balaclavas, gloves, and, often, goggles. We were aptly described at one point as looking like blown up Michelin men. Anyway, the three-hour watches with three hours breaks for sleep and eating went on pretty much the same each day. We also had to make time, at some point every day during our breaks, to mend any torn sails.

The only real problem was that we were restricted on hot drinks, to conserve water and fuel. That meant only three hot drinks a day with our meals no odd cups of coffee, which was a bit of a shame! I stayed on in Rio for a couple of weeks sightseeing, working on the boat, and generally relaxing, before coming home.

It was a funny feeling. I was elated and sad. We had all become very close during our time at sea, and here we were, going our separate ways. It was over. But it's by no means finished. I'll do it again, believe me!

"To me a big, beautiful boat is like a big, beautiful woman," said 57 year old Josko Grubic, owner and skipper of the yacht that carried young Kennedy round the Horn. The largest racing yacht in the world, *Anaconda* nearly killed the tall, tanned Yugoslav refugee with *the sun* bleached hair and pierced earlobe. At its launch in 1975, the 25 metre yacht broke her cradle, and fell on Grubic, who was drinking champagne at the time, and he suffered a broken skull, leg and ribs.

Grubic should have been in hospital for months, but in three weeks he had checked himself out and was supervising repairs to *Anaconda* from a wheelchair. While waiting on a skull operation, Grubic sailed in the Clipper Race from Sydney to London round the Horn. One stormy night, 725 kilometres south of Buenos Aires, *Anaconda* was tossed upside down by 18 metre waves.

"I was upside down too, with my head jammed against the hatch. All I was worried about was the hole in my skull. I thought I'd really had it this time, my head would be smashed. I yelled out: 'Come back, bitch!' Finally she did, threw me upright and righted herself. It was the longest minute in my life, eternity." Grubic's adventurous attitude and determination was a big help to me in organising the yacht race over what seemed like the longest three years in my life. He was with me at various stages, including a promotional tour of Australian yacht clubs.

Australia and Brazil have many similarities, but in some ways are poles apart. The most obvious difference is the language, and overcoming that will take time. Australians and Brazilians are two of a kind in the southern hemisphere, with similar seasons, similar climates and the same love of the great outdoors – harsh lands, with big coastal populations, sandy beaches, surf, the bush, barbecues, fanatical about sport, former colonial outposts, fiercely independent. Both wear green and gold as their national colours and are equally rich with resources and often competitive in world trade. Yet to make their relations more than superficial, both have found it hard to shake off the yoke of the northern hemisphere.

What was once the tyranny of distance is just an illusion fostered by northern hemisphere airlines, which have hoodwinked us into flying around the widest circumferences of our planet. Some flights from Sydney to Rio take up to 56 hours through the US, yet it 's a mere 10 hours away by 747, not as the crow flies but as the planet curves. Run a piece of string around the globe and plot the shortest distance between countries and you will get the southern hemisphere in perspective. I have flown to Rio in 13 hours through New Zealand and Argentina.

It's possible to fly from Sydney to Rio in 10 hours, but *Qantas* says it will not start a direct service because not enough people want to fly there. How can they know if the service doesn't exist?

Thanks to former Australian Trade Minister Doug Anthony, I broke through the Kangaroo route curtain in 1983, and got approval for six return flights between Sydney and Rio.

Doug Anthony was one of the few Australian politicians to comprehend the potential of an Australia-Brazil trading alliance. The Japanese have always played one country off against the other in trading of resources such as iron ore. As with the oil-producing countries of the Middle East, Australia and Brazil should maintain a ruling price for iron ore. In Brazil, Doug Anthony and I discussed this, along with a wider concept for resources trading by the three major southern hemisphere suppliers – Australia, South America and South Africa. Between them, the three regions provided much of the raw materials for the northern hemisphere. Bad management by successive governments had not only allowed the northern hemisphere to gain financial control, but to exploit the situation further through political and business dealings that maintain the status quo.

There was enormous potential for trade agreements that would enable the three southern hemisphere giants to gain a greater share of world wealth. The proposed charters in 1983 were programmed into the *Qantas* system. The first flight in each direction would have been substantially filled by government and business groups from both countries, with conferences, seminars and exhibitions being staged simultaneously in Australia and Brazil. Final approval for the flights involved reciprocal rights and at that time the Brazilian national carrier Varig had no spare capacity. Varig was hard pressed servicing existing routes, so the project went into the too hard basket and it is still sitting there.

Argentina knows the world isn't flat. *Aerolineas Argentinas* has been running a polar route service from Buenos Aires to Auckland and back since 1979. Ironically, *Qantas* flew migrants to Australia from Argentina in 707s on a polar route way back in the 60s. When *Aerolineas* started to build up its passenger loads on the Polar route, *Qantas* started limited services to Buenos Aires. *Aerolineas* has no competition from *Air New Zealand*, still haunted by the spectre of Mount Erebus; the Kiwis won't go near the Pole.

On November 28 1979 All 257 passengers and crew died when *Air New Zealand* Flight 901, a DC10 sight-seeing flight over Antarctica, flew into a white-out and crashed into Mt Erebus, near Scott

Base Mt Erebus made *Qantas* more nervous too, although it sometimes operates sightseeing flights to the Antarctic. One could ask whether they may not be more risky than regular services across the Antarctic region. Airline executives will tell you that trans-polar traffic potential is low. If there are no flights, how can there be any traffic? Tailor a product to the market and people will buy. Take that string and run it round a globe from Sydney to Honolulu, on to Los Angeles, across to Miami and down to Rio.

Or take it from Sydney to Tahiti, across to Easter Island, to Santiago and on to Rio. Then run it around from Sydney to Rio, take it on up to New York or London, Rome or Paris and see how much distance and time you would slash from existing routes. It is not just the distance and time, it is the jet lag factor and time zones too.

Flying over the Antarctic is a fascinating way to go. When *Aerolineas* became the official airline for the Sydney to Rio race, most times I flew down to south between Auckland and Buenos Aires, skirting the Antarctic up across the tip of Chile and Argentina, just above Cape Horn, leaving Auckland at night, having dinner, then sleeping and waking for breakfast the same day after crossing the International Date Line.

I was wide awake to catch the first unforgettable sight of the southernmost point of the starkly beautiful Andes. Then we were over the sparkling blue lakes at the southern tip of Chile after flying a mere seven hours. Three more hours and we were touching down in Buenos Aires. It's three in the afternoon in this bustling metropolis with its endless rows of bleak concrete blocks, the stifling ghettos of repressive juntas and regimes. After President Martinez de Peron was deposed in an Air Force uprising in 1976 there had been Lieutenant General Jorge Rafael Videla and General Roberto Eduardo Viola, a moderate, who fortunately was the incumbent on my first visit. Taking office on December 22, 1981, his replacement Lieutenant General Leopoldo Galtieri was to spread to the world stage the cancerous political violence that had been rampant in Argentina for so many years. It was Galtieri who ordered Argentine troops to land on the Falklands and South Georgia Island on April 2, 1982. Outnumbered, it was no surprise that the small Royal Marine garrison at Port Stanley surrendered. Do cry for me, Argentina.

The soaring, modern apartment blocks and offices of downtown Buenos Aires seemed incongruous amid the sprawling mix of early Spanish and British colonial architecture – grand wide boulevards and gracious avenues.

Luxuriant garden growth cascades from the balconies of stylish middle class apartments of rich reds and browns. It is an exciting, vibrant city of style and panache, distinctly European with touches of Paris, Rome and London. The Harrods store and the old railway station would look at home in Piccadilly.

Unlike inner Rio, there were no apparent signs of poverty in downtown Buenos Aires. There were two distinct cities in one, co-existing under the watchful eye of the junta of the month. Vigilant armed soldiers were everywhere and there were clear signs downtown of the unfortunate ones. Weeping mothers were shuffling silently in a meandering circle, grimly clutching the photographs of their lost sons and daughters, a few holding small protest placards.

Crossing the small concrete bridge to the causeway that led to the Yacht Club of Buenos Aires, I walked among the ghosts of their long-lost sons and daughters. There was a time when I could have faced a deadly hail of bullets on that small concrete bridge, my lifeless body then dragged the short distance to the sheds that stood there in grim testament, holding pens or the last resting place for thousands of unfortunate ones. There was no time for rest when they were thrown aboard a naval vessel or aircraft, no time at all when they were callously flung into the dark, cold Atlantic, the innocent with the guilty. There were terrible atrocities on both sides. I saw the bomb-shattered wall of the office of a naval officer. His daughter came in to take a shower in his en-suite, kissed her father goodbye and was well clear of the building when the bomb she'd planted in the shower went off. Passions run deep in Argentina. The death squads showed no mercy either, and I felt uneasy wherever I walked. Security was heavy at naval headquarters, where I was visiting an officer named Kelly.

There are many Irish, Scottish and Welsh in Argentina, so loyalties were strangely divided during the Falklands War. Many Argentine officers had served in the Royal Navy and some had been to Australia. I got the red carpet treatment and an assurance that the yacht race would run smoothly in Argentine waters. Over a number of visits I got to know Kelly and some of his fellow officers well and we drank some fine Argentine wines and ate the best beef in the world at the yacht club and in some of the many excellent restaurants.

With the sinking of the *Belgrano*, Fleet Street ran that crude 'Gotcha!' headline and I thought 'People are people, generals are generals, and newspapers are newspapers.' It was a stupid war with senseless loss of life on both sides, its redeeming grace being the swift demise of Galtieri and his goons. In the end Argentina was really a winner. They kicked Galtieri out and that was a winning goal for the blue and whites. Democracy finally came to Argentina on December 10, 1983, with the popular election of civilian lawyer Raul Alfonsin.

My yachting contact, Phillip Jenkins, had flown down from Rio for my first night in Buenos Aires, a city where he had represented British aviation interests for many years. We walked from the hotel down the main shopping mall in the centre of Buenos Aires for my first taste of Argentine beer. It seemed like only a few hours since we had left Auckland halfway around the world according to those distorted airline maps. I was feeling no jet lag at all.

The many stylish shops that were open late at night had fantastic bargains, particularly leather goods, if you had US dollars. The inflation rate changed by the hour; the currency was almost out of control and European and American tourists were everywhere, taking advantage of this shopper's paradise. Fly there and buy all your clothes and accessories, airfare included, and it would still be cheaper than shopping at home. At the time I could understand what Brazilians meant when they described Argentinans as Italians pretending to be English – so many young men dressed in Harrods suits, so proper, with a strange formality in the air, and then I remembered the samba shows in Rio, and how the Argentinans went wild because they were out of Argentina, even if it was only temporarily, out of the giant Gulag, where nobody knew who the secret police were.

I paid a courtesy visit to Brigadier General Mayo in the *Aerolineas* head office in downtown Buenos Aires. I had signed a contract with him in Auckland, making *Aerolineas* the official race airline and the management and public relations teams had been most co-operative. That was to change as the Falklands War drew closer and I became an early civilian casualty. Before visiting Argentina, what stood out in my mind were Peron and Evita, the scuttling of the Graf Spee in the battle of the River Plate, the Argentine football team and that brilliant yacht designer German Frers.

The Perons were long since gone, as was the infamous German raider; football I could see any time, but the River Plate and Frers were there. The old man of the sea was now touching 80. His son had taken over the business and was becoming just as famous. A friend of Phil's took us sailing on the River Plate and by chance he knew the Frers family. Shortly after skilfully sailing out of the narrow channel into deeper water, there they were, the old man going blind, but still at the helm, the son tending the sails in a light breeze. We sailed across to them, and talked about the race and Frers' boats, and it felt good to get that close to the legendary man.

Later, as we sailed out across the Plate towards Uruguay, I thought of Captain Hans Langsdorff and the final days of the German pocket battleship *Graf Spee*. I would later discover that the *Waltraute* was another German vessel in strife in the River Plate, but that episode had a happy ending. In 1913 the *Waltraute* was unmasted in a severe storm off the Argentine coast and had to sail under jury rig for 41 days before reaching the mouth of the Plate. Spotted by an Argentine fishing boat, *Waltraute* was towed into Montevideo harbour, but would never again carry a sail.

Buenos Aires is one of those cities you find hard to leave. On one visit I found it almost impossible. I had been given the wrong departure time for the return Polar flight and arrived at the airport as the 747 was taxiing away from the terminal, with the next flight a fortnight away. Still without a sponsor for the race, I was on a strictly limited budget and while I would have been happy to stay in Buenos Aires for two more weeks, I could not afford that or the alternative of ticketing through North America. I had to take a chance.

Realising my plight, the *Aerolineas* airport manager arranged to ticket me from Buenos Aires to Santiago at no cost, but from there on I was on my own with no tickets. I would have to talk my way across the Pacific from Chile to Australia. It was a bit risky going to Santiago as there was no connecting flight that day. On arrival, I found that LAN Chile had plenty of seats on a flight leaving the next day for Tahiti and would give me a boarding pass. The local *Aerolineas* manager had explained my situation and it was no problem, although it should have been. I spent an anxious night at the *Carrera*, settling for room service only. Fortunately, there were not so many uniforms this time.

When I got to Tahiti I discovered that the *Qantas* flight was full, but I hung around hoping and eventually was told there was one first class seat left and they would give me a boarding pass for that. I've been lucky that way. Travelling to Rio through Los Angeles on concession, I was off-loaded in Lima, Peru, when local airline staff found the flight was overbooked out of Lima.

Having an overnight bag, I didn't bother about my main baggage. Wandering around, I found a door from the transit lounge into the general terminal then strolled out into the street, caught a cab into town and checked into a small hotel for the night. The next morning I had to board an *Aero Peru* connecting flight to Rio. The Immigration official got quite agitated.

I had left the airport through the wrong door, so no entry visa was stamped in my passport. I tried to explain, but with his English and my Spanish he just gave up, shrugged his shoulders and allowed me through. Another time I might have ended up in gaol.

My unexpected stopover produced a spectacular reward, a long, slow climb over the Andes, hugging the terrain, towering peaks on either side, almost close enough to reach out and touch.

Travelling to Rio often, I logged more polar flights than the *Aerolineas* flight crews. In organising the yacht race, I went to countless meetings with government, tourist, trade and civic authorities, yacht clubs, the Brazilian and Argentine navies and dozens of potential corporate sponsors. The Cruising Yacht Club was close to its deadline for abandoning the event when I finally concluded an agreement with *Xerox* in Brazil. I had been seeking $500,000 for naming rights and overall sponsorship, but *Xerox* would commit only $200,000. The company had decided to budget $500,000, with $300,000 covering support activities including advertising and promotion.

I secured a further $10,000 from the tobacco company Souza Cruz and $20,000 from *Xerox* in Sydney.

We were unable to attract individual sponsorships, so a substantial part of the $230,000 was used to meet the costs of the race entrants. I also subsidised events and projects in the trade, tourist and cultural fields, including the first showing at a national overseas museum of the complete works of Australian sculptor Noel Gray through Professor Edson Motta, director of the Museu Nacional de Belas Artes in Rio.

Scheduled to subsequently travel to museums in Sao Paulo, Brasilia and Belo Horizonte, the exhibition encompassed Gray's entire artistic output between 1972 and 1981. It was a massive undertaking: included were 21 sandstone sculptures and two sandstone friezes, together weighing more than four tons, six painted relief panels and many thousands of framed drawings and sketch books. Sydney jewellers Percy Marks commissioned Gray to design and create the sandstone and silver trophy for the yacht race. Australia's Deputy Prime Minister Doug Anthony underscored the importance of Gray's exhibition by presenting a drawing by the Glebe sculptor to President Figueredo of Brazil.

Aerolineas, through its involvement in the Falklands war, created major financial problems for me. New Zealand Prime Minister Robert Muldoon decided that Margaret Thatcher would be antagonistic towards the Argentine airline flying between Buenos Aires and Auckland. This was unthinkable for a Commonwealth country when Britain was at war with Argentina, so he temporarily suspended the service. I was now commercially crippled, and Thatcher and Muldoon compounded my situation. The involvement of the airline in the war and the reluctance of *Xerox* to commit to subsequent races resulted in a financial debacle for Bronwyn and me. We lost our house in Sydney, despite a *Daily Mirror* story on January 27, 1982, of a joint announcement by Mayor Coutinho of Rio and Lord Mayor Sutherland of Sydney that the two cities would be involved in staging a second race in 1984.

Plans for a reverse event in 1987, timed to arrive in Sydney during Australia's 1988 Bicentenary, were abandoned. There had been other moneymaking possibilities on my many trips to Rio, but they had come to nothing. Percy Marks, the jeweller, entrusted me with $30,000 worth of opals to sell in Brazil on commission. They wanted to test the market in Rio and were prepared to take the risk of my being caught by Customs. With the expensive package of cut and polished gems and set pieces in my suitcase I got there and back undetected. I had no success with my principal target, Sterns, the biggest jeweller in Rio, and had to bring the opals back to Sydney, but went through Customs in both countries without having my suitcase opened.

Xerox did pay out some major creditors from the event, but it was left to me to pay off a $150,000 balance. I was about to fly to Auckland to fix a sheriff's notice to an *Aerolineas* 747 when Muldoon ordered the airline out. My solicitors told me I would have to go to Argentina to pursue the matter and legal costs could be enormous. The Falklands conflict was like the war in Vietnam when, along with many others, I found it difficult to support either side. I had no such problem once it was over and commercial realities had set in. By the time *Aerolineas* resumed its service, I had gone a long way down another road.

While in Brazil, I made a number of visits to Sao Paulo. Boarding an old Electra which had once belonged to *Ansett Airlines* at the Rio city airport made me apprehensive. The day before, a small aircraft had flown straight into Sugarloaf, which stands directly in line with the end of the runway. I was more than a little nervous as we taxied out and hurtled down that runway towards the looming rock, but we banked to the left a long way before Sugarloaf and headed out to sea. Turning south, we flew down the coast towards Sao Paulo, one of the world's most densely populated cities. As we banked we had a spectacular view of Copacabana and I wondered how it looked from the air on New Year's Eve.

We had been on the spacious balcony of Australian Consul Warwick Pearson's beach front apartment when the fireworks erupted at midnight. A dazzling display of bursting shells and cascading colours that had faded in comparison with the bewitching spectacle of a million tiny candles set adrift from the beach in paper boats. Voodoo chants drifted up from the water's edge as the glistening candle carpet floated on a gentle swell into the dark Atlantic.

Coming in over the mountains to land at Hong Kong's old Kai Tak airport, the apartment blocks used to seem dangerously close. Descending rapidly into the pulsating heart of Sao Paulo, the people in the apartments seemed even closer as we flew through the downtown district below rooftop height.

The first time is terrifying, like landing in a 747 in New York's Central Park would be. On landing you realise that the airport is a plateau with a sheer drop at both ends of the runway, at one end a busy main street. 'That's why they use the turbo-prop aircraft,' I thought, and then I saw the domestic 747s and 727s landing in the middle of a city, where congestion is a way of life. But when we drove on to the frantic Sao Paulo freeway system, the airport landing seemed like child's play.

I flew to Brasilia many times, visiting my family or on business, on one occasion being summoned there by Australian Ambassador Rudi Schneeman. He said it was a matter he could not discuss on the telephone – he had to meet with me privately. Rudi was a diplomat's diplomat, and had that look about him, oozing charm, tact, connections, protocol and the old school tie.

By contrast, Warwick Pearson was a down-to-work diplomat, shirt sleeves rolled up, eager to foster trade, tourism, and other interchange between the two countries and one of the most supportive people for the yacht race. When the yachts arrived after their epic voyage, it was Warwick who ran the length of a causeway waving a large Australian flag.

He helped tremendously, opening the right doors, finding the right people, and frequently bending his back for the cause. Over lunch at the Australian Embassy in Brasilia, Ambassador Schneeman confided that an Aide de Camp to Australia's Governor General, Sir Zelman Cowen, had indicated that His Excellency would like to be at the start of the event, but I wasn't to know that.

"It has to be a spontaneous gesture – that's the way these things are done, you know," the Ambassador confided. "The Governor General and Lady Cowen would love to be invited to be at the start of the race. Of course, the invitation has to come from the Cruising Yacht Club. If you can arrange an official invitation from the Commodore, Sir Zelman will accept. But simply make it a suggestion to the Commodore; don't say anything to anyone about this conversation."

When I got back to Australia I did arrange the official invitation, and Flight Lieutenant Geoffrey Squires, then Aide de Camp to the Governor General, handled the necessary arrangements for the Vice Regal presence at the start of the race.

There was a human side to this story. They did come to the start of the race and, along with other VIP guests, were on the Royal Australian Navy mine sweeper *HMAS Ibis* when the starting gun went off. I had explained to Flight Lieutenant Squires that we could not invite Sir Zelman to fire the gun as we had already invited the Mayor Coutinho of Rio to be the official starter.

To avoid any breach of protocol, the Cowens joined Deputy Prime Minister Doug Anthony and *Ibis* skipper Lieutenant Commander Welford on the bridge while Doug Sutherland accompanied his Rio counterpart to the for'ard starting gun – but the best vantage point I saved for my wife and myself.

When Coutinho fired the starting gun and thousands of green and gold balloons billowed above the race yachts and spectator fleet, we were on the radar platform, head and shoulders above the head of the acting head of state. I felt that we deserved it.

My neighbours Bill and Pat Grettan were on a small spectator boat off Kirribilli when the Cowens arrived home on the vicegeral launch and he cursed himself for not having a movie or still camera. A Brazilian band was playing loud samba music as their Excellencies walked up the front lawns of Admiralty House and it was an unforgettable sight – the Governor's lady doing a lively samba on the lawn. Not that Admiralty House was any stranger to high jinks; a previous custodian, Sir John Kerr, sometimes experienced a degree of difficulty in keeping his feet on the lawn just walking.

Kerr's sacking of Australian Prime Minister Whitlam in 1975 was a case of the Governor General dancing to Opposition Leader Fraser's tune. The Constitutional crisis that led to this extraordinary event had all sorts of strange side-effects that reverberated around the world.

When the Australian Senate refused to pass supply and the Government money tap ran dry, I was in New York seeking funding for the production of *Barney*. The Film Commission had a full time officer Jim Henry at the Australian Consulate in New York, and he had kindly allowed me to use his office. I was able to get secretarial work done there for funding for the film, but there was a catch. With the freeze on government spending, communication with the rest of the world was at a premium phone calls were limited and we were allowed only three postage stamps a day. I had limited funds at the time, but at least they were private. There was no money to pay consulate staff wages, so most of them took out loans with the Chase Manhattan Bank to cover their wages. They had to pay interest on the funds they had borrowed.

By coincidence, the Big Apple was going bankrupt at the same time, so Australia got unprecedented publicity in New York. I don't know if it was the city's pending bankruptcy or normal practice, but I was besieged by New York street prostitutes.

One night an enterprising young black prostitute trailed me to my downtown hotel room, and knocked on the door several times. When she had approached me in the street, I had told her I had no money, but she kept hammering away at the door and finally, in a rage, exploded: "Hey man, if you don't open this door and let me come in and fuck you, my man is going to stick (knife) you." The door had several chains and locks on it, but I still pushed the dresser against it, and sat quietly on the bed until she left. After a sleepless night, I moved out of the hotel and went to stay at Jim's place in Long Island.

There was widespread friction between blacks and whites in New York, and Jim explained that whites in his suburb formed a human wedge when boarding their morning train. They grouped together, rushed into the same compartment en mass and sat in a block; safety in numbers, they said. New York was suffering a spate of bomb threats and bombings and it had been that way in Los Angeles.

Worse was still to come in London and I began to believe the bombers were following me. In LA, a Puerto Rican cab driver had pulled a knife on me for not giving him a big enough tip. "I've got a wife and five starving kids to feed, man." I gladly handed over more money and he screeched off into the night.

Another cabbie proudly showed me his new security system. "Many cab drivers were being mugged and robbed, so we installed special emergency buttons on the dashboard," he said, pointing to the button in question. "When you push this, cop cars come from everywhere, sirens screaming, guns drawn. Unfortunately, while I was telling some Japanese tourists about it, I actually pushed the button. The next minute they were all lying on the pavement, surrounded by cops, with guns drawn. The cops gave those Japanese a helluva fright before they realised it was a false alarm," he told me.

I had gone as far as I could with business in New York, so it was time to head for Chicago, then on to Battle Creek, Michigan, headquarters of the cereals giant Kellogg where I had a meeting to discuss an across-America run by Rafferty. I was also off to Detroit to talk to Ford about an executive fitness programme to be run by Rafferty.

He was a big guy, the cabbie who took me to Kennedy Airport. He could still be hit on the back of the head, so I asked him why he didn't have a security screen. He suggested I look over the back of the front seat and there was a double-barrelled shotgun, loaded and cocked.

"Who needs a security screen?" he said with a big grin.

I grinned back, but my thoughts were increasingly toward how I was going to earn some decent money and get us back on the property ladder again. Unsurprisingly, I was headed back to where I had been before.

Airline becomes a Lifeline

Richard Branson's Virgin Airlines flights to America paved the way for massive deregulation of airlines throughout the world – and for Australia, it was long overdue. A new national airline was the lifebelt that the late Bryan Grey threw me in the murky wake of the yacht race. I was desperately seeking a new challenge and Grey's proposition was simple: "If I manage to buy out *East-West Airlines*, can you guarantee to keep a new national airline on the front pages?"

Nobody could guarantee it, but I knew that I could give it my best shot. What else can you say when you're broke and desperate? After mortgaging his house and becoming as broke and desperate as I was, Grey and his merchant banker partner Duke Minks finally acquired all the shares in the small regional carrier.

Bryan had three obsessions in life: airlines, horse racing and the family tree; sick bags, chaff bags and tea bags – Earl Grey, of course. For several years he had been piecing together a claim to the family title of Earl Grey.

I had my first cup of the family brew with him in 1964 on joining the Channel O team at *Ansett Transport Industries*. When the new station opened Bryan was the accountant, but he was unlike any accountant I had known. He accepted that expenses were not some figment of our imagination, but a genuine expenditure that produced results. Having a beer or two with a group of television journalists was something he understood, better still he often joined us. Publicity was something he understood more than most people in management.

As Branson and others discovered, the key to publicity in the airline business is cheap air travel. When you're hunting publicity a bird in the hand is worth more than a flock in the bush. With *East-West* the bird in question was Ita Buttrose, the Kylie Minogue of the Australian media. Kerry Packer's former right hand, Ita was flying high as editor-in-chief of Rupert Murdoch's *Sunday Telegraph*. She was the best person you could wish for to kick start the Third Airline Campaign.

To get to Ita, I approached *Sunday Telegraph* travel writer Fred Baker. Fred had left England after backing a tank through the ground floor of a barracks building on the British Army's Catterick base in Yorkshire. When he asked what he should do next, the tank commander had replied: "Do not use the bloody stairs."

Born in the north of Scotland, Fred had spent several rough and tough years as a North Sea trawlerman before his stint in the army. One of his early memories of Scotland is of his grandad's porridge being stored in a drawer in a bedroom cupboard. "We might have been poor but we never went without a feed. Mind you, a slice of it made an excellent doorstop." Once Fred had finished flexing his muscles and the army's tanks, he started flexing his mind and read English at Cambridge. He became director of the Cambridge Arts Laboratory before moving to Australia and advertising. When he discovered how little mind-flexing goes on in advertising, he joined the Royal Melbourne Institute of Technology as publications manager, later becoming senior research consultant with Australian Frontier, the only independent research organisation in Australia. While there he helped raise $250,000 to fund the independent Melbourne suburban newspaper, *The Valley Voice*. Claiming that he was 'axed in a Stalinist coup by the local Labor Party,' he moved to Sydney as associate editor of *Travel Trade*. Eventually, he went the way of most journalistic flesh, becoming a scribe in the Murdoch empire. Fred maintained his sanity by writing on travel for *Penthouse, Passport, Golden Wing, Inside Tourism, Travel Week* and *Meetings*.

Knowing that he felt old age was advancing rapidly in the journalistic world, I gave him a scoop on the introduction of the Golden Oldie Fare, a massive 50 per cent discount fare for pensioners. He agreed it would be of great appeal to Ms Buttrose as, like Fred and I, she was no longer a literary spring chicken. We kept our fingers crossed, because her boss Murdoch just happened to own half of *Ansett Airlines*. Ansett and *TAA* considered *East-West* a small fish, so nobody expected us to make any impression on what was Australia's equivalent of *Pan Am* and *United*.

From the day Ita's prose appeared, we flew the publicity pants off the big two. Australians who had never dreamed of flying suddenly found it was cheaper than driving a car. Grey became the champion of the people. Countless stories appeared on *East-West*'s battle with the big two airlines and the cartoonists had a field day as *Ansett* and *TAA* desperately tried to match our initiatives. Like Pete Sutherland, Grey let me call the publicity shots, although there were times when he was a reluctant hero. When we introduced a dirt cheap $120 return flight between Sydney and Melbourne, the Department of Civil Aviation threatened to have Grey arrested, so he sent me to Melbourne to meet the first flight.

In the finger-way at Tullamarine Airport it was like the main street of the town in High Noon. Surrounded by a large contingent of media, I walked slowly towards the Federal Police who were waiting at the gate lounge at the end of the long walkway. In the background I could hear the sound of an *East-West* Fokker Friendship aircraft as it taxied towards the terminal.

'At least I've made it to the ground,' I thought. 'Are they really going to go through with this farce? Will I end up in gaol? Grey's a bastard.' Then the Feds disappeared through a doorway and a sea of smiling passengers spilled out of the gate lounge.

From that moment the iniquitous Two Airline Agreement was doomed. Sadly, the demise of the other new airlines, *Compass Mark One* and *Two*, resulted in a return to the status quo. It was inevitable, for that crafty dealer Prime Minister Bob Hawke stacked the cards against *Compass One*, while *Compass Two* self-destructed. The latter event was quite predictable. In confronting striking pilots in 1984, Hawke returned another favour to his mentor, *Ansett Airlines* chief Sir Peter Abeles and in the process they dramatically changed the face of flying. It was quite strange for a Labor Prime Minister to use the military as strike breakers.

It would never have happened while Hawke was President of the Australian Council of Trade Unions. At that time Hawke was first attracting the patronage of Abeles. San Francisco police, who investigated Abeles' alleged association with known US Mafia figures, had Sal's Bar under surveillance in 1978 when Hawke went there as

Abeles guest. Local US Teamsters Union branch boss Rudy Tham, a known Mafia associate, allegedly arranged for Hawke and Labor Party official David Combe to be entertained at the bar. Sal's Bar was allegedly run by a Mafia identity. In the Waterfront Corruption Hearings before a US Senate Sub-Committee in 1981 a Mafia informant claimed that the Teamsters 'were receiving payoffs' from Abeles' shipping company Seatrain.

In 1982, Mafia hit man Jimmy Fratianno claimed in testimony that Tham had introduced him to Abeles. Abeles always denied that he knew Tham or that Fratianno had Mafia links, or that he ever gave either of them any money. Abeles supported Hawke during his political ascendancy and Hawke kept his mate flying during the pilots' strike. They conspired to break the strike, which many believed was precipitated by the airlines to undermine the strong industrial relations power of the pilots.

Throughout his union and political career Hawke was said to have had an ongoing love affair with the Australian public. In the nationwide consummation of this relationship, Australian pilots were among the abstainers. When the pilots' strike was over, many of them acknowledged that Hawke had finally screwed them. Hawke allowed *Ansett* and *Australian Airlines* to second seats on international flights, and made the extraordinary decision to allow both airlines to employ overseas pilots who had minimal local flying experience. The most extraordinary decision was allowing the use of RAAF aircraft for commercial passenger flights.

Despite Hawke's unqualified support for the airlines, the regular high flying army of politicians, public servants and business executives found flights difficult to get. This started a rush on video and phone conferencing facilities that for many ultimately replaced much of their interstate travel.

The mateship of two powerful men in the war on Australian pilots also led to the country's tourist industry nosediving as the chaos appalled international travel agencies and tourists. No doubt Hawke discussed tactics over a Saturday morning barbecue at Sir Pete's palatial Sydney home.

"I can't talk to you now. I've got Hawke, Neville Wran and Andrew Peacock here, we're having a barbecue," fumed Abeles when I insisted he had an urgent matter to deal with one Saturday morning.

"If you don't sign these papers, even that illustrious trio won't be able to keep you out of trouble," I said. "You could be charged if you fail to complete this application in the prescribed manner."

The overdue application was for a permit to run a raffle, and the law is strict on that – a bit slack sometimes on drugs and white collar crime, but not on raffles. This was no ordinary raffle. It was for one of Abeles' favourite causes, the Sydney Hospital Foundation for Medical Research. We had set up a giant Christmas stocking in front of the MLC building in Sydney's Martin Place and crammed it with Christmas goodies.

Carole Fahrenbeck, one of Abeles' favourite ladies, had engaged me to promote the Foundation, and himself in the process. When Carole resigned to go overseas she was replaced by one of Abeles' not-so-favourite ladies, Pixie Noble, who tried to put shit on me one day without good reason. When Abeles confronted the two of us, she went to water, and withdrew her comments. After she left I was lighting up one of my short panatella cigars when Abeles said "Here, have a real one," and handed me one of his expensive coronas. Always stand up for what you think is right, my boy," he said, as I inhaled deeply. If I had stood up I would probably have blacked out.

The raffle had to have a permit number, the only person who could sign the application form was Abeles and I was standing up for what I believed to be right. He was angry because I had called him at home and wanted to bring the form over immediately. The media would have loved that. I could see the headline: 'Sir Peter Abeles runs a raffle.' When he calmed down, we compromised and I had the form delivered to him. It was a state government form, so maybe Premier Wran dropped it in to Macquarie Street for him after the barbecue. They would do little things for each other, as we all do for our barbecue mates. If you got a phone call from a mate in trouble in a pub with some woman who had taken off with his money, would you arrange to get a few dollars to him? What's a few hundred dollars Australian or even US? But then nobody's ever proved that allegation and Abeles is dead now.

Abeles and I had a falling-out when I was with *East-West*. His airline accused me of corrupting my wife through pillow talk. *Ansett* management told my wife, Bronwyn: "You are in big trouble and you might be fired for sleeping with the enemy."

"Encourage them," I said. "We'll make a million from Sir Peter – he can afford it. Make them fire you and we'll sue."

Sadly, they backed off after giving her a warning. What really peeved those fine upstanding captains of industry at *Ansett* was that the conversation was apparently all one way. While she was allegedly divulging all their commercial secrets in the seclusion of our bedroom, they were not getting any feedback on *East-West*. Maybe that's why the bug was planted in the *East-West* boardroom.

One of Abeles' former lieutenants, Tony Bauer, had alerted us to the possibility that our phones and confidential boardroom discussions were being tapped. He told many a tale of corrupt tactics in the trucking business – of cars being run off the road by trucks, bashings and smashing of property. Bugging was a mere bagatelle. In America shootings and bombings were commonplace in the trucking business. It was Tony who found the right guy to check out his suspicions. He was in the business, so he knew just where to look. Grey and I thought he was so good he might have been the one who had planted them in the first place.

He let me find the first one, simply by demonstrating how a small bug could be inserted in a telephone receiver. Naturally, I went to Bryan's silent line and sure enough, when I unscrewed the mouthpiece, there it was – a tiny cylindrical metal bug that looked like a transistor radio battery. From there, after checking the backs of paintings on the office walls, our 'counter espionage' friend led us to the larger device taped under the boardroom table.

After he had picked up his fee and left, we all became quite obsessed and regularly unscrewed telephone mouthpieces and ran our hands under desks, chairs and tables and behind paintings and photographs. We never found another one.

*

It's just as well Reg *Ansett* didn't plant a bug in my bedroom before Bronwyn and I married. Back then they would have got it right and Bronwyn would have been for the high jump. *Australian Airlines* did not allow airline hostesses to get married. Affectionately known as 'hosties' by most, except for Sir Reg, the founder, who described them as old boilers, they resented the restriction. At 20, nobody would have called Bronwyn an old boiler. They would have quickly had a pot of hot coffee poured down their neck. That's something we had in common.

I had occasionally dropped a bowl of steaming soup into a migrant lap on *New Australia* for lesser remarks. In the air it's put down to 'sudden turbulence'; on an ocean liner it's "Sorry sir, the boat just lurched to starboard." As we were keen to get married, and I was doing public relations for *Ansett* at the time, promoting to the hostess management team various ways of lifting the image, it was easy pickings.

For too long the smirking old rogues who fell over each other to volunteer for graduation days and 'pin the wings on the hosties' tits' ceremonies had peddled the line that air hostesses were attractive to passengers because they were all 'single and available'. Many hostesses were already 'living in sin' because of the silly rule against marriage. Airline executives were too dumb to notice or simply turned a blind eye. I worked hard at getting the rule changed, and due largely to our impending wedding, it happened. Keeping two flats was stupid anyhow.

Despite the buckets of tears shed, and the buckets of dollars donated to start the next new airline, it was patently obvious there would be a repeat performance. The media had its emotional head too deep in the first bucket to notice what was going in and out of the second one. Buckets of blood, sweat and tears went into the making of *East-West* in 1983 as we worked long hours and rose before dawn to keep the media feeding frenzy going.

The first call would come about 5am from any one of a dozen aviation or travel writers asking: "What are you going to do to them today?" *Ansett* and *TAA* were reeling and the cartoonists were enjoying themselves as we delivered daily doses of discount deliverance to a flying public ripped off for years by a fat cartel cow, zealously protected by political cowboys. *Ansett* and *TAA* were bloated with executives; we knew, we'd been there. Their operating costs were up in cloud nine and the fare-paying public kept them up there till *East-West* came along and forced them to fly lean.

"$99 for a five day Gold Coast holiday and we can make a profit from it," I said to Grey.

"How much, a dollar a head?" he responded, but authorised me to fly to the Gold Coast to plead with local accommodation and restaurant owners to give it a go at cost.

They did and we made $20 a head and got another front page.

When the pilots decided to strike, Grey was in Holland, negotiating a deal on some new F28 jets and typically blunt when I told him about the strike.

"You can tell them from me that if they go out with the *Ansett* and *TAA* pilots we'll close the bloody airline down the same day. And we'll start it up again the next day with brand new pilots."

I talked to Pilots' Federation representatives and invited them in for a meeting the day before the planned strike. I asked Grey's partner Minks to the meeting to play the heavy.

"*Ansett* and *TAA* pilots will be furious," said one of the Federation men.

"We'll have to walk through picket lines in the morning." "Fine, I'll walk through with you," I said, and hurried off to let the media know that extra *East-West* flights would take to the skies while *Ansett* and *TAA* sat on the ground.

It was dark the next morning in the car park at Sydney's Kingsford Smith Airport and my apprehension increased as I walked towards the *TAA* terminal with a small group of *East-West* pilots. There were some placard carrying pilots from the 'big two' but they were just as apprehensive as we were.

One of them said: "Keep up the good work – you've got those bastards on the run." We kept the bastards on the run. When we found the bugs under the boardroom table and in Grey's phone we knew we had them rattled.

We had captains of a different kind in the Great Ferry Race on Sydney Harbour. Sydney Festival Director Stephen Hall was as cunning as the proverbial rat. The Great Ferry Race was rigged; *East-West* sponsored a ferry and won, although it was not our turn. Grey had offered free tickets to the ferry captain and the crew, and Stephen Hall was not amused. "Nor is the sponsor who thought it was his turn," said Hall.

'Stuff you,' I thought, 'You're the same bastard who let me persuade the Rio Carnival organisers to provide some of their street decorations for the Sydney Festival, and you wouldn't even pay the lousy fees to get them out of storage on the wharf. You were all smiles when I brought the Carnival costumes over for exhibition in the NSW Art Gallery. I even carried that bloody great headpiece, belonging to that Brazilian transvestite, all the way from Rio, with those knowing looks when I went through customs.'

"We know what you've been up to," said a stern-faced Hall. "If you're sponsoring a ferry next year you'll have to give an undertaking to the police that you won't bribe the captain."

"This is serious stuff," I said. "The police are in on it too, rigging a bloody ferry race."

I went to the planning meeting for the next race and promised the police and the organisers that I wouldn't bribe the captain. I couldn't speak for Grey. And yes, we beat them again that year. It was the year of my trip to Newport and Australia had won the America's Cup. We decorated our ferry in green and gold and rigged a spinnaker to fly from the mast, just for show. Grey was on the bridge, handing out free tickets to Norfolk Island, as we hit the front and dashed to the finishing line.

The captains of the other ferries were fuming as we stole the race again, especially the captain of the *Pepsi Cola* ferry. It took on so much water trying to catch us that it sank at Circular Quay seconds after the last passenger walked off. They were damned lucky. The ferry was crammed with people and could have sunk out in the harbour. I don't know if it was their turn to win, but I couldn't resist telling the Pepsi PR: "You bastards will do anything to keep us off the front page."

Pepsi did get the front page and we missed out – poetic justice. So much drama over a rigged bloody ferry race!

In the airline popularity stakes we didn't play around with the flag at *East-West*, but we did change the airline's colours to Australia's green and gold. I worked with Tommy Moeller on a new stylised map of Australia to go on the aircraft tails.

Tommy was songwriter and lead singer with Unit 4 + 2 in the 1960s and had a number one hit in the UK with 'Concrete and Clay' in 1965, beating The Rolling Stones to the coveted spot. The band often featured Phil Collins as drummer before he went on to Genesis and solo fame.

Tommy and his brother Greg wrote the musical *Leonardo, A Portrait Of Love* which played London's West End in the early 90s. Brother Billy was pop star Whistling Jack Smith in the late 60s and early 70s.

There have been no less than 35 cover versions of 'Concrete and Clay' since Tommy and his group first recorded it. One of those eternal hits that still gets regular airplay, it keeps Tommy in beer money. He arrived in Australia in 1975. When I met him he and his brother Billy were helping Minks and Grey buy out shareholders in *East-West*. A former Birkenhead bus conductor, Minks was one of Tommy's 'roadies' before he took another track and became a merchant banker. I know some merchant bankers who would have trouble balancing the books on a Birkenhead bus.

In 1984 Tommy and I produced 'Everyone Is Gold', a theme song and video for the Olympic Games coverage on the Ten Network. We also collaborated on a record for the Cruising Yacht Club, 'Heading from the Heads for Hobart', to promote the Sydney-Hobart race. One day we decided to produce a record for the airline titled 'Girls Who Fly', featuring a group of *East-West* hostesses. Session singer Maggie McKinney coached the hostesses and sang lead on 'Girls Who Fly' and the flip side, 'Song of Australia'. Maggie also recorded 'Everyone is Gold'. Taking the fledgling songbirds off line and producing the record impressed their peers. However, the three attractive hostesses got into trouble with their supervisors over a publicity shot in the *Daily Mirror*. Wearing short leather skirts and fishnet stockings was fine for entertainers, but not for airline hostesses. Grey, as he did with most things, accepted it as good publicity.

Two decades later, Virgin's 'spunky' was regarded by Richard Branson as good publicity, but it got him into trouble with the Queensland Anti-Discrimination Commission.

The Australian, May 12 2005:

On a Virgin Blue flight about three years ago, John Bastick, editor-in-chief of men's magazine FHM, noticed that the attendants serving him were a 'spunky lot', he told the Queensland Anti-Discrimination Tribunal yesterday. Cover girls, he said, were getting hard to find. "There's a dearth of young women who want to strip for a men's magazine." But the 'spunky' flight attendants serving him and checking his overhead luggage gave him a brainwave.

"It was a sort of hare-brained idea to find Australia's sexiest cabin crew," he said, while giving evidence on behalf of eight former Ansett flight attendants who are suing Virgin Blue – the airline set up by British entrepreneur Richard Branson and now majority-owned by Patrick Corp – for age discrimination.

The result of Mr Bastick's 'hare-brained idea' was a cover story in the September 2002 issue of FHM, headlined 'Branson's Angels' and featuring a cover picture of five Virgin Blue flight attendants in leather bikini-tops, short skirts and thigh-high boots.

Virgin's 'stunning and bubbly' attendants had 'put the spunk back into flying high', the story said.

Simon Hamlyn-Harris, counsel for the eight women aged from 36 to 56 who claim Virgin rejected their applications for jobs as flight attendants because they were too old, said the story reinforced their case that the airline promoted a young, cheeky image and was seeking cabin crew with a youthful look.

Mr Bastick said he also approached Qantas and Ansett with his story idea.

Qantas lost interest when it realised other airlines might be involved, while Ansett, then on the verge of collapse, was not at all interested.

He said Mr Branson later told a TV interviewer he wanted to put the glamour back into flying.

Counsel for Virgin Blue, Chris Murdoch, said the magazine spread was irrelevant because it was initiated by the magazine, not the company, and had nothing to do with the airline's recruiting practices.

After East-West

When Brian Grey sold out and walked out $25 million richer, publicity was no longer important – but one of Perth's many self-proclaimed entrepreneurs had decided I might be the one to set up the America's Cup Aussie port scam and, facing the prospect of selling our house at a loss, it was a timely assignment for me.

"There's $10,000 in it for starters, with a large share of the profits if you pull it together," said David, a solidly built, young, upwardly mobile businessman with all the pretentious style that wafted through trendy bars and nightclubs in the Perth of the early eighties.

"The product's right, the timing's right, and from what I hear you're right. All you have to do is tie up the outlets and there's a lot of money to be made. We want you to go to Newport and tie up a distributor for the souvenir port packs and some clothing we're getting together, like tee shirts, jackets and hats featuring the Aussie challenge. We can make it easy for you, because Alan Bond's got many top contacts there, and we can get you a knock down to them."

I have to give credit him for the 'Who's Who in Newport' list and for the quality of the product and the packaging. The $10,000 went to the bank to free up our house in Birchgrove so the buyer could complete a contract of sale. I took off for Newport, with Bryan Grey's blessing, to chase my $85,000 share of the potential profits from the port packs. Bronwyn hoped for success and maybe another house.

Newport, Rhode Island, is a close knit community with wealth beyond our wildest dreams: the Kennedys, the Book Club, the New York Yacht Club, the Auld Mug and the IRA! Yes, there's many a

Yankee dollar gone across the seas to Ireland and Newport was no mean contributor.

Shortly before I got there the unthinkable had happened. Some of the local Irish lads who took me out on the town told me about the clandestine goings on. The British Government had had their first off-the-record ceasefire talks with the IRA right there in Newport. It took more than a decade to make it happen. I had some impromptu talks with the local police in Newport. Fortunately not much came out of that, or I could have finished up in the state penitentiary.

They said they had found my jacket, covered in mud, at the scene of a hit-and-run accident; would I like to identify it? I had discovered my jacket missing after dinner with some locals. It was a weird night, first with the couple I went with, who were going through a bad patch. She was younger than him and that night she was ready to play. He was a good contact, so I was on my best behaviour.

It must have been catching, for later in the bar, another young woman picked up where she left off and offered to drive me back to my hotel.

When I went to leave I found that my jacket was missing from the cloakroom. The restaurant manager assured me it wasn't an anti-Australian plot; someone had probably taken it by mistake.

In Newport, reefer jackets are as popular as denim in China. My passport and $1500 in traveller's cheques were in the jacket, so I was hoping he was right. I'd had a fair amount to drink and the blonde was running hot. I said I'd come back the next morning for my jacket. A friend of the blonde said she needed a ride home, which seemed to switch the blonde off and they dropped me at my hotel.

Later, I would realise why the blonde had cooled down. American women are right up front when they've got the hots for someone and the blonde had made that clear in the bar, and when she phoned me at the hotel the next day. In the morning, when I went back to the restaurant and found there was no reefer jacket there, I started to worry and the blonde became the least of my concerns.

"It's not the jacket," I told the staff, "it's my passport and the traveller's cheques." I reported the missing cheques to Thomas Cook's and they guaranteed fast replacement. My Irish friends helped me check out the yachts along the wharf, to no avail. They reported the missing jacket to the local police and we went for a beer and Sunday lunch.

"Nothing you can do about your passport till tomorrow," one of them said. That afternoon the woman from the bar called and said she was dropping her kid off to play baseball, and she would be free to drop over for an hour or so. "Just can't wait to get into bed with you," she drooled.

"Dropping your kid at baseball, where's your husband?" 'He's working day shift at the precinct, so everything's cool," she said.

I cooled off as quickly as she had the night before. "Sorry, I have a meeting to go to, I'll have to take a rain check."

When the police called to say they had found my jacket I was with my dinner host, one of the Bond camp's most influential contacts. "We've got a jacket that answers the description you gave us," said the caller.

"Where did you find it?" I asked.

"At the scene of a hit-run accident, he replied. "Either you're a bad driver or just a lucky drunk." Was this the rich North or the deep South? I thought. This could turn a bad dream into a bloody nightmare.

The cop had a bad attitude. I had no passport and maybe it was his wife who wanted to jump into bed with me. I asked my local contact to come with me when I identified my jacket. You know how some cops just present with that 'I'm going to spoil your day' look.

"Where were you on Saturday night?" he said, eyeballing me intently.

"I was at Christie's restaurant with this gentleman and his wife," I said.

"That's what I stated when reporting my jacket missing." The cop turned to my companion, who confirmed my movements that night.

"What did you do after you left the restaurant?" the cop asked.

"Your wife took me back to my hotel" flashed across my mind and out of it just as quickly.

"I went straight back to my hotel, you can check with the front desk." He walked into another room and returned with a mud-spattered reefer jacket.

I checked the inside label and confirmed it was mine. "Look at the label, I know it's mine; I bought it in Buenos Aries."

"You wanna' take it or trash it?" said the cop.

"Trash it," I said and asked if I could go.

As we walked out I thought 'If I hadn't been with a local they could have given me a hard time. If I'd finished up with my contact's wife, he might not have come with me. If I'd come here on my own with no alibi, the Buenos Aires label could have hung me.'

There were other clothes in my wardrobe from South America, including the dinner suit I'd bought in Rio when selected as the foreign judge for Carnival costumes judging. Bronwyn, my daughter Caroline and hey boyfriend Andrew were in the studio audience for the judging on national television. The organisers had provided a translator, a Yorkshire girl who worked in Rio. The other eleven members of the judging panel included some of Brazils leading entertainment and sporting personalities. Guest judges were usually Hollywood stars or international sporting identities. It was good that the Sydney-Rio race was honoured that way. Rio had opened its heart to the event and the participants. Throughout Rio Carnival organisers extensively promoted the event and Australia generally.

The 23-metre Sydney sloop *Buccaneer*, skippered by 63-year-old grandfather of seven Joel Mace was first across the finish line on Guanabana Bay.

The Ocean Youth Club entry completed the race in 39 days nine hours.

Buccaneer, Grubic's 25-metre Adelaide ketch *Anaconda II* and the 20-metre New Zealand sloop *Ta'aroa* all broke the previous record of 40 days 16 hours for the 13,000 km course set by *Great Britain II* in the 1974 Whitbread race.

The 17-stone, 6ft 3in frame of 47 year old skipper Ian Macfarlane did not hold *Ta'aroa* back on the fast ride to Rio.

Throughout Rio the street poles and the grandstands used for the Carnival parades had large banners in four languages welcoming the yachtsmen.

On the waterfront at the Marina da Gloria city authorities staged a series of national television variety shows to welcome the yachts, crews and officials.

For several nights the Aussie crews were hailed as heroes and joined in singing and dancing with a bevy of beautiful girls.

We were all spellbound by the exotic and erotic Carnival parades, street and beach parties and the official Carnival Balls. When Bronwyn, Caroline, Andrew and I sat in a temporary grandstand along the route of the main Carnival parade, it was electrifying. At the magnificent 200,000-capacity Maracana Stadium we were guests of honour at an exciting Flamengo-Sao Paulo soccer match when the yacht crews paraded on the pitch before the game. A spectacular Sydney-Rio fireworks display crowned the exciting week of festivities. Manchete – Brazil's equivalent of Life magazine – ran a four page spread on the race, the festivities and the associated trade and tourist promotions between the two countries.

When we arrived in Rio for the finish of the race we stayed at the Intercontinental Hotel for a few days then moved into an apartment a few streets back from Copacabana Beach. It had everything, including a maid and a housekeeper. Most apartments do in Rio, where servants are still commonplace. It took us a while to adjust; we didn't speak much Portuguese and they didn't speak any English, but we managed to get along. The owners of the apartment were holidaying in the mountains at Terrazoppolis. They had obviously never lifted a finger in the apartment, not even simple things like making a cup of coffee or slicing a piece of fruit; that was for servants to do.

It wasn't our first experience with domestic help. Maggie and Miguel always had servants; essential in the life of an Ambassador, part of the family, travelling from country to country with them. It was not that we needed servants in Rio. They came with the apartment and for them it was a quantum leap from life in a favela. We probably spoilt them by making our own coffee, peeling fruit and pouring drinks for them.

When Caroline and Bronwyn went shopping in the local supermarket and cooked a meal they couldn't believe it. Living in the apartment was a chance to mingle with the locals. Tourists in hotels seldom come into contact with the real people of Rio, or any other city for that matter.

It was the theft of my jacket that brought me into contact with some of the real people of Newport. The America's Cup network was great, but it was my Irish contacts that opened the doors that counted. The day after my experience at the police precinct one of them rang me to confirm an important meeting in Boston. He had arranged for me to meet one of the East coast's major liquor distributors.

We drove to Boston and met the distributor in a hotel bar. He asked how much we thought the port packs would retail for and I said about $1200, and we could land them for $600. "We'd be interested in taking 2000 of those on consignment," he said. 'Bloody fantastic,' I thought, and told him that David Smith would fly over to formalise an agreement.

The next day, April 20, I flew to New York and went to the British Consulate for an emergency passport. It was valid for only three days. That really put the pressure on as the A4 paper clearly stated that it was conditional on me leaving by *United Airlines* Flight 5 to LA and connecting with *Continental Airlines* to Sydney. After a frustrating delay waiting for the precious piece of paper to be signed by a vice-consul I rushed out to Kennedy Airport and Flight 5.

Everything went without a hitch until I got to Sydney airport and realised the one thing the A4 sheet didn't have was a re-entry permit for Australia. When I spotted the familiar face of airport manager Barry Spencer near the immigration entry point, I knew my luck was holding. When I told him my problem, Barry took me through a side door and out to the baggage collection area. It had been an adventurous and rewarding trip. I had set up Smith with one of the biggest liquor distributors in the US, but what I didn't know then was that neither he nor his colleagues had sufficient money to cover production costs.

Few Australians even dreamed it would be the year the nation would break the New York Yacht Club's 132-year stranglehold on the America's Cup. Smith went to Newport and tried to raise money there for production. After a few fruitless days he telephoned me and said he was homesick.

"The best way to fix that is to work your arse off and raise the money," I said.

"The project is all set up, the hard work's been done."

In the end though, Smith failed to secure any money and then had the audacity to ask for the $10,000 back. I threatened to sue him for loss of potential earnings of $85,000 and he backed off fast. Watching *Australia* win the Auld Mug on television in the early hours of September 27 I thought 'That makes up for my lost passport, but not the lost opportunity. Yachts, ports and cops' wives that pass in the night!'

Harry M Miller could have taught Smith a few tricks. Harry has twice struck it rich in the entertainment industry where being an arsehole is often the only way to strike a deal. Harry M didn't go to gaol for being an arsehole; it was for being in over his head in a failed enterprise that cost people money. Other people were involved, but Harry M. was the only one to finish up in the slammer. The establishment had vilified Harry M long before he went to gaol – for being a success, a Kiwi upstart who was getting too close for comfort, especially when he was nominated to direct Australia's Bicentennial celebrations. He was chairman of the Queen's Silver Jubilee visit and a *Qantas* board member.

That was too much for the establishment in a time when the Royals were on top of the pile. Just because he was close to the Royal Family, political and business leaders, and firmly on top of the show business pile, didn't mean he was 'the right sort' for the job. After all, he had been just a white goods salesman in New Zealand. There was a well-orchestrated campaign and when Harry M eventually went to gaol the establishment said 'I told you so.'

Harry M was not just being altruistic when he decided Lindy Chamberlain, whose baby was taken by a Dingo at Ayers Rock, needed him as a manager. There's an analogy to be drawn between them, for both were found guilty and sent to gaol in the same year, 1982, both protesting their innocence. Lindy Chamberlain wasn't an arsehole, but many people blinded by their own prejudices put her down as much worse.

I worked for Harry M as manager of his telephone information service and he was the sharpest businessman I have known. Whenever he had an important phone discussion with anyone he would have his phone on speaker with a secretary taking notes. Harry M was a regular user of a blackboard or whiteboard in meetings, with the ever present secretary taking notes. Whenever Harry M put down the phone or wiped the board clean, he held the only ace, his secretary's notes.

When I left the business, we had a dispute over commissions. Harry said we had agreed on a small percentage of the net, after all costs had come out; "Remember, it was on the blackboard." I could have sworn it was a small percentage of the gross, but the blackboard had long since been wiped clean and Harry said his secretary's notes distinctly said 'the net.' Harry may have wiped the blackboard clean, but I'm not at all sure about the slate.

Not that I'm saying Harry's word can never be trusted. When he said arranging media interviews for cash for sole Thredbo mountain landslip survivor Stuart Diver would be 'ghoulish and disgusting' he was absolutely right. Before joining Harry I had been at the advertising agency Schofield Sherbon Baker working on business development. Although officially a 'suit', I sometimes wore jeans and T-shirt and indulged in Coca Cola can bongs in the 'creative' department. The whole business of dress denoting your station in advertising was bullshit.

It implied that wearing jeans and being temperamental proved you were creative, and being conservatively dressed and cool said you were only cut out to be an account executive or a media buyer.

I have known some in advertising who were not cut out to be either; they just happened to be somebody's good idea at the time.

Another good idea - Let's Buy *Oriana*

From his yacht on *Mary Blair* on Sydney harbour Charles English Henderson III strode noisily into my life in Sydney's conservative Menzies Hotel in late 1985. The Northern Territory cattle rancher wanted me to arrange a meeting with Bryan Grey. I knew how to get to Grey, and it gave me an opportunity to get away from Harry M. Fred Baker and I were having a beer in the elegant first floor lounge of the Menzies when, in the distance, we heard a loud American voice.

"That's Charlie," said Fred.

Charlie was a long way past his prime, a big man with hands likes plates of meat, penetrating blue eyes and a square, jutting jaw, greying, slightly stooped, and constantly racked by a wheezing cough. A well-tanned, lived-in face with a sceptical, up-curled mouth. Precise and slightly arrogant, a military man with a grip that said: 'Don't play with me, buddy.' Gnarled fists had left their mark in many a bar-room brawl – but beneath that tough exterior sat a Virginia gentleman.

Charlie was Lee Marvin with style. "I hear you know something about the tourist industry," he thundered. "You've worked with the airlines – with Grey, I want to meet Grey. Can you arrange it?"

I told him I'd like to know why. It was the right approach with Charlie – give back as good as you got. He told me about Bullo River in the Northern Territory and his plans to open a tourist resort there – not too much, just enough to get me interested. Bullo River was a million-acre cattle spread on the banks of the Bullo and Victoria rivers, 200 miles west of Darwin in the tropical north of Australia. "God's million acres," said Charlie. It wouldn't be long before I was agreeing with him.

We talked about airlines, the tourist industry and my time with Australia's domestic airlines, particularly *East West*; he talked about his background and what he was attempting to do at Bullo River.

Charlie was a flier from the old school – not a pilot, a flier. Pilots mucked around with switches and computers and all those new-fangled things. Fliers flew aeroplanes. Charlie flew like a bat out of hell, especially in the Pacific during World War II. He was a pioneer in perfecting near-suicidal night landings on US Navy carriers, pitching and rolling in the unpredictable Pacific swell. He needed the unerring accuracy of a bat. Charlie had it then. Commissioned in 1940, he served as a deck and engineering officer aboard the battleship *USS New Mexico*. He moved to Pensacola to become a naval aviator and served three times aboard *USS Enterprise,* rising to command of VT(N)90, a 27-plane night-bomber squadron.

He sank two ships at the Japanese fleet anchorage and air base at Truk in 1944 during the first low-level attack at night, in which 11 aircraft sank 12 ships. As a bomber pilot, he shot down four enemy planes, including one of the agile Zero fighters. Using TBF radar and a system of his own development, Charlie achieved the first air-to-air night intercept and kill, a Kawanishi H8K1 'Emily' flying boat. It was the same night he sank a cargo ship and disabled a destroyer with eight rockets.

Charlie was the youngest CO of a carrier squadron in the first night carrier air group, and his decorations include Silver Star and bar; DFC and four bars; Air Medal and six bars. At the end of the war Charlie resigned and went with UNRRA to Shanghai, as Assistant Director, Air. Then he was involved in a number of shipping ventures, culminating in the establishment of Henderson Trippe, trading out of Manilla, Hong Kong, Tokyo and Sydney. Henderson Trippe became one of the biggest steamship agencies and charter brokers in the Pacific. In Manila it held more than 150 agencies, including Fiat, the Rootes Group, DKW, Piper Aircraft, Bell, Pratt and Whitney, as well as the monopoly of the Australia-Manilla live cattle trade.

This enterprise became a casualty of the political turmoil in the Philippines and of malicious litigation that ultimately failed. After the death of his friend President Magsaysay, he rebuilt the business and operated a fleet of eight light tramp steamers and time-chartered tonnage on a Pacific berth service, carrying copra for Paxmo. Trouble with grain giant Cargill brought about the demise of his shipping operations.

As well as a pilot's licence, Charlie held a Panamanian Master's ticket and a Chief Engineer's certificate. I addressed him as Charles, but talked of him as Charlie; he had that presence of command. You deferred to him whenever it was appropriate, as when boarding his beloved *Mary Blair*, a 38 foot white wooden-hulled older style yacht, on which Charlie now spent most of his time. That's where he forced visitors to use the Navy phrase "Permission to come aboard, sir." I compromised and settled on *"Mary Blair*, permission to come aboard." "Permission granted" was the abrupt reply to both. *Mary Blair* sat in Sydney Harbour's Rushcutters Bay near the Cruising Yacht Club.

From our new rented apartment up the hill at Darling Point I looked down on the club and the bay. *Mary Blair* was clearly in sight and, with Charlie in shouting distance, a fact that led to some of my neighbours becoming quite enraged.

"Ahoy there, *Mary Blair*," he would bellow out at the top of his voice and his "crew" Jane Newbecker, a buxom, laughing young Australian girl, would row the little inflatable dinghy ashore to take him back aboard. I know it's bad luck to change the names of boats, but it should have been called *The Jane*.

Softly spoken, gentle, but rock-hard when she wanted to be, Jane was all things to Charlie and *Mary Blair*. A former nurse, Jane had fallen in love with boats and had sailed much of the Australian coast. She was a born sailor, a fine cook and housekeeper and a bright young companion for Charlie. Charlie related well to young girls. He didn't have too much time left on earth and was enjoying life while he could.

When we had finished our first short meeting in the Menzies lounge, we moved to a nearby bar and had a few beers. That's when I met Jane who, despite the innuendo in Sara Henderson's first book, was simply a loyal crew member and companion to Charlie. They talked about the Bullo River Special and promised to introduce me to it at Bullo. "The best damn drink you'll ever get," said Charlie. He had convinced me that the only way to evaluate his tourist project was to visit Bullo. "Until you see it, you don't know what the hell I'm talking about," he said. His wife Sara and three daughters would love to have us visit them.

Bonnie, his second eldest daughter would be happy to put on a show for us in her Pitts Special plane. One day she was going to be world champion aerobatics pilot in open company.

"She's one hell of a flier," said Charlie, "almost as good as me." But he was worried about Bonnie. "She's got herself involved with some smart young bastard."

Charlie was strictly an old-fashioned father, one of the reasons why he had gone to the Northern Territory in the first place. He had found one of the most remote, inhospitable parts of the world to rear three daughters, away from the evils of modern society. ABC TV had produced a documentary about them called Henderson's Daughters. I was keen to see it and was Charlie and *Mary Blair* lucky enough to meet the family first.

Charlie's idea for Bullo River was to acquire an ocean liner and park it in the Victoria River to give Australian and international tourists the best of both worlds. A modern, air-conditioned resort with restaurants, bars, discotheques, swimming pool, and a host of other amenities, moored in the heart of one of the world's last great wilderness regions. It was an imaginative and potentially lucrative venture that appealed strongly to Fred and me. When we discovered that the P&O liner *Oriana* was for sale, we got really serious. *Oriana* would add an important dimension to the project.

The impending sale of *Oriana* was not public knowledge. We heard it from an inside contact in P&O and decided to visit Charlie to put a proposition to him. We took a flight from Sydney to Darwin through the legendary Alice Springs. It was my first visit to Darwin, the city so dramatically devastated by Cyclone Tracy. From films of the Northern Territory, including several documentaries that David Waddington had produced, I had this impression of a flat arid land, transformed each year by seasonal rains.

Overnight it became a vast wetland populated by hundreds of thousands of water birds. During the 'wet', floods would sweep through the Territory and down south. We had seen the effects at Cooper's Creek during Rafferty's run up the Birdsville Track. Arriving at Darwin airport we went straight to Flight Facilities and met 'the young bastard', Arthur Palmer. We didn't take to him at first. He was uncommunicative and seemed to regard us as intruders. We had to push hard to get any response as we flew the 200 miles along the Timor Sea coastline to Bullo River. The country looked totally inhospitable, our view badly clouded by the huge pall of smoke that stretched al most from Darwin to the Victoria River. Smoke from hundreds of bushfires that were burning out of control in the thickly vegetated country.

God's million acres, Bullo Homestead

A regular natural phenomenon that no one bothers much about, no roads, impossible to get in there, so the fires are left to burn out. It has been this way for countless thousands of years. As well as regenerating the land, the fires provide birds with a feast on the run as countless ground creatures flee the advancing flames. It is not inconceivable that birds could start fires with sparks from dropping small rocks onto others. Some species do drop shellfish onto rocks to expose the flesh of their prey. Catching sight of the Victoria River, we got our first real understanding of what Charlie was on about. It was a magnificent, wide river with a gaping entrance dotted with islands and sandbars, a muddy, brown, fast-moving stretch of water, its existence known to few.

It had not been surveyed since Charles Darwin sailed along the northern coastline in the 1830s on his round the world voyage aboard *HMS Beagle*. Darwin had sailed from Plymouth to Brazil in 1831 and on to Terra Del Fuego, Patagonia and Tahiti before sailing around the Top End. We touched down at Bullo River just before sunset on a wide grass strip, taxied through a gate and directly to the front of the homestead. Charlie, Sara, his eldest Marlee and youngest Danielle were waiting to greet us. Danielle took us for a drive in a pickup truck with me in the cabin and Fred on the back. The youngest of the Hendersons asked what I did for a living, where I lived and if I was married. I told her I was separated and lived alone in a flat. (By now, Bronwyn and I had amicably separated.

"You don't have a girlfriend?" she asked. "What you need is a good country girl."

"Danielle, I think we should go back now; we've got lots to talk over with your father," I replied. Charlie had told us about the parties down near the creek and the helicopter pilots who were after his daughters. "I'm always chasing them off the property." I could imagine Charlie in hot pursuit with a shotgun so I was not going to flirt with his youngest daughter.

Charlie and his family were still building the homestead 20 years after leasing the property. It was a long, sprawling stone and timber complex, with spacious rooms and tiled floors. A huge fire was blazing in a wide fireplace in the lounge room, which opened onto an expansive tiled patio. We sat back sipping our Bullo River Specials as th orange glow of the setting sun gave way to the yellow tinged horizon of dancing bushfires and the fiery night sky seemed ominously close. A few hours earlier, Marlee had been bulldozing a firebreak close to that volatile horizon. Bullo reminded me of Maggie and Miguel's farm outside Brasilia. A clipped grass strip ran across the front of the homestead. Beyond it the ground sloped down to the Bullo River, up again and off into a distant range of hills.

The Victoria River was out of sight to our right. The area immediately surrounding the homestead was cleared and cattle grazed to our left, outside a wire fence guarding the air strip. When the grass got too long on the strip they simply let the cattle in to graze. The RAAF regularly used the 5000-foot strip, which accommodated up to eight Hercules transport planes on exercises.

There were other regular visitors to the remote homestead. Many people simply drove off the nearby highway and dropped in for a cup of tea and a chat. Some came from as far away as Texas – tourists who were in the same business, running cattle in a state that in many ways resembles the Northern Territory. Texans readily point out that

Australia's Northern Territory has the same development potential as Texas.

Charlie already knew of the enormous economic growth possibilities. He had worked zealously over many years to tap that potential, but to no avail. Only meagre support had come from the Federal or Territory governments. He was a regular correspondent with politicians including Prime Ministers, Treasurers, successive Territory Administrators and subsequent Chief Ministers. Like others before him, Charlie was wasting his time. Most of the politicians spent more time up themselves than up North. It was a good time of the year at Bullo, with warm, sunny days, pleasantly cool nights and no rain. Charlie was holding court in front of a huge blazing fire. It got so hot we had to move out on the patio. Above us those wonderful outback stars; a myriad flickering lights in the sky. Luckily, the smoke from the bushfires was blowing in the opposite direction to where we sat.

Charlie was a God-fearing man; before dinner someone had to say grace, and then it was on with the roast beef, country style. What happens to beef between the abattoir kill and the butcher or the supermarket shelf? Beef on a cattle property is so superior. The girls had big appetites. Marlee had been driving a huge bulldozer all day clearing fire breaks, while Danielle had shared domestic chores with Sara. The Henderson daughters were strong, healthy and deeply tanned, while still retaining their feminine charm. Each of them had a beguiling attractiveness, an earthy, animal sexuality I had never observed before. Everyone was talking animatedly across a range of subjects, everyone but Arthur who seemed sullen and reticent; not surprising, with Charlie breathing down his neck. The Bullo River Specials had a kick like a mule. Combined with the fine red wines served with dinner, they had a rapid soporific effect on Charlie, who retired early.

When Charlie left Arthur started to come out of his shell. An anthropologist and a working pilot, he was an interesting character. Light aircraft provide the lifelines in the Northern Territory and many Territorians learn to fly at an early age. The girls had been flying for as long as they could remember. They were just as adept with horses, motor cars, tractors, bulldozers, and graders. They had to be, in order to carve a million acre cattle property out of what was virgin scrub. Building, fencing, making roads – whatever it was, the girls and Charlie had done it.

But they couldn't have done it without the Aboriginal stockmen and Dick Wicks, the station hand. Affectionately known as Uncle Dick, he had joined us for dinner that night. Uncle Dick was a cunning old fox. It's an acquired art in the Territory, where it's a lonely life and a quiet one for a man getting on in years. Uncle Dick was in his fifties and had lived a hard life. The drink gets you up there, together with the heat and the debilitating wet. People fly south for the duration of wet, if they can afford to because the tropics can wear you down.

I had experienced the wet briefly in the jungles of South America, and the greenhouse climate of Papua New Guinea. It is more like having a shower than standing in a rainstorm, the tap's on full bore and the tanks never seem to empty; it just keeps on coming. It's great fun if you experience it in a holiday resort – working in it is different. It goes through to your brain, makes you drink a lot. Maybe it's the thought that you might balance it up by getting as wet on the inside as you are on the outside.

Uncle Dick had beaten the system. He definitely got wetter on the inside than the outside. Whenever he got away from Bullo River homestead it was one hell of a job getting him back. On the homestead the Hendersons could limit his intake. Let him loose in Katherine or Darwin and he would be on it for days. Charlie would fly off the handle, then fly off and find Uncle Dick, truss him up like a turkey, throw him in the back of the aircraft and fly him back to Bullo River. They had a few punch-ups but they respected each other, for Bullo was home to both of them.

Every isolated cattle station needs an Uncle Dick, a Mr Fix-it, particularly for the generator, the only source of power and light. You just have to keep them running. It was the same in Brazil. Off at the same time every night and on at the same time in the morning. For the rest of the time it was candles or flashlights. No sense wasting fuel. With the need to transport it over great distances, fuel is a costly item in remote areas.

Uncle Dick was one of the best in the business. He kept things running when anyone else would have thrown them on the scrapheap. He got on well with the 'Abos', a word used affectionately by Uncle Dick. They were people you couldn't do without in the Territory. Charlie was the Captain, the girls were the First Officers, Sara the Cook and Steward, Uncle Dick the Engineer, and the Aboriginal stockmen the deck crew.

"Have another beer," said Uncle Dick, as we sat on the patio staring into the solitude of a Territory night.

"Cunning old bugger," confided Sara, "he'll keep drinking as long as you do. You're a guest, so he knows we won't ration you. He's found a friend."

Uncle Dick wanted more than a friend; he wanted a Filipino wife and believed I could get one for him. Charlie had told him so. He asked Charlie if he could go to the Philippines and pick one out himself.

"Imagine letting that old bastard loose in the bloody Philippines," Charlie thundered. "We would never see him again; he would drink himself to death, or worse. Let him loose among all those women, it would finish the poor bugger off."

Charlie told Uncle Dick that I had arranged for two or three candidates from the Filipino bride agency in Sydney. I would arrange for him to meet them and make a choice.

It didn't take long for Uncle Dick to see another opening. "Whereabouts do you live in Sydney?" he asked.

"I live on the harbour at Rushcutters Bay." I replied.

"Maybe I can come down and stay with you for a while," ventured Uncle Dick. Warming to the weather beaten face and appreciating the loneliness of his existence, I gave him my phone number in Sydney.

"Don't give him your address whatever you do," said Sara. "He'll just turn up there, and you will never get rid of him." Uncle Dick kept me talking and the beer was flowing freely.

"Have to make that the last beer, it's time for bed," said Sara. I lit one more cigar and sat quietly on the patio, staring into a clear night sky, one of the things Uncle Dick would miss in Sydney. Loneliness does have its compensations.

Awake before dawn the next day, my first sight was of a gaggle of water birds flying, silhouetted against the rising sun at the back of the homestead, where the live-in Aboriginal families were already going about their early morning chores. There were four or five families living there, with other workers coming from nearby mission stations or from itinerant groups that roamed the Territory. We were going for a tour of one section of the property to see some of the natural attractions that might lure the tourists there.

After a hearty breakfast we would discover a world that few whites have seen, from huge expanses of rock-hard ground through dense patches of gum trees, to tropical palms and rainforest with natural springs of ice-cold fresh water, gushing freely as it had done for countless centuries. – a lost paradise of gorges, waterfalls and miniature lakes, surrounded by spectacular carpets of wildflowers. There were delicate dancing brolga; ducks, geese and colourful parrots; massive wild Brahman cattle; fierce crocodiles. Not a bushfire in sight.

Bird life was prolific on Bullo in more ways than one. A young girl there on a working holiday was walking around with a brolga egg between her breasts, hoping it would hatch. "I'm a nature lover," she said. "Besides, it satisfies my maternal instinct." It would startle the hell out of a helicopter pilot if he started to get amorous down near the creek, I thought. The egg was still there when we left and she may still be carrying it around.

They say that a dog is a man's best friend. It's a toss-up on a cattle property. I would go for the dung beetle. Charlie had been one of the first to introduce them to the Territory and they had worked well for him. By destroying the larvae of the bush fly in the dung of the cattle, they prevent the flies from breeding. Tourists find bushfires frightening – no worries at Bullo. Snakes and spiders are only a problem in the wet. Not being too keen on it either, they head for the high ground and away from all that soaking rain. Homesteads are usually on the high ground, so they move in with you during the wet, another good reason for going south. Who wants to share their homestead with snakes and spiders? The circular metal rat catchers on *Oriana*'s mooring cables could double up for snakes and spiders, although Dan Fitzhenry would probably go one better and design some special ones.

A marine surveyor and salvage expert, Dan would visit Bullo to prove *Oriana* could get up the Victoria River under her own steam.

He would give the Australian Navy a helping hand at the same time. Dan had a big reputation in marine salvage. In 1980 he had pinpointed the location of a Beech Super King Air plane which disappeared after take-off from Sydney with 13 passengers and crew.

The country was incredibly diverse, with practically every type of topography found on the continent. There was abundant water cascading downhill which could easily be diverted by laying a few pipes to take it directly to *Oriana*. This was the dry season. A million-acre health farm the Japanese would love.

We were bubbling like those fresh water springs when we got back for our roast beef sandwiches and cold beer lunch. I was on holiday already. We had brought a plan of *Oriana* with us and Charlie was taken aback. Built by Vickers Armstrong in Barrow-in-Furness, Cumbria, and launched in 1959, *Oriana*, a London-registered 41,910 tonne vessel, was 245.06 metres long, 29.57 metres wide and her funnel was 51.21 metres above her keel. She carried up to 1540 passengers and 801 crew and her facilities included four swimming pools.

Oriana – holder of the speed record for the England to Australia voyage

When we came around to discussing the deal, Charlie said, "*Oriana*; I was thinking of something a little bit smaller, but you're right. She's as Australian as the Melbourne Cup. Must be hundreds of thousands of people who have travelled on her, and she is known all around the world, and bloody beautiful. Let's take a look at where she is going to be berthed. You two like flying, do you?"

At that, we just knew we were in for a rough day. Charlie was like that, always had been; he had to prove something, to see if we had balls. We were wondering if we would still have them when we got back.

Charlie mustered cattle with an aeroplane, before switching to helicopters. His daughter Bonnie could take incredible G forces – higher than the average male pilot – before blacking out. Fortunately, Fred and I had both been up with some other terrifying pilots, most notably Bobby Gibbes in Papua New Guinea, and survived. Fred was lucky he had the camera equipment. He wanted to photograph *Oriana*'s future location and other interesting parts of the property. He was smart. While I was up front with Charlie Fred stretched out across two seats in the back. Charlie banked the light plane over the homestead and headed out towards the Victoria River, and then the fun began.

He was like a kid with a new car doing wheelies, only it was a Cessna, not a Ford. It was like being on a surfboard turning on a wave; my knuckles went white, but it was exhilarating. We got such a close look at the Victoria River, we almost touched it. Up and over the cliffs and the mooring site for *Oriana*. Then, skimming low across the range surrounding the Bullo property. It looked for all the world like a lunar landscape with giant boulders strewn along the tops of the peaks. Dozens of Stonehenges end on end.

"We call them The Marbles," said Charlie.

We wondered if he was losing his, the way he was flying. We knew why he had created Bullo River Specials, for I needed one right then, the biggest one you could pour. That's exactly what we got when we landed, because we had balls and Charlie hadn't flown them off. We had seen enough to know that Charlie had a gem of an idea.

All we had to do was get *Oriana*. That was not going to be easy.

Charlie and Sara went walking after dinner and they looked like teenagers in love. Sara seemed happy and contented with life on Bullo. She gave no indication that life with Charlie was anything but rosy. Surrounded by bushfires, she had obviously learnt how to put up a good smokescreen. Charlie said he couldn't pay us much more than expenses until we had *Oriana*. All the funding had to be in place, and that required a syndicate.

We would each get a five per cent share of the project, in return for our work. "You have to take some of the risk too you know, and five per cent could be a lot of money, you could probably retire on it."

We did the deal and the next morning flew back to Darwin. Charlie and I were up front. Fred was smart; he took the back seat again. The bushfires were still burning, the pall of smoke seemed thicker, Charlie got lost twice and Fred wasn't awake when we tried to land on an oil tanker. I didn't realise Charlie's eyesight was going so quickly until he asked if that was the Darwin strip up ahead. I looked up and said "No, Charlie, it's an oil tanker." Maybe he was joking, but I wasn't sure. When we fence-hopped on the approach to the main Darwin runway, Fred was suddenly wide awake.

Charlie had arranged a meeting with the Chief Minister for the Northern Territory, Ian Tuxworth. We prepared a submission outlining the project and our plan to acquire *Oriana*. We knew we would get no financial assistance from the Northern Territory Government. They had had their fingers burnt with other tourist developments including the casino and an Alice Springs hotel development. We needed their support in other ways. Tuxworth was a mate of Charlie's. Charlie had good mates in many high places, and he could cut through red tape like a Ghurkha cuts through throats. We had a long session with Tuxworth and his PR man. While they regarded buying *Oriana* and bringing it to the Territory as a somewhat ambitious idea, they promised us whatever support they could, other than money.

Back at the hotel Charlie introduced us to his young and nubile hairdresser, who was giving him a body massage. Charlie said he was feeling much better now. He drove us to the airport the next day and as we waited to board the 727 aircraft he turned and said: "You know, I never feel safe in those things."

When we got back to Sydney, I parted company with Harry Miller. Charlie brought *Mary Blair* down to Sydney, moored it in Rushcutters Bay, and life for me was never the same again. He moved in and my wife moved out. We decided to have a break, do our own thing. Bronwyn transferred back to Melbourne, and Charlie and I set about acquiring *Oriana*. My apartment became the project headquarters.

Each day Jane would bring Charlie ashore in the inflatable dinghy, and he would walk ever so slowly up the hill. His cough was getting much worse now. His chest was giving him hell. Often, I would look over the balcony and see him, sitting on the edge of the lawn, coughing his heart out. He would make it each time, although he got slower and slower. When he arrived in the apartment he would slump in a chair, wheezing and coughing; then it would slowly wear off, and he would be ready for action. With Charlie it was non-stop. Whether he was furiously taking notes or talking loud and fast on the telephone to a multitude of people. Tuxworth, Murray QC, the Chief of the Federal Police, Major General Ron Grey, the Chief of the Defence Forces, Lieutenant General Sir Phillip Bennett, He got them all excited. It wasn't just a tourist project, it was much more.

It was part of Charlie's grand plan for the North of Australia; ultimate control of the shipping lanes between the Indian and Pacific Oceans. The Russians didn't bother him – the Chinese were the problem. They would take over the world eventually, according to Charlie. "What other nation has so many of its citizens strategically placed around the world? Just think of how many Chinese live in the cities you know. It is the grand domino plan, a Chinese takeover. And we are wide open in the North. You have to develop the North and control the shipping lanes; it's the only way to stop them." Charlie could never get the Australian government to accept his theory, but he had in the Liberal Party a staunch ally who Labour luminary Gough Whitlam described as 'a lovable ratbag'. Billy Wentworth predicted the Japanese war in the Pacific in 1938 and believed China to be the greatest threat to the region. Charlie and Billy had a lot in common. Billy had spent considerable time in the Northern Territory and, like Charlie, he was well aware of its vulnerability and also believed Canberra was too complacent about Australia's Achilles' heel.

I don't know if Charlie ever talked to Billy, but he was talking to the Pentagon, the Australian Defence Forces, and even the Russians. All Fred and I wanted to do was sail *Oriana* up the Victoria River. Many people listened to Charlie and some agreed with him sometimes. John Keldie MC, a brigadier in the Army Reserve, whose exploits in Vietnam were legendary, knew Charlie through Bullo River. It was the location for most of Australia's Army Reserve exercises. Keldie and his troops knew the Bullo property well. Like Charlie, he knew how vulnerable Australia was in the North, with only 400 miles of sea between it and Timor. An enemy could land 10 divisions up there and no one would know they were there. They would simply come ashore unnoticed, and then melt into the surrounding countryside.

This took on new meaning when, in 1994, a group of Asian boat people did just that, then contacted authorities from a public phone box to let them know where they were. Charlie had the ear of the Minister for Defence, too. If we built a new airstrip on Bullo for the *Oriana* project, a strip capable of taking 747s, it would be perfect for Australia's F18 fighters, exactly 200 miles from Darwin, the main base in the North. *Oriana* could be extremely important to the Defence Forces. With radio, radar, accommodation, and fully equipped hospital facilities, Keldie agreed that even for normal peacetime exercises, it would be an excellent base for officers commanding troops in the area. Keldie was a soldier of great distinction. He had flown to Saigon to take over command of A Squadron, 3rd Cavalry Regiment in South Vietnam in 1968, when it was involved in the bloody battles at Fire Support Bases Coral and Balmoral.

When John Keldie returned home from Vietnam he was invited to Buckingham Palace to receive the Military Cross for conspicuous bravery. He spent several months attached to a military unit at Buckingham Palace and became friendly with the Royal Family, particularly Phillip and Charles. Charlie said we held a good poker hand, a couple of Queens at least: "The Queen of the realm and the Queen of the oceans." Early in our negotiations for *Oriana* Keldie had sent a preliminary report on the project to the Palace, and had been advised that when we finally floated *Oriana* up the Victoria River, Charles and Diana would officially launch the venture.

Charlie, as usual, was optimistic about getting the Queen. Prince Phillip had expressed interest in my proposal that a lower deck of the vessel become a Northern Territory base for the Outward Bound movement, of which he was patron.

After I mailed a comprehensive project plan to Buckingham Palace, one of his aides advised that Prince Phillip would be happy to make an official visit to *Oriana* on behalf of Outward Bound. We had other worthwhile schemes for the lower decks of the vessel, including free scientific research facilities for the CSIRO, other organisations and individual scientists and students. As there was ample fat in the revenue figures, one lower deck would be available to general students at concessional rates. Two fast catamaran type motor vessels, a supply boat, offshore fishing boats and a fleet of aircraft, including amphibians, DC3s, light aircraft and helicopters would be ancillary to the project. The aircraft would perform dual roles, flying passengers from Darwin and operating tours.

Ashore, four-wheel drive vehicles would move people about the surrounding wilderness. Tourists would enjoy the best of both worlds; air-conditioned luxury accommodation and facilities, with one of the world's last frontiers at the foot of the gangway. The plan entailed considerably less expense than building a hotel. Unlike a hotel, we could tow the vessel away and sell it for scrap if the project failed. *Oriana* came with its own power, communications rooms, dining and entertainment facilities, ready to receive guests as soon as it arrived. The air-conditioning on *Oriana* was designed for passage through the Middle East. In the Territory the vessel would require only 60 per cent of its cooling capacity.

A regular supply of fresh, potable water existed 500 metres from the mooring site, with a further permanent supply 4000 metres away, and neither needed pumping. The vessel had a sewage treatment plant, capable of coping with 2500 people daily, and we were planning a maximum 1400 aboard at any time. The sewage system discharged biologically inert effluent. The river, flowing at speeds of four to nine knots, would remove the effluent rapidly. If this was unacceptable, we planned to barge it into the open sea, ensuring maximum dilution.

Despite its ruggedness, the Northern Territory has one of the world's most complex and fragile ecologies. But mooring a vessel in the middle of the wilderness would present fewer environmental risks than the construction of a hotel. Environmentally and financially, *Oriana* was the safest option for this early eco-tourist venture.

At that time, the cost of providing a motel bed at the Darwin Sheraton was $82,000. Our cost was $32,000 per bed on 250 used, $16,000 on 500 used and $8000 on 1000 used, the top occupancy on *Oriana*, leaving 750 unused.

The benefits for the Territory included a unique world tourist and convention facility, increasing projected tourist inflow by up to 20 per cent, increasing tourist revenue by up to $35 million per year, with consequent increase in tax receipts, providing at least 250 jobs, and more through multiplier effect, additional traffic for other tourist attractions, stimulation of local industry, a new navigation facility and powerful radio communications for commercial and defence use, and a research station and education facility. P&O was extremely proud of its baby and wanted it to be adopted by the right people in a stable home. When we first contacted them the company did not believe the vessel could sail up the Victoria River. We had to prove it could and then negotiate a price.

Charlie never doubted *Oriana* would get up the Victoria River under her own steam, but P&O refused to accept his word and asked for irrefutable evidence. The only way we could provide that was with comprehensive charts, and the last person to chart the coastline around the Victoria River entrance was John Stoke on *HMS Beagle* back in 1849.

The mouth of the Victoria River had been discovered on 12 September 1819 by Philip Parker King. Captain J C Wickham arrived there in *HMS Beagle* twenty years later, in 1839. Wickham and his crew went more than 200 kilometres upstream into the hostile territory.

Now the Australian Navy was too busy with the America's Cup defence to get involved in a feasibility survey for getting *Oriana* up the river and that really got to Charlie. Many of the available Navy hydrographers were in Western Australia assisting with plotting of the course for the America's Cup defence. "What about defending Australia?" bellowed Charlie. In fairness, in recent years the Australian Navy had re-charted much of the Australian coastline and that is continuing today. Yet the vulnerable North is the poor relation and even a yacht race got priority over it. We did get some support from the Australian Navy Hydrographic Office in North Sydney, including some old charts of the river itself that we sent to P&O. The only way to convince them was with a new survey of the entrance and the river up to the selected mooring site for *Oriana*.

The best man for this was Dan Fitzhenry. Dan had many notable salvage achievements: he helped the Americans find the black box from the ill-fated South Korean 747 aircraft shot down by a

Russian air to air missile, with the loss of all 269 passengers and crew. Dan worked with the latest technology in the salvage industry, including underwater video cameras and electronic depth-sounding gear. He would plot the course for mooring *Oriana* and provide a complete underwater profile on video. Nothing could be more detailed than that. I was working through the night and my telephone bill was astronomical with numerous calls to Singapore, New York, London, Southampton, Italy, all Australian states and Katherine radio telephone, the only link with the isolated Bullo homestead.

I became the conduit in the rapidly deteriorating relationship of Charles and Sara Henderson. I was the demilitarised zone in their continuing emotional pitched battle. "Get Sara to ask Marlee if she's rounded up those cattle. Tell Sara I have to talk to Bonnie. Good staff work, that's what you need," Charlie had told me when we started work on the project. The domestic staff work I could do without. "How's Charles' cough? Why won't the old bugger talk to me? Tell him we need some money." The link in the family chain, I became a regular on the Katherine radio telephone service.

Charlie avoided Sara like the plague, frequently dumping me in the firing line as their domestic hostilities continued. They agreed on one thing – Bonnie was a problem. They had both worked their three daughters into the ground at Bullo.

The Henderson daughters were the most deserving candidates for an award for hard work in the bush. When I stayed at Bullo, Sara and Charlie spent most of the time pottering about the house while the girls did all the hard work. Most of the three-way radio telephone conversations revolved around daily instructions for the girls and Uncle Dick. Apart from that, most of the talk was about money, or the lack of it. We had meticulously planned every detail of the *Oriana* project, except for the most important one, money. Charlie kept saying he had all that under control.

He had failed to get Grey involved, but he had a formidable team, including New England grazier and former Chairman of East West Airlines, David Wright; Brigadier Keldie, who ran several successful businesses in between Army manoeuvres; Adrian Powles, a senior partner in the law firm Allen Allen & Hemsley; Murray QC; Peter Cooper and Barry Lancaster from leading accountants Coopers & Lybrand; Jonathan Jones, Commander RAN; and Charles Siefried, a

New York shipping consultant. While Charlie was trying to arrange an offshore loan, I sent proposals to Kerry Packer, Alan Bond and Sir Peter Abeles and for various reasons they declined. Timing was one of our biggest problems. Crocodile Dundee had not yet hit America; Australia was not yet tourist flavour of the month. Charlie remained optimistic, and there were always the Russians.

Thank God money is not the real yardstick of success in life. For if it was we would be infinitely poorer in the things that really matter like art, music, literature, the environment, the fauna, the flora and life's great characters. While Charlie Henderson died poor, which made his wife richer, without him none of it would have existed. I would rather have known Charlie Henderson briefly than a dozen wealthy men forever. The support of wealthy men can make life easier. It is more rewarding to share a unique experience with someone larger than life.

Charlie's yardstick for fixing a price for *Oriana* was the ruling scrap price around the world, and that's where Charlie Siefried came in. He and Charlie had worked together in shipping. He knew everything that was happening in the world scrap markets, receiving daily reports on prices being offered and likely fluctuations. He had also found some investors in New York, but Charlie Henderson didn't want to know them. "Those bastards will take us over, finish up owning the whole damn thing, and we'll just be working for them. I would rather deal with the Russians than the bloody Yanks," said Charlie the American war hero. The Russians operated ocean liners around the Australian and New Zealand coasts and throughout the Pacific. They were keen to build up tourist trade, with *Intourist* opening an office in Sydney.

Russia had been trying for years to sell hydrofoils to Australia and they would be ideal for shipping passengers and cargo from Darwin to the Victoria River. There was the chance of a package deal – buy a Russian ocean liner that was going out of service, with a hydrofoil or two thrown in, and that would open the possibility of the Russians operating a fly/cruise programme in and out of Bullo. We opened discussions with a captain from a Russian shipping line.

Like many World War II servicemen, Charlie had a grudging admiration for the Russians. He liked their guts and revered their sacrifices. They appealed to him as individuals, particularly seagoing Russians, and the best way to talk to a seafaring man was on a yacht after a hearty breakfast of kippers. Charlie's Russian seafaring friend was a non-smoker, loved kippers, and had been on North Sea convoys in the War. He and Charlie would get on famously. He didn't have time to go sailing so Jane cooked the kippers, then left Charlie and his guest sitting at the mooring.

Charlie didn't tell us too much about their discussions and nothing came of it. They probably talked about the war and the Chinese. We were starting to run out of time, but there was no shortage of Russians. Charlie was forever charming young women and inviting them on board *Mary Blair*, and no doubt the previous owner had been of the same mind. He had bought the sleek white yacht from Shirley of Little River Band fame and he and the yacht had been a magnet for young women.

Charlie, who said he was just following tradition, had met a White Russian, a young Brisbane schoolteacher, and she turned up one night for drinks with one of her teenage students. An attractive blonde woman in her mid to late 20s, she had travelled through China before coming to Australia. I'd never met a White Russian. Her student, a pretty, dark haired teenager, had won a talent quest in Brisbane and was in Sydney for the finals at a television studio. Charlie had just bumped into them in the city and invited them for drinks on *Mary Blair* and, as so often happened with him, a major drama was about to unfold.

The relationship between the White Russian and her young student was not entirely academic and I suspect that Charlie had already worked this out. The student's family had, as I was to hear later from the White Russian.

It was a beautiful sunny day on Sydney Harbour as Charlie, the White Russian, her teenage lover and I sat at the stern of *Mary Blair* enjoying our Bullo River Specials. We were animatedly discussing every other subject but student-teacher relationships. Charlie as usual had Jane below decks preparing a range of nibbles. *Mary Blair* bobbing gently at her mooring near the Cruising Yacht Club just before sunset was hard to beat. Eventually, the visitors decided it was time to take their leave. Jane rowed them ashore and they promised to return the following night. "There's more to them than meets the eye," said Charlie with a knowing wink. Subsequent events would prove him right. One day the White Russian turned up alone and confessed all to

Charlie. Not only did the family know what was going on, they had caught up with her.

Always one to indulge in melodrama, Charlie, with this juicy football under his arm, was running for a touchdown. "There's no room on *Mary Blair*, but John's got an apartment and you can hide out there," he told her.

I drank copious Bullo River Specials and tried to remain calm. I was contemplating jumping overboard and swimming for shore because I had this feeling that while Charlie had been scoring his touchdown I'd been jumped upon by the American footballer nicknamed 'The Refrigerator'.

One of Charlie's finer qualities was the ability to remain gallant in the face of the most extreme adversity. Not wanting to have him feel superior, I withstood the fierce tackle and stood my ground. There was another reason for me agreeing with Charlie's noble gesture. I had been threatened with a rather large kitchen knife by the partner of a young lady to whom I had been paying too much attention, after discovering that I had a predilection for certain lesbian women. Despite a narrow escape from this potential crime of passion, I found the White Russian's young lover attractive.

A phone call to my apartment from Brisbane two days later created what I can only describe as carnal confusion. Charlie had given my phone number to the student as a contact point and she had given it to her parents.

When we received the telephone threat from the student's father it brought upon a sudden rush of gender bending by the White Russian. I had not bedded another woman since Bronwyn had left; in fact I hadn't done much at all with other women since Bronwyn had left. The White Russian found it difficult to sleep after the student's father threatened her and in the emotion charged atmosphere, heterosexuality took on a great deal of appeal. I left my large, lonely double bed and slid into the lower bunk in the second bedroom. The next day I called a cab to take her to the airport, destination unknown, but possibly White Russia. I've not heard from her, the student or her father since.

In London, Adrian Powles had talked to P&O and found that the company chairman was making a business trip to Australia, not about *Oriana*, but on other matters. The cruise business was not going too well, which was one of the reasons for pulling *Oriana* out of service. In a telex from London on March 7, Adrian advised: 'Our advice from independent sources here is that the amount offered (A$5 million) is close to the value of the vessel in its present condition and in current market circumstances.'

Adrian was a mild-mannered man in his late 40s who was always stressed out, talked fast and had a nervous twitch. Charlie said Adrian was hiding something. "I've tried to contact him in London a few times without success," Charlie said. Whenever Charlie raised the subject, Adrian would twitch a bit more and laugh nervously. "There's something mysterious about your trips to London. I think you've got a mistress over there, Adrian." It wasn't a female Adrian was having an affair with; it was with the wickedest mistress of all, that lustful femme fatale – gambling. Gambling seduces rapaciously, stealthily, and without shame. It was the ultimate fatal attraction which led Adrian to his bankruptcy, being struck off as a solicitor by the Law Society and a seven-year gaol sentence for fraud. Adrian had been with the prestigious 172-years-old law firm for 26 years and was the last person anyone would suspect of misappropriating close to $1 million.

In Sydney in 1985, the Chairman of P&O said he did not have the time to go to Bullo with Charlie. Charlie had said: "It is the only way he can assess it. Go there, see it for himself."

The Chairman compromised and agreed to lunch and a sail on the harbour with Charlie on *Mary Blair*. At Bullo, Charlie had you at his mercy; on *Mary Blair* you could at least jump *Oriana* – holder of the speed record for the England-Australia voyage off and swim ashore. We lunched at the Australian Club with the Chairman, P&O Operations Captain, John King, one other P&O executive, Charlie, Adrian, David Wright, John Keldie and myself. The Chairman said we could have *Oriana* if Fitzhenry's survey was acceptable and we had the money; it was ours for $6 million. My staff work had been painstaking and, thanks to Allen Allen & Hemsley, I had amassed mountains of telexes – those Allen's sent for me and those I got back from P&O and Sembewang Shipyards in Singapore, whose people knew *Oriana* down to the last rivet.

We had discussed a complete refit, from Teflon-coating the keel to new gold taps, and a good price for everything they would remove from her in Singapore. Adrian arranged for me to work through his secretary in compiling reports, making phone calls and sending and receiving telexes. He also provided a room at Allen's whenever we had a meeting of all the 'partners' in the project. I found Adrian to be a meticulous man who took pride in his work and spent long hours at the office. Of all of the people involved in the venture, he was the most concerned about the right financial structure being put in place. He resisted several attempts by Charlie to pursue overseas borrowings for both the *Oriana* project and the Bullo property.

We had surveyed, prepared plans and costed a new airstrip at Bullo capable of taking 747s and the F18s of the RAAF. With help from the police based upriver at Timber Creek, we organised a boat for Dan Fitzhenry, and he flew North with Charlie. Being a salvage expert, Dan convinced Charlie that the best way to prove *Oriana* could get up the river was to reverse the situation and treat it as a salvage operation, starting from the premise that *Oriana* was up the river and demonstrating that it was feasible to salvage the vessel from the mooring location, thus leaving no doubt about getting her to the mooring. Together with Marlee, Dan and Charlie comprehensively charted, surveyed and videoed the entire stretch of the Victoria that *Oriana* would have to negotiate to reach her new mooring, and it confirmed what Charlie had believed all along. There were a few tight turns, but she would get there under her own steam.

Dan designed, produced and costed plans for the complex mooring facility, right down to crocodile-proof cages for maintenance work under water. She would sit on the bottom, so tides would not be a problem. We planned overnight camps, bush pavilions, boat trips and other activities, ever mindful of not disturbing the environment.

Present day prices and activities at Bullo station, which is now owned and operated by Marlee and her husband, Franz, indicate we were not being fanciful with our costings or our planned tourist attractions.

The property has twelve motel-style double rooms and is owned and operated by Marlee and her Australian husband Franz Ranacher; it attracts wealthy celebrities like Greg Norman. Marlee has written her own book about growing up on the property – Bullo – the

Next Generation. Adult single occupancy in motel-style units is $735 per night, adult twin $657, child share with adult $350, child single $450, helicopter hire capacity three and pilot $830 per hour.

Activities include river cruises up the spectacular Bullo River Gorge to fish or spot crocodiles; guided tours to local aboriginal rock art; introduction to the hundreds of bird species that call Bullo home; cattle mustering or horse riding, depending on riding ability and the station's mustering schedule; optional helicopter trips for aerial sight seeing; river and coastal fishing, with unique access to untouched local areas by boat or helicopter The vessel would fuel and store in Singapore and after that would be supplied from Darwin by barge. We would retain the P&O principal crew, but make a large dent in Darwin unemployed by providing local hospitality and maintenance training. *Oriana* would provision from Darwin, but the resort would aim to become self-sufficient in produce. We planned a Vietnamese village – a market garden community. We believed that some of the growing Vietnamese community would like it too. It would be more like home than Sydney's outer suburban Catamaran.

If anyone in Canberra had any vision, that is where they would settle some of the Asian refugees – in their own kind of country, doing something they do well, small communities farming a territory bigger than their homeland. Israel has been doing it for years in much worse conditions. You could grow anything in the Territory if you put your mind to it. Not the massive multi-million dollar schemes like Ord River, but traditional peasant farming. We call it market gardening.

As the ambitious project began to take shape, Katherine radio-telephone was running hot on the domestic scene, with me doing most of the talking. I stayed strictly neutral with Arthur and the Hendersons. From observing Arthur and Charlie at Bullo, I believe much of Charlie's ranting belied the respect the pair had for each other. Bonnie also maintains that her father and Arthur had a good relationship. She says her mother's books *From Strength to Strength* and *The Strength in Us All* are built on fantasy and exaggeration.

In an extraordinary judgement on a man she had never met, Jane Fraser, writing in *The Australian Magazine* in April 1994, said of Charlie: 'He seems destined to be remembered, if at all, as a somewhat pathetic creature, hopelessly innumerate and profligate, abysmally self-centred and endlessly priapic. Oh, and not without a certain boyish charm. This, at least, is how he is portrayed in his wife's extraordinarily popular autobiography.'

Fraser added the words: '...his own lacklustre lifetime performance and somewhat unremarkable death.' What a shocking judgement of a man who had played a heroic part in helping to fend off the planned Japanese invasion of Australia in World War II. But then, Ms Fraser is a rather lacklustre and somewhat unremarkable writer. Interviewed by *New Idea* in July 1994, Bonnie said many of the anecdotes in Sara's books were based on Bonnie's own experiences, not Sara's.

Under the headline My Mother Betrayed Me, Bonnie told *New Idea*: "I hope that while people enjoy the books, they also recognise them for what they are: virtual fantasy. Through the two books Sara has made me public property on her terms, but I can no longer sit back and allow her to betray me and my family. We haven't spoken in five years. The cheque Daddy made out to me for $50,000 for wages was stopped by Sara. She also refused to have a reading of the will, so I am unsure of Daddy's other wishes. Not any of our children have ever received a birthday or Christmas card from Sara. She has never ever played with her grandchildren. When Georgie was born with neonatal blindness, Sara did not call."

Arthur told *New Idea*: "People get the wrong impression from these books, that it was Sara who built up Bullo. In reality it was Bonnie, who worked like a dog for five years as head stockman to fulfil her father's dream of making Bullo the property it should be. When I went to Bullo to get Bonnie off the station when she was 21, she needed a major jaw operation which resulted from grinding her teeth from stress since she was a little girl. Midway through the surgery, Sara rang, screaming at me to bring her back, there was work to be done. Bonnie was treated like a working dog, but she didn't go back." Gus Trippe, cousin and business partner of Charlie for many years, who probably knew him better than most people, in a letter to Bonnie and Arthur in June 1993 said: "I'd still go to hell for Charlie as I have done over the years. But I would not cross the street for Sara." Bonnie and her sisters are as strong-willed as Charlie and Sara. It was the way Charlie brought them up, to fend for themselves and make their own decisions in the harshest possible conditions – ride like the wind, cut them, brand them, muster them, fence them, shoot to kill, butcher them and fly like a bat out of hell. Bonnie had put on a show in the Pitts Special when we first went to Bullo. I could hardly bear to watch; the tiny plane was like a yo-yo on a string, twisting, turning, looping, banking, stalling, dropping like a stone; she scared the hell out of me. Charlie and Sara might take out Arthur, but not the Pitts Special; it was her second skin.

Bonnie had gone to Darwin and moved in with Arthur, as I knew she would. I had talked to her when I had gone there on my second trip, along with Adrian and his son. We had met in a bar in the Darwin Travelodge, because Charlie loved her, and he wanted me to let her know that he did, but he and Sara were not going to back off. Bonnie said she already knew that. "I love Arthur and I want to marry him and have a life of my own," she said. "They keep threatening to take my plane. If they do that, then I'll never go back to Bullo." We talked generally about life at Bullo and the tourist project. Like Sara, she was excited about *Oriana* and was hoping that it would solve Charlie and Sara's problems and take their minds off her and Arthur.

Bonnie eventually broke the leg-ropes her parents had tied on her from an early age and then bolted out of the family stockyard. When Sara grounded the Pitts Special and sold it, Steve Hart, a friend of Arthur and Bonnie, bought it and sold it back to Arthur. Bonnie eventually married Arthur in 1986 and, in Henderson tradition, they have three daughters: Amelia, Georgina and Harriet. Their property is a modest 65 hectares just south of Darwin, where Bonnie breeds Waler horses and Arthur continues his anthropology work.

Bonnie's own story has been told in Debi Marshall's *Her Father's Daughter* published by Random House. There are two sides to every coin and families drift apart with depressing regularity. Charlie was no angel, but he did not deserve the opprobrium heaped upon him after his death by so many women seeking to justify the myth that all men are bastards.

Ironically, Bonnie and Arthur have split and now she lives alone with her daughters. In Her Father's Daughter, Bonnie has to some extent set the ledger straight about both men. Her revelations about her father's numerous aircraft 'prangs' made me realise how lucky Fred and I were to survive our flights with Charlie. I took some pictures of likely Filipino brides for Uncle Dick, but he was not impressed with any of them. He was still planning to go to Manila, and make his own choice, but Charlie said: "Over my dead body."

We set out in two trucks. I was with Uncle Dick, who loaded the beer on, and we took off first. Marlee, Adrian and his son were charging along behind wondering about Uncle Dick, the beer and me. He was a good talker, but I set him straight early: "No beer until we get there." We were going to the hallowed site where the majestic white *Oriana* would sit at the foot of the red cliffs, and we were going to climb those ancient cliffs to see it all at first hand. Nobody but the Aboriginals had been there before. That morning Marlee had rowed me out in a small dinghy in a secluded gorge with sheer, towering walls, the damp morning mist rising slowly off the water, the mist the Aboriginals had seen 40,000 years ago. It took us three hours to get to the point where we had to abandon the vehicles and go on foot across the broad, grey salt flats, where giant crocodiles roamed. With Marlee leading with a .303 rifle slung over her shoulder, the 'crocs' didn't stand a chance.

We walked through thick mangroves and over rocky outcrops, then climbed and scrambled through dense undergrowth and rock-strewn crevasses. Exhausted, we sat on a wide rock ledge on the edge of the cliffs, looking down at the berthing point for *Oriana* and pictured it there. Nobody could come here and not feel close to the land, nor understand what the Aboriginals mean about the timeless land, infinity on earth. We had left Uncle Dick with the vehicles but not all the beer – just a couple. I sat there drinking a Fosters and wondered if anyone else ever would.

No white had been there before. The Hendersons hadn't, and the locals knew of nobody who had. I left the empty Fosters can there, propped in a small crevice, and I thought of Spike Milligan, but I wasn't littering; I just wanted to let someone know I had been there. Maybe in another 200 years someone might find it and wonder how the hell it got there. I once thought Birdsville was a long way out but now it seemed a long way in. This was one place where Rafferty wouldn't run, unless those wild cattle came upon him.

In country too inaccessible to round them up, they may run wild for ever, adapt and survive. Like the wild cattle found in Brazil, grazing on a beach, eating only shells, not looking too healthy, but surviving. The wild cattle of Bullo didn't have such problems; the wet saw to that with plenty of good grazing and nobody within a bull's roar.

We picked our way slowly back across the salt flats, keeping a wary eye open. If a mob of them charged, none of us would stand a chance, not even Marlee with her 303. Adrian's son hadn't seen a crocodile, but it didn't bother me or Adrian. Next day Charlie took Adrian and his son up in the Cessna to show them around. I stayed on terra firma and talked to the girls. It was good to be out of Sydney, as my neighbours were becoming restless, and not just about Charlie bellowing off the balcony. I seemed to have many people coming and going. Charlie was always noisy, whether he was coming or going. I didn't realise it at the time, but Charlie was nearing death.

When *Oriana* sailed out of Sydney Heads for the last time, bound for her final destination, Japan, trailing her long paying-off pennant, many people phoned radio talk back shows and wrote to newspapers and asked why. Tears were shed, some crocodile and some real. When Charlie left town, I tried some alternatives for *Oriana*, like a permanent home at Circular Quay. Sydney hotelier Leon Fink did have the money for that, but the relevant NSW government minister Laurie Brereton didn't have the will, despite his excellent masterminding of the development of Circular Quay and Darling Harbour. The best Brereton could offer Leon was a short-term berth at Darling Harbour, pending completion of that development. Fink backed off, leaving me with nowhere else to go.

Oriana was part of Australia's heritage, but it went to Japan where it became a floating hotel-convention centre, berthed in Beppu Bay on the island of Kyushu. So the Japanese finally got the better of American war hero Charles English Henderson III. Worse, *Oriana* went from there to China.

In early July 2004, during a severe storm, *Oriana* broke free of its mooring in Xinghai Bay in northeast China and at first it was feared she had sunk. Later reports said *Oriana* had listed badly, but she had been saved.

Oriana now takes pride of place in the Chinese resort city of Dalian In Strength to Strength, Sara Henderson dismisses Charlie's dream in a few sharp words: "To solve our half million plus debt, he was going to borrow some twenty million more. Not to mention the headache of a thousand tourists and eight hundred staff on *Oriana* out in the middle of nowhere." On my visits to Bullo, in Darwin and during our inspection of *Oriana* at Circular Quay, Sara was ecstatic about the project. She made it clear to all of us that she would be playing a major role and that in terms of interior decor she was the expert. Like the rest of us, Sara liked the good life and had many ideas for entertaining tourists once the vessel was moored on the Victoria River. Sara also came with us to lunch at the Wrights' property near Armidale and for dinner with the Keldies on Sydney's North Shore, and on both occasions we discussed the *Oriana* project in detail. The Japanese paid $13 million for *Oriana*, and spent another $20 million on fit-out.

We could have got *Oriana* for $6 million and the potential returns from Charlie's dream would have put the Japanese venture in the shade. Charlie and *Oriana* – dreams and ships that pass in the night.

After a long illness, Charlie died in June 1986 in a house in Sydney's northern beach side suburb Palm Beach, with his beloved *Mary Blair* moored within sight of his bedroom. Marlee married a helicopter pilot named Charlie in 1988, but tragically, later the same year, he fell off a motor bike, broke his neck and died. In 1992 she married again. Danielle married in September 1993 and lives in Queensland.

Charlie has four sons from his first marriage, Jack and David who live in Australia, and Hugh and Fraser who live in the US, so the Henderson genes will be around for some time. Perhaps, after all, we should leave the last words about Charlie to Sara Henderson: "For all his faults, there is no doubt that on the 15th of June the world lost a remarkable human being."

Paint the Bastards White

It was appropriate that I met John Abels during the celebrations for the 75th Anniversary of the Royal Australian Navy. A former assistant to the Federal Defence Minister in the Australian Liberal Government, he was selling port from a stand on Sydney's old Woolloomooloo Wharf. Colin Barnes of the Sydney Visitors Bureau had asked Fred Baker and me to sell stand space on the wharf for the marketplace associated with the anniversary. It was set up for the sale of souvenirs to tourists and crews from overseas vessels.

Abels was selling Hunter Valley souvenir port in pottery decanters. Fred's wife, Jan Lamont, had a stand to raise funds for the restoration of the barque *James Craig*. Jan was a formidable woman who the distinction of being chief of her Scottish clan, which meant that on formal occasions Fred would have to walk several paces behind her, cutting a handsome figure in his kilt. Eventually he got too far behind and she ran away to Queensland with a sailor, which Fred saw as evidence of amazing presence of mind. Jan was public relations manager at the Sydney Maritime Museum which was faithfully restoring *James Craig*.

In keeping with Sydney's convict history, prisoners from Long Bay Gaol were allowed out to assist with the restoration, which involved plating and riveting the hull, using the original construction methods and tools. Jan, Fred and I ran a number of promotions to raise money for the restoration, including the Marching of the Masts Ceremony. This traditional maritime event brought Sydney's main city thoroughfare, George Street, to a standstill several times. The massive Oregon masts, which were shipped from Canada, required four timber jinkers and a low loader borrowed from the State Electricity

Commission. The march also included a steam traction engine which frequently had to stop for water and for Jan, naturally, a pipe band.

The barque James Craig

James Craig had been rusting away in Recherche Bay in Tasmania before being towed to Sydney by a museum crew. It is now fully restored and has visited a number of Australian ports. The day the crew turned up in Recherche Bay to encase the hulk in concrete for the tow, a fist fight had broken out with an American crew over ownership of the vessel. The Americans not only lost the fist fight, but also the ensuing court battle. I can't say if that's what led to the American battleship *USS Missouri* coming to town during Navy Week.

We talked to Abels about a fleet of safety buoys for Sydney harbour and then met with him and his partner Rick Carroll an advertising executive and restaurateur. They agreed to fund a company called Oh Buoy to construct a fleet of buoys and sell advertising contracts. While commercial shipping lanes and hazards are clearly marked with buoys, beacons and lighthouses, recreational boating enthusiasts are mostly left out in the cold and often in the drink. Sydney harbour, like most recreational boating zones, has many hazards but precious few marks, despite the increasingly heavy traffic from surf-skis to maxi-yachts and gin-palace cruisers.

Maritime authorities worldwide have little or no funds for the marking of recreational boating hazards. I had discovered this some years previously and set about rectifying the situation, with an eye to the revenue potential that could flow from corporate sponsorship of safety markers. The initial inspiration had come from Brazil, where I had seen large inflatable buoys marking a circuit for sailboard races near Rio de Janeiro. The markers advertised the South American cigarette manufacturer Souza Cruz's Hollywood brand.

When returning from the finish of the Sydney Rio race, I brought back some photographs of the marker buoys. When *Oriana* made her final graceful exit from Sydney Harbour my mind turned back to the buoys.

"What good is a good idea unless it gets off the ground or in this case into the water?' I asked my friend Norm Bennell, an executive with the Maritime Services Board of New South Wales. Norm agreed to organise a meeting with the Harbourmaster. The prospect of gaining safety markers for harbour hazards while reaping a profit from the venture was a project that delighted former seafarer Captain John Briggs.

The world of commerce would provide the buoys, saving any capital outlay by taxpayers on what were essentially community assets, and contribute a considerable sum to state revenue. This was New South Wales Premier Nick Greiner's policy of corporate funding of government enterprises in action. From May 1986 I met with Bennell on a number of occasions to discuss the safety buoy project and drafting of a contract with the Maritime Service Board (MSB).

Then I continued the negotiations over a contract with Briggs, who had advised the board he needed the buoys for two major reasons.

The first was for crowd control, particularly for the annual Sydney to Hobart yacht race; the second was to mark hazards on the harbour and other NSW waterways. Briggs was contemplating moving the start of the yacht race outside the Heads because of safety problems with the huge and sometimes unruly spectator fleet. After much deliberation and discussion on designs, anchorage and other technical details, we settled on an eight foot, spherical, hollow fibreglass buoy, with internal steel bracing, mast and road traffic style signs, and sand and polyurethane for ballast and flotation.

The MSB approved the buoys and asked my solicitor Barry Geraghty to draft a contract. Work on a contract for advertising on litter bins in the city of Sydney some years previously had alerted Geraghty to a number of pitfalls. There would be substantial capital outlay on buoys, maintenance, insurance and sales activities, so Geraghty advised me to go for a five-year contract with a five-year option.

"They've given you the opportunity to get a long term contract," he said. "With so much development work and money to go into this to make it work, you need plenty of time to get your investment back and make good money yourself."

I submitted the draft contract to the MSB legal department, and subsequently to the MSB board. Bennell told me: "It has to get board approval. The MSB will also have to get Transport Minister Laurie Brereton's okay on this."

I got the draft contract back with some proposed MSB amendments and took it to Geraghty who said it required some further negotiation. After a number of phone discussions, Briggs eventually said: "The board has approved your contract." When I got the final contract back and a letter asking me to sign it and return it to the MSB, I caught a harbour ferry to the Mosman Rowers Club, an appropriate venue to celebrate with friends.

Later, Fred and I took a launch out on the harbour with a number of regular harbour users to pinpoint permanent safety marker locations. Our first meeting with Abels and Carroll was in a flat in the inner Sydney suburb of Petersham, not far from Abels' main business. The Lolly Trolley employed young people to sell bags of chocolates, sweets and nuts in city and suburban business districts. Abels employed the unemployed, school kids and sometimes kids who didn't make it to school. It was a good cashflow business, keeping many kids in pocket money, but it could not have funded the Harbour buoy project. Abels assured us he had money coming from the sale of wine and other goods and that Rick had good cashflow from his restaurant. Together, they were in a good position to fund the operation.

Fred and I had come up with some designs and Bob Peachey of Fiberglass Australasia agreed to manufacture a prototype. Carroll said he had had discussions with Coca-Cola and they would like to see a prototype with their logo on it. We asked Peachey to go ahead with production of the first buoy.

Soon, Peachey's Minto factory was flat out producing the fleet of 50 buoys, while Fred and I were dispatching proposals to potential buoy advertisers. While there were a number of genuine enquiries about advertising on the buoys, we found it was a difficult proposition. New outdoor advertising locations need a long lead time to establish themselves, as most people wait for someone else to make the first move. When it's successful they all scramble to get aboard typical of big business. Far from being movers and shakers, many people in marketing worry about doing anything that alters the status quo. Many are terrified about making a wrong decision and losing their jobs, and tend to stick to what they regard as safe, mainstream advertising.

Abels started to sweat, for he didn't have the money and neither did his partner. When Peachey asked Abels to put his money where his mouth was, Abels gave him a series of post-dated cheques, and they started to bounce. Briggs, the MSB and the boating public and spectators were the only winners at that time. Come Sydney-Hobart time, the famous blue water classic would still start on the harbour. Imagine the race starting outside the harbour and losing much of its excitement and spectacle. The Maritime Services Board laid the buoys on the morning of the race and they worked like a charm, making life infinitely easier for the Cruising Yacht Club, the Water Police and the MSB.

Having discovered that Abels and Carroll were broke, we had to shelve the project for a while. We were reluctant to get involved with any more dubious financial partners. However, we met two businessmen, John McAuley and Warren Brain, who seemed financially sound, and once again we set out to fund the buoys and a new magazine called *Waterways*.

You would think that we had got it right by now. McAuley was an uncle of Christine Bookalil, fashion editor for *Vogue* magazine, who shared a small inner Sydney terrace with us and Canadian PR consultant Iain Macintosh. Many a client must have had his impressions of the PR world vindicated when he walked through the front door to be confronted by half-naked female models, frock changing for fashion shoots for *Vogue*. Working with Macintosh and us was Sharon Zaunmayer, 'Z' as she was affectionately known.

While things were booming on the waterfront, we had negotiated for Bennell to take a $60,000 advertising contract with *Waterways*.

The MSB worked with us on editorial content. The magazine would target boating and fishing enthusiasts with articles on boating safety, licensing, regulations and developments on the water and around the foreshores. It also provided an excellent promotional vehicle for the safety buoys. With McAuley, Warren Brain and Fred Baker, we discussed lodging my buoys contract and the MSB advertising contract in a joint venture company. This time we set out some basic conditions about the level of investment and what we'd be paid.

"The only reason we're talking to you is that we have no money to continue developing the two projects," I told McAuley and Brain. "Our previous financial backers have fallen over, because they didn't have the money they said they had."

McAuley said: "We have quarrying interests, we're buying the Canberra Rex Hotel, and there are other interests, so there will be no problem with money. I do work for Alan Bond and Laurie Connell, so I know what I'm doing in finance, particularly in taxation matters. I fly over to Perth regularly to look after their taxation and other financial matters. Money will not be a problem."

You would think we had it right this time. At McCauley's request Fiberglass Australasia re-issued Oh Buoy invoices totalling $80,880 to McAuley, on his assurance that he would pay all the money owing on the manufacture of the buoys. Later, McAuley said: "It would be better if you assigned the contract to a public company that we can form. The contract would be the major asset of the public company. That and the advertising contract with MSB for *Waterways* would be an attractive package with which to float a public company."

I said: "That sounds like a good way to do it, so Fred and I could get a substantial shareholding. We've put considerable time and money into setting up the safety buoys and the magazine."

McAuley said: "The only way we can establish the safety buoy and magazine projects in other Australian ports and overseas is with a public float.

There's a lot of money involved, especially to cover overseas ports." After our earlier experiences with financiers, before the launch of *Waterways* we insisted on a trust fund for subscription money. Because the magazine was well accepted, readers were sending us subscriptions for up to two years.

Then along came the crunch. McAuley and Brain failed to pay our salaries in December 1987 and production of the magazine stopped abruptly early in 1988. On Christmas Eve 1987 Warren Brain said: "John and I are in financial trouble and the magazine has to go. We have other interests that are more important to us."

I said: "Warren, this magazine is becoming a great success, and what about the buoys?"

Brain said: "John and I are not going to put any more money in, we just can't afford it."

That seemed to be it, so I negotiated for production and distribution of a final issue of the magazine then took on a Bicentenary assignment for a Melbourne public relations company to enable me to survive financially.

*

It was the Flag Inns Cross Australia Balloon Challenge, in which I represented the sponsor. Although McAuley had talked of using the subscription money, all subscriptions in the *Waterways* trust account were returned to readers. McAuley and Brain seriously jeopardised the safety buoy project when they failed to honour their financial obligations to the company.

Armed with the MSB contract I had flown to other Australian ports: , Hobart, Adelaide, Perth and Brisbane and to Auckland, New Zealand for meetings with maritime authorities and water police. The consensus was that once the safety buoys were in operation on Sydney harbour, all would have negotiated similar contracts.

Safety was paramount during the Bicentenary Balloon Challenge, but the unexpected can always happen. It was like the *Hindenburg* disaster when a wayward balloon hit the roof of a house and caught fire in the middle of Broken Hill. In an on-the-spot broadcast a local radio announcer turned back the pages of history with the words "Oh my God, oh no, the balloon's caught fire; this is terrible; oh no!" The reason he was on the spot, at roughly the same distance as the radio reporter at the scene of the *Hindenburg* disaster in New York, was a challenge from the outback mining centre of Broken Hill.

Built in Germany in 1936, the 804-foot long rigid airship *Hindenburg* was the world's first transatlantic commercial airliner. Fitted with four diesel engines the airship could reach a top speed of 82 mph. On May 6 1937 the airship's hydrogen ignited while *Hindenburg* was manoeuvring to land at Lakehurst. The fire caused by the invisible gas destroyed the airship and thirty-five passengers and crew died.

In Broken Hill the city fathers dared the balloonists to fly as close as they could to a cherry-picker crane with a pole extending from the top of it holding a $10,000 silver ingot. Whoever could grab the ingot from their balloon basket could keep it. The pilot of the balloon that hit the roof and wrecked the rooftop air conditioning unit was the only one who managed to fly that day. Strong winds had deterred most of the others from trying, but the young American balloonist had a strong motivation he was broke and we were still a long way from Sydney. A large crowd had turned out to spur him on and a film crew had accompanied him to a launch site out of town and were in the basket with him as he headed at low altitude across Broken Hill.

With some expert manoeuvring he managed to get down to the height of the ingot, but he was about 50 metres off course. As he drifted past the elusive ingot he turned up the gas burner to gain height; the roof was in the way and the impact turned the gas burner on to the balloon itself. Flames licked up the side of the balloon and disaster loomed in full view of the cameras in the basket and on the ground. Miraculously, the flames died as the balloon bounced clear of the roof. Then, as he attempted to land on a road on the edge of town, he struck power lines and the balloon dropped like a stone.

The pilot suffered a broken leg and arm, and his crew and passengers were cut and bruised as the strong wind swept the downed balloon along the road. It could have been much worse.

While that drama was unfolding we were out of town with the Flag balloon and a hastily mustered ground crew from the local football club. We had seconded them to add some weight as we attempted to launch in the howling wind on the protected side of a hill. Somebody had tied off the balloon basket to a towbar, instead of to the front bull bar on a four wheel drive vehicle. As we wrestled with the slowly expanding balloon there was a sharp crack like a gunshot and I felt a glancing blow to the right side of my forehead. I fell to the ground, along with several burly footballers, knocked down by the shattered towbar and shackle as it was whiplashed through the air on the tethering rope.

The wind swept the balloon up the hill, with only the pilot in the basket as the few ground crew who had not been knocked to the ground hung on grimly. The last thing we wanted was a solo pilot up in the air in a half inflated, half-rigged balloon in what had become a howling gale. Fortunately the errant balloon came to a halt at the top of the hill. On the way to hospital with our 'walking wounded' we heard the "Hindenburg report" on the car radio. Our escapade seemed minor in comparison, but if any one of us had turned at the sound of the tow bar breaking, we might have died in a balloon accident before we'd even got off the ground.

We had more than our share of problems from the day we left Perth on the epic journey. It was the largest number of people and vehicles to cross the continent in one group and there simply wasn't enough accommodation in many places. The organisers planned to fly all of the balloons across the city of Perth to start the challenge, but fierce winds put a stop to that.

Not even the impressive line-up of outside broadcast equipment and the accompanying media entourage outside the Burswood Casino lift-off point had any effect.

God the man and nature the woman are equally fickle; boats are all female; and what about 'She's blowin' a gale' or 'She'll be right?" Predictably, Richard Branson's Virgin balloon entry had a female pilot. As the sponsor's representative, I had the best vehicle in the road fleet a double-decker bus with bar and gaming room for entertaining the media. It was 'piss and poker' all the way for the hacks, with an occasional break for cheese and biscuits.

Buckets of booze always accompany sporting events, particularly when they're out of town, and you're the most popular guy around when you've got the key to the bar. Flag management had excelled by providing the 'booze bus' and a wad of 'letters of credit' for bars and restaurants at Flag properties along the way. A round of drinks could set you back $300. It's a wonder we didn't set fire to all the balloons just by breathing close to the burners. The pilots and crews put in some excellent flying and special manoeuvres at various points along the route, and nowhere better than in South Australia's Barossa Valley.

That morning sight alone of dozens of multi-coloured balloons rising slowly from a vineyard in a misty vale made the event worthwhile. It was just like an enormous bunch of technicolour grapes hovering over the vines Apocalypse Now without the whacking of helicopter blades. After the winery celebration party the night before, a 'booze balloon' patrolling among them would have had some early pickings. Some of them were still 'basket cases'.

Smoking can drive a man to ballooning. Our Flag pilot had convinced his wife, who was in his ground crew, that he'd given up smoking cigarettes. The only place he could light up without her knowing was way up. I watched amazed as, standing close to the gas tanks, he lit up a cigarette. "Is that really safe?" I asked nervously.

He gave the burner a blast and said: "That's safe, so's the cigarette. Don't tell my missus, or she'll kill me. She thinks I gave up smoking years ago. This is the only place I can light up without her knowing."

"When in Rome," I said as I lit up and scanned the surrounding sky, just the same as yachting watch the horizon, not the waves; don't look down, enjoy the wind. We were not being pushed by the wind, we were in the wind; we went where it went. No passing air, no sound other than the burner.

Then we went leaf gathering. Vineyards or orchards are best, for you can pick the fruit from the basket as you glide along. We were out from Dubbo in western New South Wales and had to settle for gum trees. As we floated across the tops of the trees we leaned out and grabbed a handful of leaves. Landing with a few bumps and scrapes, the balloon came to an abrupt halt with the basket on its side. As we crawled out and stood up, the next excited group of passengers began running across the paddock towards us. The ground crews keep the balloon in sight, or in radio communication, at all times for the safety of crew and for fast passenger transfers. Pilots, crew, ground support, drivers, officials, media and others worked hard at making the event a success and were rewarded by the keen interest and hospitality all along the route.

*

While Prime Minister Bob Hawke mouthed platitudes about reconciliation, my son Chris and some Koori friends talked of how best to protest the Bicentenary celebrations, which they felt endorsed the dispossession of the Aboriginal race. They had limited resources, but the buoys, sitting high and dry on a wharf, would come in useful. When the MSB asked if I could send the buoys to Botany Bay for First Fleet Re-enactment crowd control, it was too good an opportunity to miss. Graffiti would have been appropriate, but restraint in the face of conflict often brings its own rewards.

We decided friendly Aboriginal motifs and signs were appropriate decoration for the buoys that were, like the convicts, being transported to Botany Bay, albeit by land. It was a rare opportunity to gain valuable coverage for the Aboriginal cause, a chance to contribute. So we all got up to our elbows in paint while drunken white businessmen on harbour cruises drifted by, yelling abuse. "Lazy black bastards," they ranted. "Why don't you get a real job?" We had three days to complete our task before the transports arrived to take the brightly coloured buoys to Botany Bay to await the arrival of the fleet. The truck drivers did not see anything unusual about the freshly painted buoys. "What the fuck do you think you're doing? I'll get sacked if I float these on the bay!" said the agitated MSB official who phoned late at night. "We can only use them if we take them back to their original colour, white," he said.

"Well, you can't bloody use them at all," I responded.

Chris talked with his mates and they said "Your old man's business is at stake. They're not going to use them as they are, so tell him to let the bastards paint them white."

On Australia Day, Chris marched with his mates in the Aboriginal protest in the city, while Hawke and Keating and their mates were sucking up to the Royals. Symbolically, down at Botany Bay a fleet of large white buoys held black protesters at bay while a real-life descendant of Governor Phillip Gidley King was poncing around in a silly outfit, muttering about the financial disaster of the fleet re-enactment. In 1793 Captain Phillip Gidley King was reported to have become 'a little addled again', but nevertheless he was appointed third Governor of the Colony of New South Wales in April, 1800. Descendant Jonathan King, journalist, writer and historian, spent 10 years working on the re-enactment and was inclined to be 'a little addle-pated' on more than one occasion.

Sir Donald Trescowthwick and I had tried to scuttle Jonathan's self-perceived second coming of the King family for good reasons. We felt the project would create considerable ill-feeling between blacks and whites and that some of the vessels King had found for the long voyage presented unacceptable risks. Trescowthwick had piloted the First Fleet Committee through a crucial period and I had organised funds and promotion at a critical stage. As a member of the First Fleet Committee I had attended meetings in Trescowthwick's offices in Melbourne, liaised with The Australian and other media, and briefed Brazilian Government ministers and officials in Brasilia and civic authorities in Rio. In his book, Battle for the Bicentenary, King suffers from selective amnesia and for a historian makes a number of elementary mistakes.

He says: "I set out to ask the Brazilian Government to support the fleet's visit in 1987 praying that the ABA had not got there ahead of me." He is aware, as is Brazilian Ambassador Marcos Cortes and Sir Donald Trescowthwick, that, armed with official letters from them, I went to Brazil to promote the project weeks before him. I met with politicians, public servants, tourism officials and others to seek their support, an endeavour financed by East West Airlines. My brother-in-law Miguel and other government and business connections from the yacht race arranged a series of meetings on the re-enactment in Rio and Brasilia. These meetings inadvertently paved the way for King's visit in August and provided him with the right contacts.

The other claim that King makes is that when the fleet arrived in Rio in 1987, suddenly the 'obscure country' of Australia mattered in Brazil. Brazilians have a clear recollection of the extraordinary impact of the Sydney Rio race and associated Australian trade and tourist projects five years earlier. Around the time of King's trip to Brazil, Trescowthwick entered the following direction in the minutes of a committee meeting: 'Integrity and precise communications are essential'.

Trescowthwick and I had problems with King over integrity and precise communications on a number of occasions. The worst example was his lack of commitment to an event that did so much to ensure the re-enactment project would, despite Australian Bicentennial Authority opposition, retain a high profile. I had recommended to Bryan Grey that we sponsor a First Fleet 'dummy run' with the brigantine Golden Plover from Airlie Beach in Queensland with seven Australian youngsters selected through a newspaper essay competition.

Among the winners flown to Airlie Beach for the Golden Plover voyage to Sydney were two Fletcher Christian descendants, David Magri and Patrick Petch. Also aboard were Penny Oxenbridge, Toni Hutchinson and John Fraser, who crewed on the Bicentennial re-enactment voyage, and Bernadette Nunn, now a television news journalist. It was about this time that I began to doubt the commitment and ability of King, who had failed to organise various aspects of the project assigned to him. There was no insurance cover on Golden Plover or the contest winners. The owner of Golden Plover was unable to contact King to finalise 'pressing matters' with him.

When King failed to appear, Bronwyn and I had to fly to Queensland with the young crew and act as chaperones at Airlie Beach. It was there that we learned that King had failed to arrange the insurance cover, which almost ruined the event. He just disappeared when a number of people connected with the important project, not the least the owner of the brigantine, urgently needed his presence. According to the owner and skipper of *Golden Plover*, Gert Jacoby, King had a history of broken promises and he flatly refused to sail from Airlie Beach until King was tracked down.

After a series of frantic phone calls to Trescowthwick and another committee member Wally Franklin we managed to pacify Jacoby and an insurance cover note was taken out. In his book King blandly glosses over this near disaster with: "Franklin insured the ship and children with Sirius Insurance run by Arthur Weller and talked News Limited into supporting the event through Channel 10." On the voyage south, all the teenagers had 'kissed' the top of the mainmast in true sailing tradition. It was a wonderful experience for them and a vital promotion for the First Fleet venture.

Always there when media were present, King was prancing about in period dress when the TV cameras appeared. It is difficult to take his book seriously when he says: "I was dragged on to a series of TV programmes." That's like saying 'Madonna has never sought attention.'

King says in his book that Trescowthwick resigned from the committee because of a feasibility study, by finance manager Terry Heap, which questioned the financial viability and other aspects of the project. Certainly, that was one reason, but King himself, and strengthening resistance from the Aboriginal community, were others. When the committee eventually disbanded, King went ahead with the project, gaining sponsorship support from Australia Post and others.

In the end, the general public was forced to rescue what was essentially a failed private enterprise which devalued the original epic voyage. The project created enormous financial and emotional problems for many people. I became involved in the first instance because, like King, I believe the original voyage at that time in history was equivalent to Armstrong's journey to the moon. It was a remarkable voyage that helped to open the southern continent to the world and was the forerunner for the migration of European and Asian settlers. Unfortunately, it signalled the death-knell for the Aboriginal tenancy of the land as they had known it for countless thousands of years.

Jonathan King deserves recognition for his tenacity. Ironically, his greatest contribution to the Bicentenary was to unite many Aboriginals and white Australians in the ensuing protest against the oppression of the indigenous race. Of all the Bicentennial events, it was the first fleet re-enactment fiasco that made Australians more aware of the Aboriginal cause. Since January 26, 1988, there have been a number of milestones in the reconciliation process – yet most Aboriginals are socially and economically still no better off.

Aboriginals played a leading role in shaping the life of my son Chris. After being accepted by Australia's National Institute of Dramatic Art, Chris found it was too stifling a discipline for him, so he quit and joined an acting school in William Street, Sydney, run by Aboriginal Brian Syron. That's where he became friends with a number of Aboriginal actors, including Rhoda Roberts, Ernie Dingo, and Justine Saunders. Since the mid-70s actor and director Syron had been pushing for the emergence of a black theatre. Selected by Syron, Chris was among 40 participants in the first National Black Playwrights' Conference in Canberra in January, 1987. There, Aboriginals and non-aboriginals work-shopped nine plays and five film scripts by Aboriginal writers. In theatre Chris appeared in *The Keepers, The Lower Depths, The Maids, Hay Fever* and *The Importance of Being Earnest* and worked in Theatre in Education for Jigsaw Theatre and Creative Arts Theatre. He performed in benefit concerts at Belvoir Street Theatre for the Aboriginal National Theatre Trust and his film and television work included *Fragments of War, Simpson* and *Land of Hope*. Eventually, Chris decided acting and part time waiting was losing its appeal so he got a job caring for street kids, and became a player in the theatre of life. Later, he would become a drama teacher.

I was about to lose the Darling Point flat that Chris had been sharing with me, and was in grave danger of becoming a street adult as the recession started to bite. When Bryan Grey threw me the *East-West Airlines* lifebuoy, it enabled me to mount the Third Airline Campaign. When the harbour buoys and magazine came adrift, Bryan's son Michael threw me another one, but the lifeline was not secure. Although I did some early PR work for *Compass*, there was no place for me on the management team.

Looking back at what happened with deregulation of the Australian airline industry and the launch and sad demise of *Compass Mark One*, it was a blessing in disguise.

Dennis O'Connor - That's our Buoy!

When Denis O'Connor, regarded as one of the world's finest yachtsmen, struck a rock in Sydney harbour while competing in a 12 metre yacht race, I thought I had struck oil. Instead, it triggered a chain of events that would leave me high and dry. Connor's gaffe dramatically highlighted the lack of safety markings for hazards on the harbour.

For me, it was an opportunity to dust off the safety buoys and get the project under way again. The race in which Connor hit the rock was sponsored by the ANZ bank, so I contacted the bank's marketing department and over the phone secured sponsorship of a buoy to mark the spot. When the MSB launched the ANZ buoy in the presence of a large media contingent on the harbour, the board issued press releases about long-term permanent safety markers and a list of permanent locations for the buoys.

Captain Briggs poured champagne over the buoy and said: "This is the first of many permanent safety markers to go on the harbour. It is something that Sydney Harbour badly needs. If Dennis Connor can run aground here, what about all those less experienced people?" A photograph of the Harbourmaster pouring champagne over the ANZ buoy appeared in the Daily Mirror and that's when the 'buoyshit' began.

On his way to work by car early the following morning New South Wales Transport Minister Bruce Baird took a phone call from radio talk back host Mike Carlton. Carlton asked the Minister if he was going to allow advertising on the harbour. The Minister told Carlton on air that he would ban the safety buoys, without having seen my contract, the buoys or the charts on which harbour hazards were marked.

He also appeared not to be aware of the considerable sums of public money spent on pulling boats off sandbars and rocks. Later an MSB staff member said the minister had said of the safety buoys "Bottoms will be smacked over this." After the minister banned the buoys there were a number of boating accidents on Sydney harbour. One man drowned after his yacht struck a rock, which was listed to be marked with a permanent buoy. Baird's action was contrary to harbour safety needs, the Harbourmaster's directions and New South Wales Premier Greiner's policy to save taxpayers' money.

Greiner had appealed to private enterprise to come up with schemes to save capital expenditure and return a profit if possible; this was just such a scheme. It is interesting that the same minister endorsed advertising on freeways, which many people regard as creating a new road safety hazard and an eyesore. Carlton, of course, was being provocative by pushing it as an aesthetic issue rather than a safety measure. He asked if the minister favoured advertising on the harbour; the same Carlton who makes his living from commercial radio which, like the safety buoys, could not exist without advertising – the same Carlton who solicited $800,000 from the public to sponsor a fleet of vessels from Rio to Sydney in 1988, with advertising emblazoned across the sails of one vessel. Carlton personally went out in a boat to meet the giant floating billboard, which was on Sydney Harbour for several days.

At least two men have died, one lost at sea from one of the vessels sponsored by Carlton and others and another who drowned when his yacht hit the rock in Sydney Harbour. Meanwhile, Carlton continues to make his living from advertising, having denied other people the right to do the same – typical of talking heads on television and radio who espouse causes only when the issues don't affect them. Carlton also failed to say anything about the many other people who benefit from advertising on Sydney harbour, including commercial radio stations, without any safety benefits or returns to taxpayers.

A minister carries heavy responsibilities and it is Baird who should be accountable, for his action in banning the safety buoys sight unseen was at best reckless.

*

Melbourne was the worst-hit Australian city in the recession, but I had decided to become a bigger fish in a smaller pond with some good friends and contacts. But prospects looked bleak until Michael Quist asked if I would consider washing cars. With more than a million Australians out of work, I would have gladly shovelled shit. I had been close to the fan on many occasions when it hit. From day one I set out to turn every menial task into something of benefit.

Employed as a general hand in the maintenance department, I had a self confessed arsehole for a boss. "Everyone says I'm an arsehole, so I may as well act like one," he boasted. "It's the best way I know of cutting through all the bullshit."

It's a symptom of the authoritarian executive mentality that pervades the corporate world. Much of it came from the returning officers of World War II, a lot of whom got into management simply because they were top brass in the military. Since then it has bred its own, helped along by a mass exodus of public servants into business, large and small, taking with them a heap of authoritarian baggage. The 'rule with an iron fist' approach continues to exclude many wise men and women from management.

It's a mentality that is at the very heart of male-female relationships, marriage and parenthood. Sadly, it's continually fostered in so many aspects of our lives. When people go to work they should check in their personal baggage before they clock on. My boss was like many who had been moulded by the system. One minute he would bawl you out unnecessarily in front of others, then the next he would discuss intimately his father's suicide and his own father-son relationship.

Apart from washing cars, my tasks included car detailing, cleaning leaves from gutters, taking out the garbage, sweeping the driveway, pruning the trees, pulling out weeds and being pleasant to the Japanese. I hated them in World War Two, but in peacetime bore no grudge. "Computergate" was just a distant memory as I adjusted to being on the bottom of the heap at Mazda Australia.

Occasionally I did think of the anomaly of composing messages for the Japanese Prime Minister one day and washing cars for 20-year-old Japanese trainee executives the next. Sometimes I became despondent, but never revealed my private thoughts to anyone, not even 'fuck'n Les'. He would have been an avid listener, but in a car wash it is easy to keep your head down and arse up, which brings its own rewards.

When Quist threw me the new Mazda 121 car release information from which to prepare a media kit, he was doing me no special favour. The PR Department was under pressure and he knew I could handle it. I had been in many high-pressure situations with the nephew of the famous tennis player and been 'Adrian Quist' with him and his wife Ginny often when they came from Adelaide to try their luck as smaller fish in a bigger pond.

We often joked about Quist needing a white cane. What nobody realised was that he had worn his contact lenses so long that they were sharp as razors and cutting into his eyes. Eventually he had to have corneal transplants in both eyes. His eyes were giving him trouble in his job as a consultant with Howard Bull & Associates; Howard became exasperated, as he was wont to do, and said Quist had to go.

When his father Bruce flew to Melbourne from Adelaide, he invited me for a drink to discuss the nasty thing being done to his favourite son. "He can't help it if he's having problems with his eyesight. It's a bastard of a thing to do to a young man at the start of a career in PR. Why don't you stand up for him?"

"Don't fight it, Bruce, it's probably the best thing that could happen to him," I said. "He's a bit of a passenger right now. Howard's chucked him in at the deep end and he's going to sink or swim. I think it will be the making of him."

Bruce took my advice and went back to Adelaide, and a half-blind Quist was left to fend for himself in a harsh world. Mike had his ups and downs, but went on to become the best PR in the Australian car industry – and he has never needed a white cane. His daughter Jackie is one of Australia's most talented television current affairs reporters and his son David is a computer industry executive.

Meanwhile, I was in the car wash. The PR department at Mazda was always under pressure; that's the nature of the business. I was grateful, for that generated extra money for a few more beers with Peter and Michael and their Greek cab driver mates at the Victoria Hotel. Cab drivers have a rich fund of stories and none better than the one I heard on an *East West Airlines* promotion in Adelaide, when I hailed a cab outside the Casino.

"You must pick up some interesting customers from here, winners and losers alike," I said to the driver.

"I'm going to tell you a true story that is really incredible," said the jovial Aussie driver. "I was sitting on the Casino rank late one night when I noticed a guy who was under the weather trying to get a cab. I was about fourth in line and I noticed everyone else refused to take him. When he got to me, I asked him where he wanted to go, and he named a hotel that was only about a mile away, if that. He could have walked there just as quickly, and that's why the other drivers didn't want to take him. I wanted a break, so I said I'd drop him there. He had been drinking heavily and just slumped into the seat. A few minutes later, I said 'We're here,' but he refused to budge.

'We can't be here,' he said, Perth's a long way from here.'

"Then he told me the full story. He had won $40,000 in the Casino and was worried about getting home without being mugged. Rather than fly to Perth, he had decided to get a cab to take him straight home. The hotel he was referring to was one with the same name in Perth. I rang base and got a quote on a round trip to Perth, drove home picked up a change of clothing and told my wife where I was going. We drove to Perth, staying at a motel on the way, and when we got there he took me to dinner. Then he booked me into a top hotel, bought me an airline ticket and arranged for my cab to come back to Adelaide on the train. He paid the fare and gave me another $200.

When I got back to Adelaide I couldn't wait to get to the Casino rank and tell the other drivers who had knocked the passenger back."

*

Another passenger, this time on an airliner, was of great interest to me when I realised I would be sitting next to him one day on a Sydney to Melbourne flight. Australian Trade Minister John Button and I talked at length about my experience with Ian Sinclair, leader of the National Party and Defence Minister in the Fraser Government. I had flown to Brazil in the early 80s for discussions with Varig and civil aviation authorities on my proposed polar charter flights and with Embraer on the Tucano trainer aircraft. The Brazilians were trying to interest the RAAF in the Tucano, but were meeting strong resistance from some 'top brass' who wanted side by side, not tandem seating in a replacement trainer aircraft.

In discussions I had with Embraer representatives in Australia, they had thrown in a sweetener. If I could get the Australian Government to override the seating objection, a deal could be struck with the Brazilians for a co-production agreement and a sales and servicing contract for the Asian region. Australia needed a replacement trainer for the RAAF, the EMB-312 Tucano trainer was a proven aircraft, and the turbo-prop Bandeirante had established a first class reputation for Brazil's aviation industry in Australia, the US and other countries.

The Bandeirante was flying on commuter routes in Australia and the US, and was one of the few aircraft to be imported by the Americans. Most importantly, Brazil-Australia co-production of the Tucano and other aircraft would help to build a viable Australian aircraft industry. Once established, Australia could supply the whole of Asia with Tucanos, Bandeirante and other aircraft, and the attendant aircraft servicing would boost Australia's aviation status in the region.

The Tucano EMB-312 first flew in 1992 and was put into service in 15 countries. The EMB-314 Super Tucano is an enhanced version, with more speed and altitude. The main missions of the aircraft, in addition to basic and advanced pilot training, are border patrol and counter-insurgency operations. Following preliminary discussions with the Brazilians, Bryan Grey gave me leave to negotiate with Embraer in Brazil.

East West's aircraft maintenance base was in Tamworth, an ideal decentralised location for establishing a co-production facility. Grey was interested in *East West* having a stake in the project, and was ideally placed to provide land, other facilities and expertise. Belatedly in mid-1997, Prime Minister Howard made a big song and dance about his government's initiative in setting up a similar sounding deal with a British aviation group.

My trip to Brazil was timely, as *East West* was about to upgrade its fleet to Fokker F28 jets, and there was some possibility that

I could find a buyer for some of the airline's aging Fokker F27 fleet. As the *East West* representative on the First Fleet Committee, I could also pursue Brazilian Government and City of Rio support for the Australian Bicentennial project.

It was a busy schedule, but an enjoyable return visit to what had become my 'second world'. I made good progress with the First Fleet agenda in Rio, but lack of Varig capacity rendered invalid the charter agreement I got from Brazilian civil aviation authorities. It was ironic, for *Qantas* and trade and tourist groups in both countries had become enthusiastic about the flights. From Rio I flew to the Embraer aircraft factory and was impressed with what I saw of the achievements of Brazil in aircraft manufacturing.

There was universal admiration for Brazil's civil aviation prowess and Varig had won many international awards. The country's rapid advances in airline operations and aircraft manufacturing was due in no small measure to its earlier experience as an aviation captive of the Northern Hemisphere.

During my visit to the manufacturing base I saw assembly lines and jigs for new aircraft, including a Brazilian 'Jumbo'. In talks with top officials, I secured a preliminary agreement, subject to an RAAF order, for the Tucano, to establish co-production, sales and servicing facilities in Australia, with Tamworth as a likely base. That done, I flew to Brasilia for talks with government officials and a visit to Maggie and Miguel and their family at the Santa Antonio farm. In Brasilia I received strong assurances of support for the First Fleet re-enactment voyage and found keen interest for the aviation project among trade and defence officials.

On my return to Australia I contacted Ian Sinclair's office and arranged to meet him. Unfortunately, the RAAF boffins were still pushing the side-by-side seating plan for instructor and trainee, and Sinclair was not going to cut across them. "Those boys know best, you know," said the Minister. "They've assessed the Tucano and believe it is not the right aircraft to meet their needs."

Canberra, like Brasilia, Washington and other capitals of bureaucracy removed from the mainstream of life, tends to deaden the minds of politicians and bureaucrats to the realities of life. The best input from the Minister for Defence for a project of such enormous domestic and international significance for two countries was to refer me to his junior minister, Howson, who was even less enthusiastic and just as subservient to the RAAF top brass thinking.

None of us have the time to pursue every opportunity that life presents, no matter how worthwhile they may seem, so I moved on to other things that were easier to get off the ground. Labour Senator John Button saw it in a totally different light.

"Your first and last mistake was approaching Sinclair, and I don't say that in a political sense," the physically diminutive but larger than life Senator confided. "You should have started with the unions because it was a chance to create new jobs on a large scale. The government aircraft factory at Fishermen's Bend has never reached its potential. That would have been the best location, and with union support you could have made it happen. The unions would have put the pressure on the politicians."

I said diminutive because I could not help noticing that the good senator's feet were not touching the ground as he sat on his seat on the right hand side of the *Ansett* first class cabin. John Button is a short man with big thinking, who does not fit the 'chip on the shoulder' mould of so many. My recall of our side-by-side configuration is a result of the indelible impression made by the businessmen who offered me varying amounts of money and other incentives to swap seats. Business is a bloody rat race at times. They were breaking their necks to pin the minister in the window seat and bash his ear. It's one occupational hazard I had not given too much thought to, having acquired a somewhat cynical view of politicians over a period of years.

Flying first class is not only a fringe benefit for politicians; it's a chance to escape the unwelcome attentions of the 'travelling salesman'. I had waited for Button to open the conversation, if he wanted to, not because he was a senior figure in government; it was something I normally did myself as a form of self defence. There is nothing worse than sitting in a window seat and getting your ear bashed, particularly on a long flight, no matter who you are. I got great pleasure from telling all of the would-be Button 'fellow travellers' to piss off. I wanted to rub it in by letting them know I was travelling on a free industry ticket, but the airline would have copped a serve.

"I've done my leg skiing, so I'm going home to rest up," said my fellow passenger. He had noticed me looking intently out the window at the snow-capped mountains below. We started to talk, and I said my brother was now in his department, he asked me about his background, and I mentioned the Brazilian connection.

"He speaks Portuguese, then? That's useful, because there weren't too many people who could speak another language fluently when I got the trade portfolio. Not one who could speak Japanese fluently – can you believe that?" I said I could believe anything about Canberra and that was how we got on to the discussion about Sinclair.

All that Australia has seen to date in debate about its future is the same old pot pourri of politically correct faces, the last people who deserve another audience or another free lunch. It is time to give some of the rich and famous, and the media circus that surrounds them, a swift metaphorical kick up the arse. What is needed is a cross-section of working citizens who could draw up a blueprint for the future management of a country, so rich in resources and talent it should not brook a day of poverty for a single citizen. 'Fuck'n Les' would agree with that.

He'd been at the bottom of the work heap for a long time, but 'Fuck'n Les' was a long way up the people ladder. His nickname comes from every second word he utters. Les is the epitome of the working class man; for him everything else is "fuck'n bullshit". Swarthy, bearded, small but nuggetty, no bastard ever worried him. Les makes good sense about things like company bonuses. "How can they fuck'n justify paying fuck'n bonuses based on fuck'n salaries? It's just not fuck'n fair. Every fuck'n one of us works just as fuck'n hard to create the fuck'n profits. Then in a rare moment, adding significance to the point: "The total fuck'n bonus payout should be equally divided between all fuck'n employees."

That's hard to argue with. It is a common practice with employers that if you earn $200 a week and the bonus is 10 per cent you get $20, while someone on $2000 gets $200. Every executive should spend some time each year on the bottom of the heap and get some homespun 'Fuck'n Les' philosophy about what makes their business tick and see how a few simple changes could radically improve relations between management and workers. But it seems that the battle-lines remain drawn on the industrial relations front, with the same old rhetoric mankind has suffered through countless political conflicts, many of which have scarred and depleted generations. Neither side of the outmoded, disgraced, irrelevant party political system displays any real grasp of what new generations aspire to change.

Becoming a general hand at the age of 56 taught me a lot. It was physically demanding and improved my health and fitness markedly. The dearth of mental stimulation was good for a change. I had always found that painting fences, mowing lawns, cooking or cleaning house was excellent therapy for those constantly using their wits in the business world. Your mind concentrates only on the job at hand. I enjoyed cleaning cars, trucks and buses, pruning trees and watering gardens, and even climbing on the roof and clearing leaves out of gutters had its finer moments.

It was relaxing strolling around the roof of the Mazda plant, finding a quiet corner and enjoying a cigarette in the warm spring sunshine. The plant building was a no-smoking zone, so even the bosses had to stand out in the street if they wanted to light up. While washing cars or watering the garden on steaming summer days, I would often turn the hose on myself. Hot and flustered executives would wander by muttering under their breath as they sweltered in suits and ties. A hard day's work was a hard day's work, the equivalent of a full workout by an athlete or a footballer. I had a miniworkout before and after work as I walked to and from Mazda and my new home, a single room in the Victoria Hotel in the beach side suburb of Albert Park. Between times I painted a house and built a driveway.

*

The Victoria was a long drop from that 32nd floor luxury apartment in the heart of Sydney. My room was just slightly more roomy than my *Coulgarve* cabin. A single bed, small wardrobe, bedside cupboard, chair and small table; a short walk down the passageway to communal showers and toilets. As with my job, I decided to make the hotel work for me. I thought of the whole splendid old Victorian building as my apartment, and my room as just a bedroom. Despite being on a marginal wage of just under $300 a week, I lived remarkably well. Odd jobs after hours, including sessions with market research discussion groups, supplemented my income.

I walked about ten kilometres a day between the hotel and work, and on weekends, when I built a brick driveway for a friend in

Brighton, I walked four times that distance. A pleasant form of exercise, averaging 80 to 100 kilometres a week. Sometimes I worked from 8am to 4. 30pm at Mazda, then walked around to my friend's house in Port Melbourne, pulled out the ladders, paint, brushes and rollers and worked till sunset. It was autumn and the days were getting shorter, so sometimes I managed an hour's painting before starting work.

Life at the *Victoria* was entertaining, and with the staff and the other permanent and casual guests, I constantly felt part of an extended family. You could always count on the unexpected.

Along with other guests I was regularly tailed along the beach road on my way to the carwash. Some mornings it was fairly obvious and I would turn and give a friendly wave to the squad car. When a tennis ball flew through my open window one night, I rattled it and found it was definitely not hollow – an excellent way to deal in drugs without having to go into the hotel. I was going to cut the aerial 'post pack' open, but decided the dump bin out the back was the best place for it.

Leaving for work one morning I noticed through a window thick black smoke in the kitchen, so I went back into the hotel and woke the young apprentice chef. "Can't do anything about it mate, they won't let me have a key to the kitchen, so we'll have to wait until the chef arrives," he said, and promptly went back to sleep. Fortunately, it was only oil in a pan that had been left on a live electric stove overnight.

Another Mr Williams, who had lived in the hotel for several years, became seriously ill one night and staff called an ambulance. Mr Williams hated doctors and hospitals and refused to go. Staff called the police and they supervised his removal; he fought them vigorously, but finally was carried struggling to the ambulance. We all knew he would die that night. The following night we were having a farewell drink for Mr Williams when bartenders Glen and Dirk suddenly decided to go upstairs to check his room.

"Looking for the name of a relative to notify?" I asked.

"No, we know he took a lottery ticket every week and it might have been a winning one."

Every night when I got to the hotel I'd have one beer and then go upstairs for a shower. Most of my life I had woken up, had a shower and gone to work; now it was get up, go to work and shower when you finished. It is amazing how you can adapt to a complete change in work and lifestyle; it's all a matter of attitude. Mr Schultz, the owner of the hotel, had an unusual attitude. He rarely related to his permanent guests, and seemed to believe he was doing them a favour, especially me. We never did get on first-name terms; it was always 'Mr Williams' and 'Mr Schultz'. I don't think he ever forgave me for knowing Ernest Forras, the previous owner.

From what I could gather Ernest was paid much more than the hotel was worth, at least according to Mr Schultz. Ernest would have found that funny. He had a great sense of humour.

A former cavalry officer in the Hungarian military, Ernest arrived in Australia in 1951 after escaping from occupied Hungary and living a gypsy like existence throughout post-war Europe. In his book *Ernest Escapades* he relates many wonderful stories of his remarkable and frenetic life. Always obsessed with fitness, Ernest grew up in Vac on the River Danube, 30 kilometres north of Budapest, and attended a school run by strict Catholic monks. In 1939 he attended a four year military course at the Budapest Military Academy, studying many subjects, including how to kiss a lady's hand. I can vouch for his prowess in the latter.

Ernest trained hard in swimming, equestrian events, cross-country running and pistol shooting and gained selection for the 1942 Tokyo Olympics, but World War II put an end to that, so Ernest devoted most of his time to cross-country skiing and caught the bug. Later, in Transylvania. he tried downhill skiing for the first time and spent most of the time bouncing off trees and bushes.

Not long after meeting Ernest at Victoria's Mount Buller, I ended up with cracked ribs, but not from laughing. On my first day on skis, I did a spectacular somersault outside a shop called Ski Rescue on Bourke Street. The more I got to know Ernest, the more risks I took. In 1944, in Transylvania's Karpat Mountains, Ernest and his fellow officers held endless parties in the officers' mess, and it was no different on Mount Buller.

I was promoting Mt Buller when I met Ernest and Austrian ski instructor Hans Grimus. When I began staging promotional fashion parades I suddenly became popular with the ski instructors, who were always eager to buy me a drink when I arrived with a new group of girls. Grimus became one of the mountain's success stories, opening his own first class commercial lodge, aptly named Pension Grimus.

From humble beginnings in 1951 as a porter and skiing instructor at Victoria's Mt Buffalo, Ernest became one of the pioneer developers of Australia's snowfields. From Mt Buffalo, he went to Falls Creek to open a ski school and manage a lodge; then followed a canteen at the top of Mt Buller's Bull Run, a ski school and in 1953 a commercial chalet. He called it Kooroora, Aboriginal word for happy gatherings, and it always lived up to its name. Ernest sold Kooroora and worked on many other developments at Smiggins Holes and Thredbo in New South Wales before returning to Mount Buller in 1964. Two years later I was introduced to Ernest and the other legend of the mountain, Captain Morgan.

The Captain Morgan legend had started in 1954 when Ernest and some friends drank a bottle of the fine Jamaican rum one night and the following morning found heavy snow where it had been scant the day before. "It had to be Captain Morgan's doing," said Ernest, who immediately ordered two dozen cases of the 'magic formula'. The following year the Melbourne Herald ran a front page story: "The old Captain has done it again. He has brought the snow to Mt Buller. After scant ground cover late last week there is now more than 30 centimetres of the stuff!"

Ernest specialised in another drink, a Hungarian red, Egri Bikaver, 'Bulls' Blood from Eger', which Ernest imported from Hungary. He was fond of saying that 'Bulls' Blood' would make a man achieve anything, but I suspect that depended on the quantity. When the Ottoman Turks had the town of Eger under siege in 1552 the citizens drank red wine to give them courage to fight the enemy. The wine spilled over their armour and their beards and the superstitious Turks believed the Hungarians were drinking the blood of bulls to make them fierce. The Hungarians led by Istvan Dobo stopped the Turkish advance across Europe, giving Eger a hallowed place in history. Today the famous Bulls' Blood wine is still produced from the 500-year-old recipe that created the legend.

We took Ernest and Bulls' Blood on face value when Grimus and I decided in the early hours that we would climb the steep north face of the mountain one weekend when hundreds of people would walk to the summit to aid a local charity. We had issued a challenge to mountaineering clubs to climb the north face as part of the fund-raising effort. Nobody volunteered, so after a night on Bulls' Blood we talked ourselves into it, along with Ernest's son Tony and another young friend of his. Trouble was, Grimus and I were not crash-hot when we woke up, and it was the first time I forgot my healthy respect for the Australian bush. Ernest drove the four of us together with Grimus' dog, Captain, to the foot of the mountain.

The dog was noted for its ability to ski down the steepest slopes on four mini-skis that Grimus had made. Without the dog we may not have survived. It was sheer foolhardiness that led us to set off into the dense undergrowth in mid-summer without food or water and dressed in shorts, T-shirts and runners. There were abundant streams and springs, and it was fun crossing logs and pushing through the bush as we slowly made out way up the lower slopes. Then we hit the serious part of the climb and there were no streams or springs, just thousands of March flies and the heat.

Suddenly, the fun turned into drama as our throats burned dry, and our scratched and bruised bodies attracted the March flies. Mountain man Grimus urged us on and we reached a rocky outcrop, two-thirds of the way up to the summit where, from the shade of a small cave, we watched the smoke rising from the local sawmill. From our high vantage point it looked like a matchbox toy.

We had reached the point of no return. Our options were to head back down, find a stream, quench our thirst and follow the water, or press on and try to reach the top before nightfall. Grimus suggested a compromise: he and the dog could move faster than the rest of us, so they would head to the top and get help. As they disappeared into the bush, our tongues were beginning to dry and swell so we started sucking on small pebbles.

It was dark and the burning sun and biting flies had left us to sit and ponder our fate. Back in Melbourne, *The Sun* was following up a story on three people missing on a mountain in north-east Victoria. At the top of the North face of the mountain, Grimus was lying exhausted as the dog sought attention down in the village. We saw the lights bobbing at the top of the steep rocky face; a search party was on its way down.

Ernest, with an overstuffed backpack, was one of the first two to reach us. "We thought it would be best to come down to you, stay the night and then climb out at daybreak," he said, hugging his son. "Have some of this chocolate. The guy with the water chickened out and couldn't tackle the climb down in the dark. Someone else is bringing it down. I've got plenty of food, but all I've got to drink is red wine."

My mouth and throat were so parched I couldn't wait; I sipped the red wine and nearly choked. Ernest's Bulls Blood was indeed the colloquial hair of the dog. Refreshed, but feeling the cold of the night air in our own blood which was congealed in streaks all over our arms and legs, we voted to climb out, rather than wait for daybreak.

It was an eerie feeling climbing up that steep rock face in the dead of night, but it was good to be alive. Ernest would swear to this day that it was the *Egri Bikaver* that got me to the top. "How do you think the Hungarians stopped all those Russian tanks in Belgrade?"

*

Apart from my merchant navy training days, I've never been one for uniforms, but in my financial circumstances I was glad of the free ones at Mazda. When I got my first issue, I struggled into a 36-inch waist. At the end of twelve months, I was comfortable with a 32. Most people I knew over 40 had a beer gut. At 58, after a year of hard physical work, I lost mine and felt as good as I did when I was a teenager.

"It's shit, fuck'n work, but it sure keeps you fuck'n healthy," said fuck'n Les. "Think about all those fuck'n stressed-out bastards in mahogany fuck'n row. Half of them won't make fuck'n retirement age." Before joining Mazda I had spent plenty of time in the business stress zone. My new occupation may well have stopped it claiming me. Under stress, many executives drink more, lose their appetite and start to fall apart.

I had changed my lifestyle completely and I was walking for 90 minutes to and from work every day. My drinking was generally limited to a small carafe of red wine with dinner and my appetite had become enormous. Thanks to generous helpings and extras from Debbie and Joan, the girls in the canteen, and the chef and staff at the *Hotel Victoria*, I managed to satisfy it.

Herald Sun journalist Geoff Easdown wanted to do a story on how a former highly paid executive, forced by the recession to work in a car wash, is coping. I wasn't interested in the publicity, as I didn't plan to stay there forever.

On balance I'd have to say I was 1000 per cent better off than the average highly-paid executive – fitter, healthier, with zero stress level. There were interesting sidelights to the job such as driving vehicles to auction, setting up stages and tents for outdoor promotions, working on the Mazda stand at the Motor Show, country trade shows, ferrying new vehicles to and from Sydney and even a television commercial. People go from jobs down the credits to become directors and producers; I reversed the trend. From co-producer on *Barney* to car detailer on the 929 television commercial was a sharp drop down the list, but just as satisfying. We shot the commercial in a small country town and the luxury car was mine for the duration.

Mazda hired the Sandown racetrack to let some VIPs and selected dealers loose in the RX7 that won the Bathurst race, and I drew gate duty, checking them in and out. When it was over an executive threw the keys to me and said "Go for it." I'd never been on a racetrack in my life. I hurtled down the back straight at 200kph, braked hard and threw her round the S-bends, improving with every lap. Next, a 'burn' in the MX5 with the top down; on the tight circuit it was competitive with the RX7, as I kept thinking: 'I've only ever seen this on television.' Whenever possible I shared my unexpected pleasures around, giving my daughter, friends and staff at the Hotel Victoria a drive of new model cars.

On weekends I had the key to the best workshop in town – the Mazda maintenance section. Over a period of weeks I sanded and re-varnished fittings for a houseboat, borrowed ladders and paint brushes to paint the house and the houseboat. You can do anything if you put your mind to it. I owe a lot to Mazda, as does Eduard Volchek. Eduard played piano in the faithfully restored Victorian lounge room of the *Victoria*. Each night I would take a can of Fosters and sit alone in that magnificent room and listen to a recital by a wonderfully talented young pianist.

It never occurred to me that one day I would be responsible for getting him back to Russia, to study at the Moscow Conservatory of Music. An opportunity came for him to attend a summer school at the place where Tchaikovsky, Rachmaninov and many other great Russian composers had studied. To fund his trip we had to seek the support of Mazda's general manager, Malcolm Gough. After hearing Eduard play, Quist was impressed with the 19 year old Russian's talent, but Gough was fanatical about sport and Quist could not simply say "We need $20,000 to send a pianist to school in Moscow."

Quist booked a motoring writers' luncheon into the *Victoria*, introduced Eduard who gave a short after-lunch recital which impressed the motoring writers; Gough took to the idea, unaware that it involved the general hand from the carwash. Eduard played piano with a maturity way beyond his years. It was an outpouring of sadness and grief, joy and happiness from an entire Russian Jewish family. Such emotional renderings could never come solely from one so young.

Thanks to Gorbachev's *Glasnost* policies, Eduard and his family were allowed to leave the Soviet Union, along with many other Jewish families. Some settled in Israel, while others went to Canada, the US and Australia. The money Eduard made from playing at the *Victoria* and other venues at night kept the family going during the recession. During the day he studied at the college, which had nominated him for a six weeks intensive study course with the top professors at the Moscow Conservatorium. He had the advantage of speaking the language and that was to prove extremely useful in the events that would unfold.

He got lost in Moscow during the abortive coup, along with students from the US, Britain and other parts of Europe. It was impossible to contact him on the phone and we knew he didn't have a passport, just a visa. If the coup had been successful we may never have seen him again. When the world welcomed the peaceful outcome, we breathed a sigh of relief for Eduard and his fellow students.

On his return we organised his first public recital, a $50 a head black tie dinner at Miettas, a leading Melbourne restaurant, on April 29. He said: "Good, it's my birthday. " I said: "No, it's my birthday. " Then we realised we had been born on the same date, albeit many years apart, and if there hadn't been a recession and I hadn't moved to Melbourne to find work I may never have met him. But coincidence keeps turning up in my life. By chance a passing motorist gave me a lift to work one day; it was Tony Rafferty, who I had not seen for years. He had married a music teacher from St Catherine's school, and they came to Eduard's recital. Mazda subsequently commissioned Eduard to write a theme piece called *Alpine Cycles* for a video of a bike tour through the Snowy Mountains and provided the funding for him to go the Julliard School of Music in New York for an entrance audition. Eduard couldn't afford to live and study in New York, but he was reunited there with his childhood sweetheart.

The last time I saw him he was playing in a piano bar at the Park Grand Hotel in Sydney. When he first came to Mazda I was washing a car and he asked me if it was mine. "Where's your office?" "You're standing in it," I replied.

He couldn't understand why I wasn't an executive, but it was the last thing I wanted to be, especially when the bike race was on. I took two weeks holiday and headed off to Canberra in a racy 323 for the start of the race from Australia's new Parliament House on November 5, 1991. For several weeks I had been telephoning radio stations across the country offering voice reports on the inaugural Mazda Alpine Tour. Why not? I had no connections with any stations, so most of them had said yes; it wasn't costing anything at a time when advertising revenue was down. I was given the newsroom phone numbers for a network covering over 200 stations, big coverage in anyone's language; big coverage for Mazda. The PR man had come in from the wet, flushed back out of the drain.

It was a wild ride, in more ways than one – the next best thing you could get to the Tour de France. It was a ride that took us through Banjo Patterson country and for my young Japanese trainee friend Steve it was a chance to see 'real bloody fucking Australia'. He also got to wash my car for a change. The Kamikaze Kid was headed for the Snowy River and wild horses couldn't hold him back. He had been working on another event for Mazda in Western Australia and had tended to stand back and observe, getting a bollocking when he returned to Melbourne.

The Kamikaze Kid was a nickname that came from the race construction crew, as he went hell for leather at everything to make amends. Not since the production of *Barney*, the yacht race and the Perth to Sydney balloon challenge had I been involved in a spectacle of such proportions. In its inaugural year, the event had world championship points status and had attracted a number of top riders from France, Germany, Italy, the US, Japan and Britain. Race Director John Craven had just run another successful Victoria Health Herald Sun Tour and most of the Alpine riders had competed in that event. It was the end of the season for the European riders, but they had precious time to relax before Australia's toughest road race.

The race was over 932 kilometres across the Snowy Mountains through Khancoban, Thredbo and Cooma, then up the Pacific Coast from Bega to Narooma and Bateman's Bay to Sydney. Cycling is a demanding sport, involving monotonous hours of training, and few ever share in the glory or the awards. Most of the finer moments of road racing occur far from the public eye on deserted mountain roads or endless flat stretches of country road.

It is a rare privilege to be part of a tour entourage. Even motorists who, by chance, intersect a tour in full flight are pushed aside by police escorts, as if it were a Royal Tour or a Presidential motorcade. A road cycling race takes off like an ejaculation in a vagina, with riders, officials and media penetrating a travelling womb. The strongest sperm constantly try to break out and race off along a main artery. When rider sperm break through, parental cells give chase to protect them against speeding vehicle cells. As more and more rider sperm break clear, more parental cells rush after them, others dropping back into the vagina to encourage the feeble to remain with the seminal stream.

The first rush down a steep mountain descent at 100 kilometres an hour provides the orgasmic part of the equation. When you're in a car descending at a maximum 80 kph ahead of the cycling bunch and someone asks: "What if they catch up with us?" The answer is the end of the life cycle: "You'll just have to drive over the bloody edge". Standing at the side of the road on one descent through a forest of stark, white snow gums we watched three European riders flashing down. As they came close one threw his hands in the air and yelled "I love this bloody country."

"Get your bloody hands back down or you might become a bloody part of it!" I yelled, as they hurtled into a sharp curve.

It was on the notorious Brown Mountain heading down to the New South Wales South Coast that one of them slammed into a metal guard rail and somehow survived. It's not a sport for the faint-hearted.

The inaugural Mazda Alpine Tour lived up to the promise of Craven to make it the toughest in Australia. It was another steep learning curve for me; the radio coverage was extensive and the sponsor was happy. The Kamikaze Kid found sharing a room with me was a harrowing experience, waking each morning at 5am to find me churning through endless voice reports for radio news services across the country. Mazda had provided a manual typewriter and it was that, not an alarm clock that woke Steve each morning. "Fucking bloody typewriter," he'd say every morning as he tried to bury himself under the sheets.

Once he was on his feet, he was a tireless worker, collecting my daily news-sheet for tour personnel and arranging photocopying and distribution. Every day he washed my car, which made me feel better about the daily routine at Mazda. A huge crowd turned out for the I would do another Alpine Tour, hand over the daily news-sheet to someone else and add photography to my assignment. The second time, heavy snowfalls made racing through the Snowy Mountains more hazardous, while transmitting up to 40 voice reports a day was becoming easier to handle.

There isn't anything that's beyond any one of us, no matter how late in life. Three or four short paragraphs, modulate the voice and go for it. Two years later, when I went on the *Victoria Health Herald Sun* Tour there was no place in the media team, so I joined the construction crew. Slinging heavy metal barriers, towing a trailer, tying ropes and hanging signs at the age of 59 involved another learning curve, but to do it brought satisfaction and a few extra dollars. I had just lost a job when Craven made the offer for me to go on the 1390 km race around Victoria and Tasmania. "Can you handle construction crew?" he asked. "I'll ride a bike if you want me to," I replied.

The construction crew threw me in at the deep end and gave me a hard time, but all in fun. "From chocolates to boiled lollies, they said. It serves you right for being a bloody Pom." We drank in public bars, backed horses and whinged about bosses – up the workers! One early morning in Myrtleford we were setting up barriers and hoardings for the finish of a tour stage when an angry local in a truck drove up and loudly abused us for anti-smoking advertising signs.

"The weather's fucked the tobacco crop this year and you lot come to town telling people to stop smoking," he ranted. He was a tobacco farmer who looked mad enough to take a shotgun to the lot of us.

"Not me, mate – I'm with you," I said and lit up a cigarette. Later, I thought it was a bit rich going into a depressed tobacco growing area with a quit smoking message, particularly as some of the people manning the campaign booth occasionally would duck round the corner for a quiet smoke.

A week later we were in wine country and I was back to doing radio on the inaugural Mazda Winery Tour. "From piss to plonk," the construction crew said as we wound our way through the wineries of South Australia, and 'The Tour de Plonk' became the unofficial name of the race.

It started from a wine cellar on a vineyard on Melbourne Cup Day. We'd stood around a vineyard for hours that morning, but nobody thought to back the Irish horse Vintage Crop and it won by a country mile. Luckily, I'd drawn it in a sweep, so I was $80 in front, and I slung a few barriers and bought watermelon for the construction crew. "You can tell he's back with the silk department," they said. "Fucking watermelon." So it was back to the public bar, betting on horse racing and putting shit on the bosses. I'd learnt a lot from Fuck'n Les, even if he was a 'bloody Pom'. They were the salt of the earth, the construction crew. Syd Salt would tell you that himself, which he often did. It was Australian mateship at its best, for Jeff Dew, Luke Drummond, Billy Toleman, Harry McCaig, Geoff Burrows and Gavin Hill came from a variety of occupations from police sergeant to public servant, and the tours were a big escape for them – an escape from tedium at work or at home, a chance to be yourself away from all the bullshit, and boiled lollies last a lot longer than chocolates. Thirty thousand people turned out for the final criterion in the centre of Adelaide because it was Grand Prix eve and the city was jumping.

*

I left Mazda to take over as editor of the Melbourne city lifestyle magazine *Melbourne Agenda*. Two years of physical work had given me a hard edge, and it felt like starting all over again, without the illusions. The magazine relied on advertising for all its revenue, so it was mostly 'advertorial', with space for real editorial at a premium. It was an opportunity to be in the PR and media scene, and maybe get into something else at a later stage. Having learnt at Mazda, I gave it my best shot, making the city my 'patch' and closely monitoring its heartbeat. We did a deal with a photographic retailer in return for a new Nikon camera and I discovered a whole new creative world. Another learning curve, although I'd directed enough shoots in advertising and PR, now I had my finger firmly on the button of a new career path at 59.

Betty Friedan says in her book *The Fountain of Age* 'There are choices we can make, along the journey we all sooner or later must take, that truly open surprising new possibilities.' To be booked as a wedding photographer for the first time in your life as you're nudging 60 should really be no surprise, as long as you have reasonable eyesight and believe in yourself. At 60 you should have a lot to draw upon in recording the commitment, aspirations and dreams of two people just starting out in life. It is the same with fashion photography.

I covered a number of fashion shows and I tried to capture the totality of the event, not just the garments, but the movement and exuberance of the models who made the garments come to life. The majority of our readers were female office and shop workers, so much of the editorial/advertorial focussed on fashions, cosmetics, health and fitness. I found myself wandering around cosmetics counters picking up leaflets and brochures on new products and the cosmeticians must have wondered about me because I became quite a regular. 'Poor old dear, it's probably how he fills in his day.' I also had a body beat, checking out the latest in weight reduction, plastic surgery and aerobics routines.

The body beauty industry has plenty of money-grubbers who exploit the fears of young and old women alike. Privately, some of them ridicule many of their clients, while publicly giving them false hopes of acquiring hourglass figures to snare or hold their man. One salon owner clipped photographs of women from international magazines to use for endorsements in advertising. 'Look what six weeks with Madam X has done for my figure.' She got into trouble when one of the attractive young women turned out to be the daughter of a diplomat transferred to Melbourne.

I wrote a story to make people think about another angle, sexual harassment of males. Men seem to take a more philosophical view, though some women might offend and embarrass us. The story about how I was abused was written tongue in cheek. "She was pissed!" the publishers yelled at me.

Does that mean that anyone who sexually harasses someone while drunk is excused? I was starting to understand how a woman would feel; I was the victim, being made to feel guilty, and my anxiety level increased when they said: "She'll probably punch your lights out."

It was not the threat of physical violence but rather the vehemence with which it was said that increased my anxiety. Everybody's entitled to criticise and I was quite happy to cop some flak; publishers, as well as readers, had the right to put their point of view in the magazine. It was the week that distinguished radio commentator Alistair Cooke in his *Letter From America* had been moved to 'put aside the disintegration of the former Soviet Union as the major story of the week in deference to the issue of sexual harassment'. Every public figure in America, Cooke reasoned, was now living under the threat of a sexual harassment charge, real or imagined – another bonanza for shonky lawyers. It was motivated largely by the charges brought against a nominee for the American Supreme Court, a black judge, whose former assistant had accused him of sexually harassing her over a number of years.

In Australia legislation has given people the right to press sexual harassment charges for a wide variety of reasons, including the way another person looks at them. Some commentators and columnists are claiming that it is now open season on men. One male academic in Australia was accused by a student of sexually harassing her by reading to her certain passages of a book. In my case, I was physically harassed by two women within a matter of days, one a high profile media identity with her hand on the inside of my thigh at lunch and another grabbing at various parts of me at dinner. The second occasion was quite embarrassing for me, and for other males and females seated opposite me. Now, the female publishers of the magazine were attacking me in a more damaging way, attacking my right to speak out.

They had every opportunity to constructively criticise my story in the next edition of the magazine. Instead, they arbitrarily sacked me, demanding that I leave the premises immediately. I wandered about in a daze for some time. I got angry and lodged a complaint of unfair dismissal, established a prima facie case and was given a substantial financial settlement, the details of which I cannot disclose. What disturbs me more than sexual abuse of males is the general lack of knowledge of the growing discrimination against men in business by female 'networks'.

When I was offered the job with Victorian Cycling Incorporated most people I knew in the cycling world said: "Don't do it. It's like so many sporting bodies, fraught with warring factions," said one promoter. "The amateurs and professionals have been at war for years. When they came to merging, it got completely out of control and finished up in a Supreme Court battle. The two rival groups will never bury their differences." I had no choice. After my sacking, I was finding a job hard to come by.

On the surface I seemed to have arranged a good deal, with a three year work agreement on a basic retainer of $28,000 a year, plus 10 per cent of all sponsorship money I raised, all conditional on their accepting that the first twelve months would be spent planning and starting major initiatives.

"While I'm keen on the 10 per cent," I told them, "don't expect any sponsorship money for six to twelve months. Every man and his dog are out there knocking on corporate doors for money." In recent years, the list of door knockers has doubled and many companies are now questioning the morality of putting money into sport when so many people are out of work and living below the poverty line. Cycling is a sport that lives below the poverty line. It can and will improve, but lead time is vital. It was another challenge. At first it worked out well and when I addressed my first full council meeting on plans for marketing the sport long-term I was roundly applauded.

When the national championships were held in Adelaide, a meeting was arranged there with the national governing body, the Australian Cycling Federation. We met in the Adelaide Super drome and the Australian Cycling Federation endorsed plans for a major project which linked cycling medal winners at the 1996 Atlanta Olympic Games with a new indoor cycling track for Melbourne.

Suffice to say that at the time both got screwed up by internal and external wrangling and stupidity. Lack of professionalism within the administration of cycle racing in Victoria led to the chain falling off frequently. Maybe one day someone will get the sport back on the right track.

Judge for Yourself!

Justice and the legal system do not necessarily go hand in hand and judges are just as fallible as the rest of us. There have been as many of the corrupt, immoral, absurd, stupid, greedy, bizarre and incompetent within the legal fraternity as outside it. And a university degree does not guarantee intelligence or wisdom. Having said that, we have what we are given and have to make the best of it. But there are times when as a community we have to make a stand, and time was the essence of my stand against the procrastination of New South Wales Supreme Court Justice Vince Bruce.

Fred, Bob Peachey and I had been locked in the legal process with the Maritime Services Board over the safety buoys and had painstakingly recorded all of the events that led up to the contractual agreement. We had gained an early hearing date, but our QC, former Australian Attorney General ,Tom Hughes, blew it. *Williams v Maritime Services Board* was in the commercial list, but a sudden and unexpected withdrawal by Hughes meant we could not get another QC up to speed in time and we had to let our listed date go by and fall into the crowded civil list where we would languish for five years before we finally had our case heard. Hughes withdrew from the brief to fly to Perth for businessman Laurie Connell, who was, according to Hughes, 'a much bigger fish'.

Our case was a relatively paltry $1.8 million, whereas the high flying merchant banker's case was a multi-million dollar gilt-edged brief for Hughes. After many debilitating hours of recording every single relevant fact about the case, we had been given an audience by Hughes and his junior, Ventry Gray. I had asked our solicitors, Malcolm Johns & Co, to get the best and they had secured Hughes, whom I had seen perform brilliantly in a number of defamation cases that I covered as a journalist. The MSB thought I was not in a financial position to fight the case, but I had been backed by Peachey in return for a percentage of the damages for breach of contract by the MSB.

To set the MSB back on its corporate heels, I had demanded Hughes and also the services of Touche Ross, one of the best accounting firms in the country, to assess quantum for damages. Touche Ross had sub-contracted an advertising media buyer to assist and they had come up with the figure of $1.8 million. This did not take into account the revenue potential from other Australian capital cities and Auckland, New Zealand, where I had obtained agreements in principle to establish the safety buoys. After a one-hour meeting with Hughes we appeared to be in a strong position to tackle the powerful MSB; then he dropped his bombshell and took off for Perth.

We demanded another top QC to replace him, but we were forced to appear in court and say we were not fully prepared for the hearing. Ironically, Connell and the Rothwells merchant bank finished up taking one of the biggest corporate dives in history, while I splashed down in the civil list.

At a later stage we ended up in the Appeal Court of NSW in what can only be described as a Shakespearian tragedy, in which our QC fell upon his own sword. In an inexplicable move, the MSB had said it would like us to consider going to arbitration. We said we would love to go to arbitration. The MSB lawyers said we would have to get Sir Laurence Street, the former Chief Justice of NSW, to arbitrate. 'Wink, wink, he couldn't afford Street at $3000 a day." So our enterprising young solicitor, Joseph Jacobs, went out and got him. When advised of this, the MSB suddenly decided arbitration was not their preferred course of action. Jacobs advised us to take the matter to the Appeal Court.

The bench of three decided two to one to reject our appeal for arbitration on the grounds that as a minister of the Crown was involved, the matter had to be resolved by the courts. What I was thinking in the body of the Appeal Court was that arbitration decisions automatically go back to the court for final ratification. Secondly, the case was not against the minister, so it was not a test of his authority; the only things it would test about him were his credibility and intelligence.

Even such a distinguished person as the former Chief Justice would have to abide by the court's subsequent ruling on his arbitration, and he surely had enough credibility and intelligence to realise this. Our QC waffled on about everything but the fundamental issues and was politely told to shut up and accept the court's decision. The dissenting judge, who was considerably younger than his fellow bench men, said I was getting a raw deal. I agreed, but as the plaintiff I could hardly jump to my feet and say so.

That's the remarkable thing about the law; it's mostly got nothing to do with you. Sometimes in court you wonder: 'Do they really need a plaintiff and a defendant? I'm sure they would be much happier left to their own devices.'

The MSB solicitors had cost us a lot of money by leading Jacobs up a blind alley. We would have been far better advised to push harder for a court hearing and stay out of the mustiness and murkiness of appeals legalese. Eventually we got our day, or as it turned out, our week, in court, but we then had to wait a further agonising three years for a judgement from Justice Bruce. The public needs to jump up and down and scream and shout about the legal system, because most of the time the only people who seem to get justice are those who can afford it. And it is quite reasonable to say there are stupid judges and stupid lawyers.

July 4, 1997, Independence Day in America and in Australia a hint of independence for me with receipt of a letter from barrister Ventry Gray to solicitor Michael Grey. It was the first tangible evidence that our case had been heard in the NSW Supreme Court two years earlier.

'I have just been informed by the President of the NSW Bar Association that Mr Justice Bruce will not be sitting to hear any further cases until his outstanding arrears of undelivered judgements (including his judgement in the Williams case) have been brought up to date. You will not be surprised to learn that there are many such undelivered judgements, but the Judge had not long been appointed before he heard the Williams case and the judgement in this case must be amongst the longest outstanding. Unfortunately I cannot tell you either: (a) where the Williams case ranks in the list of undelivered judgements, or (b) whether judgements will delivered according to ranking. "There is really nothing more that can be done. I can only express the hope that the delay which has occurred, and which Mr Williams has all endured with such resigned patience for nearly two years, is rewarded in the

near future which, I suppose, cannot mean anything more hopeful than by the end of the present calendar year.'

One week earlier I had bet on a horse called *Have Patience* which won at good odds. I don't know if Vince Bruce bets on horses, but while he was on the bench he was certainly heavily involved in sport, particularly Rugby League. It appears he spent a great deal of time involved in the judicial process for that code while a scrum of litigants patiently waited for him to throw in a ball or two. He also found time to go to the Atlanta Olympics as a member of the Athletes Appeals Tribunal and later put up his hand to head an inquiry into the appointment by Athletics Australia of East German coach Ekkart Arbeit. Announcing that Judge Bruce was joining former champion athlete Herb Elliott on the review panel, Martin Soust, Executive Director of Athletics Australia, said the panel 'had as long as it wanted' to reach a decision.

A month or so before Ventry's letter arrived, we had decided that almost two years was a ridiculous time to wait for a judgement, so we had made a formal request to the NSW Bar Association to investigate what many members of the legal profession had described as 'a bloody disgrace'.

All sorts of reasons had been put for the inordinate delay, including the proposition that Judge Bruce was suffering from 'professional paralysis'. Barristers had a code that one could not make a direct approach to a judge, not even to inquire about his health! While it is fair that nothing should be done that could be seen as an attempt to influence a judge, there should be some line of communication open in such unusual circumstances – otherwise litigants have no representation. As the third anniversary approached, we decided to bite the bullet.

Justice Vince Bruce became the first judge in the State's history to be invited to Parliament to show cause why he should not be dismissed after he was found to be a 'procrastinator.' In a majority report, the NSW Judicial; Commission said Justice Bruce was unfit to continue as a Supreme Court Judge.

The verdict came after the commission subjected Justice Bruce to a series of time-trials on his completion of cases, following numerous complaints about delays in his delivery of judgements.

Attorney-General Jeff Shaw said the commission had found complaints against Justice Bruce substantiated and that his incapacity to perform his judicial duties had been proved. "These matters could justify Parliamentary consideration of the removal of Justice Bruce from the office of a Judge of the Supreme Court of NSW," he said. "It is my intention to invite Justice Bruce to appear before the Bar of the Legislative Council to show cause why Parliament should not request the Governor to remove him from office."

Premier Bob Carr said judges should be treated no differently to the rest of the community when it came to work standards. "The ordinary Australian out there knows that he or she will be sacked if they refuse to work," he said. "We need judges to pull their weight, it's as simple as that, and if Parliament has got to assert that principle in this case then we'll do it."

The historic move came after five of Justice Bruce's colleagues unanimously dismissed an injunction by him to stop the Government tabling the damning report. The panel of the NSW Court of Appeal was told that if the report was tabled, the judge's 'future life could be destroyed'. Barrister Dick Conti, QC, said the reputation of the judge could be 'severely damaged' if the report was allowed to be debated in Parliament.

But, relaying the unanimous decision, Justice Keith Mason said Mr Shaw was legally entitled to table the document.

The commission's report said Justice Bruce was given more than 10 weeks leave in 1995 to reduce a mounting backlog of cases. By December he had halved his outstanding judgements. to 11, plus the massive NutraSweet case, but by February this year it had climbed back to 22. "The division thinks that there was also operating as a significant factor what clinical psychiatrist Dr Gilandas called 'procrastination'," Justice Mason said.

Sydney Morning Herald 27 June 1998:

"The 24-16 vote in the Legislative Council on Thursday night has saved Justice Bruce's immediate position. But it has, in no sense, resolved doubts about his future. From being a judge whose removal from office the Judicial Commission thought Parliament should consider, he effectively has

become a judge on probation. Not only that, the system for maintaining the integrity of the judicial system has been placed under heavy strain.

According to the Attorney-General, Mr Shaw, Thursday's vote by the Legislative Council means there will be no similar motion put to the Legislative Assembly. That is his interpretation of section 53(2) of the Constitution Act, which says a judge can be removed by the Governor, 'on an address from both houses of Parliament in the same session'.

"The shadow Attorney-General, Mr Hannaford, says he hopes the matter will still be considered by the Lower House. That is not likely to happen. But it must be said that the spirit of this most important constitutional safeguard surely is that the fate of any judge, when allegations of unfitness are raised, is in the hands of Parliament, not just one part of Parliament.

"As Mr Hannaford points out, the members of the Upper House make up only one-third of the total number of parliamentarians.

"It wrongly implied that the proposal to remove was a proposal to punish rather than to protect the public and the integrity of the judicial system. It allowed sentiment to overwhelm what should have been serious doubts about inconsistencies in Justice Bruce's own speech.

"The truly sad thing about this case is not that a person who deserved punishment has managed, by appealing for sympathy, to escape his just deserts. This case was never about punishment for wrong-doing. It was always about protection of the public and the integrity of the court from incapacity in one of its judges. As Mr Shaw said, judicial independence from the executive and legislative branches of government is vital, 'but the separation of powers does not mean that a judicial officer found to be incapable of exercising the duties of the office can remain in that office'.

"What happens now? Justice Bruce will continue his work as a judge. It must be hoped that there will be no further instances of delay in his delivery of judgements. There can be no excuses for that if it happens. If the same old pattern of delay does continue, those parliamentarians who voted against his removal will have been seen clearly to have failed their most difficult test. They will not have done what is right for Justice Bruce."

On the night that the Legislative Council accepted Justice Bruce's submissions that his depression was the most relevant factor affecting his work, the President of the Council, Max Willis, and others were not in a fit state to perform their duties.

Willis and others were seen tripping backwards and forwards from the Council chamber to a party in an adjacent function room. The judge survived and a leading politician, Max Willis, who had been involved in judging him, was forced to resign for being drunk in the House.

Justice Bruce took 1000 days to hand down a 13 page judgement rejecting our case, which he delivered in a matter of seconds with no apology for the delay.

But Justice Bruce had lost credibility and soon followed.

The Australian was moved to comment that in the time it took him to deliver the judgement "Jesus Christ turned the world on to Christianity and John F. Kennedy energised a generation and flirted with nuclear war." *The Australian* also noted that "Seconds after handing down the decision, Justice Bruce grinned as he left the courtroom".

Now, in 2005, as another yacht hits another rock – this time right next to the Opera House – another of the major players in the Vince Bruce saga Supreme Court Justice Jeff Shaw has been forced to resign in disgrace.

The *FT Spirit* was on a charter sail for the *Financial Times* and had 12 people on board, most of them experienced sailors.

"We came in too close and hit the bottom and as we did the boat pivoted on the keel and it ripped the big 20-tonne of lead that keeps the boat upright right off," said Deckhand Benny Mawson.

"No one was injured, everyone's just a little shaken." Spirit is an international America's Cup Class yacht from the 1992 San Diego Challenge.

"There was a huge crash, the bulb keel which keeps the boat upright fell off and she capsized," said London visitor Richard Long.

He said the top of the mast crushed one of the lights on the walkway which kept it on its side. His wife Jan Long said the boat had been sailing close to the shoreline. "It was very close, it hit a rock," she said. Jan said the yacht was sailing towards the Opera House.

"There doesn't appear to be a marker there warning about rocks on that side," she said.

Meanwhile I'm still dealing with words and pictures in the business world as I enter my seventy-second year.

It was fortunate that from the age of 60 to 64 I worked with an IT consulting group in Melbourne, which enabled me to become proficient with both PC and Macintosh computers.

At times it was daunting – such as when I walked into the IT division of a corporate giant like BHP and discovered myself surrounded by 25-year-old super-nerds.

Compounding that was the assignment – educating senior executives in the use of a new remote mail system. We managed, even getting the essential user manual details on to a postcard.

I was more at home producing videos for the roll-out of new software programmes for the Education Department and promotional videos for the Anti-Cancer Council, although that landed me in hospital for major surgery. When I was asked by the client whether at my age I had had a PSA test for prostate cancer, I replied in the negative. Fortunately for me that turned into a big positive. I was lucky that the simple blood test led to further, more invasive tests which showed that I was in big trouble.

I was forced to put the cancer videos on hold while I underwent a three-hour operation to remove my prostate cancer shortly before it would have removed me from the land of the living.

The surgical team advised me that I had come into their expert hands in the nick of time, so to speak. During the lengthy recovery period a backpack was essential for carrying special pads and other paraphernalia needed as I walked the streets with a tube up my penis and a bag on an inner leg. My target was to get fit enough to play nine holes of golf, which I managed to do and I've been reasonably fit and healthy since then. I still carry the same backpack, but for other reasons.

At 64 I was I was also fortunate to meet up again with Fred Baker in Tasmania. Living in a small cottage on the bank of the

Derwent River in Lower Sandy Bay and walking to Hobart and back each day for six months did wonders for my health.

Looking out from the back deck of the cottage I was aware that there was nothing between there and the Antarctic; which meant I was breathing in the purest of air. It was the same on the top of Mt Wellington where we loaded casks with pure mountain water for Fred's home brew; both the mountain and the home brew may also have been good for my health.

My voyage to Tasmania and back on the Bass Strait ferry *Spirit of Tasmania* reminded me that from my time at the *Vindicatrix* Sea Training School back in 1948 to the present day I'd never really been far from the sea or the travelling that I loved.

Semaphore may or not be my final port of call. Peter Everitt and I have both signed on for the November Vindi Reunion so we may float around in the Barossa Valley for a while.

Meanwhile I'm operating a 'business in a backpack' with no overheads; I use the flash drive on which this book is digitally stored for print design and production on a public computer at the Semaphore Library in Adelaide. I've spent much of the past year at the library completing this book.

To supplement my pension, I've produced a number of items including a set of six house wine labels for Semaphore's Café Saltwater.

I produced the artwork for the labels at the library and sent it by email to the printer in Adelaide; they in turn sent back an electronic proof which the client approved before printing went ahead. How technology has changed our lives.

Emboldened, I moved on to produce a set of Semaphore souvenir cards for tourists and residents. The State Library of South Australia gave me permission to publish images from their library of historic photographs.

Then came the hard part; calling on businesses in Semaphore to sell them – and I did, making a small but handy profit. Now I'm preparing to produce and sell prints for framing and a set of greetings cards. I'm again working with Fred Baker, who is doing final production and printing in Hobart; once again, it's all handled by computers.

Recently, by chance. I noticed some workmen at the top of the timeball tower and I talked my way up, giving me the chance to replicate a 1925 photo taken from the same location. I had to climb up four steel ladders inside the tower, which took me back to *Coulgarve* days, carrying sacks of potatoes up and down steel ladders.

Forgive me for harking back, but it goes with the territory when you've reached 'time-on' in the second half of the game of life. Some things are clear as daylight, while others are but vague memories.

In the absence of a merchant seaman's discharge book, which was the result of my jumping ship in Sydney, I have no memory of actual dates of my sea service, other than jumping ship in 1953. Fortunately, as this book was going to the printer, I received from the National Archives in Kew photocopies of my records including discharge book and identity card. More than 50 years on I had thought that it all started in 1948 or 49, but I was dead wrong. Thanks to researcher Henry Parker I was finally able to set the record straight.

Dates apart, my recollections of most of my experiences are clear and I've tried to present a true picture of the good, the bad and the ugly.

When in old age you become increasingly aware of your own mortality, you tend to do that; consider a balance sheet of life while you're still capable. And yes, you do occasionally wonder how long there is to go.

Fred Baker and I have a German friend about my age in Hobart who does wonder.

Otto told Fred he asked his doctor the other day how long he thought Otto had left. "The doctor said 'ten'," Otto said. "Ten what?" I asked. "Ten years? Ten months?" He looked at me for a while then started counting 10, 9, 8, 7 6 and I fell off my chair laughing."

THE END

Afterword

I first started writing this book in the early 1990s and gave it the title *The Seventh Wednesday* due to me being born on a Wednesday and I thought the title was mysterious. I was in Melbourne at the time and, despite book launches and other promotions, it sold very few copies. As my employment prospects dried up as well, I moved on with life and in 2000 or so, I decided to move to Adelaide and to be closer to my son, Chris.

By then, I'd qualified for the Aged Pension and was supplementing this by providing some IT and internet services within my local community. I was also working closely within the aged and veteran communities. My previous book was a distant memory and then, on Anzac Day, April 25 2004, I began to make new connections with my past after watching a small group of men parade in the annual Anzac Day march with a banner which read '*Vindicatrix* Association'.

This prompted me to pop the name into an internet search engine and discover the extent of the world-wide network of Vindi boys. On June 29 2005, I finally joined that network when I attended my first meeting of the *Vindicatrix* Association South Australian branch at the Seafarers Mission in Port Adelaide.

Not long after the 2004 Anzac Day holiday, I had met by chance the first Vindi boy I had seen since December 1953. Peter Everitt, a deck boy from a class of 1951, was about 100 yards from the time ball tower in a café-bookshop, appropriately named Pathfinders, run by his daughters Diane and Lorraine.

Peter recalls two things that stand out from his training on *Vindicatrix* – a song:

They say that on the Vindi the beds are really fine.

But how the hell would they know, they've never slept in mine.

And blankets:

"*One day when some government people were inspecting the camp we were all issued with new blankets and told to put them on our beds. As soon as the government blokes left, we were told to give the blankets back*".

Nevertheless, Peter also said he enjoyed his time on the *Vindicatrix* and that it was a turning point in his life.

After his time on the ship with three names Peter went straight to another vessel that had three names, *Port Vindex*, although the 16 year old deck boy didn't know that at the time.

"Older crew kept saying that *Port Vindex* had been an aircraft carrier during the Second World War. And I can remember seeing some reference to that on the ship's bell. But I could never imagine aircraft landing on such a small ship." I did some research and was able to let Peter know that originally *Port Vindex* was an uncompleted refrigerated cargo vessel, Port Sydney, which the Royal Navy bought in 1942 and converted to a small aircraft carrier.

Launched in May 1943, she was commissioned in December of that year as the escort carrier HMS Vindex, a twin-screw vessel with enclosed hangars and a long steel flight deck. Vindex served as a convoy escort in the Atlantic and Arctic in 1944-45 when her aircraft sank a number of German submarines. After service in the Pacific, Vindex was sold by the Navy in 1947 and operated as *Port Vindex* until she was scrapped in Kaohsiung in 1971.

Peter vividly recalls one particular experience on *Port Vindex*.

"It was my turn to be 'Peggy', you know serving meals to deck crew. When I put down one guy's meal he said 'Where's the butter?' I was hurrying and said, 'It's in the cupboard right beside you,' and went back to the galley. When I got back he said 'Where's the butter?' and I said 'Right beside you.' With that, he jumped up and knocked me down. When I got up he knocked me down again and I ran off to my cabin. None of the other crew had tried to help me, which as a 16-year-old I thought they'd do. Later, the same guy became my mentor and at the end of the trip he was standing next to me at the rail as we came into port. He said: 'Well, you left home a boy and came home a man.' He was right, because when I joined the ship I was brash and cheeky and I should have put the butter on the table."

After a first trip of fifteen months I can easily relate to 'left home a boy and came home a man.'

A view of the Time Ball Tower Circa 1990 (Port Adelaide Enfield Local History Photos)

Unlike some of the Vindi boys, I do not have many clear memories of my time as a trainee, other than my canal swim and subsequent cold, wet time 'under the clock'. In the absence of a discharge book, which was the result of my jumping ship in Sydney, I have no idea of actual dates of sea service, other than remaining ashore in December 1953. Our senses seem to be the best memory triggers we have. While I have only a vague memory of arriving at Sharpness and leaving there, I clearly recall standing at the foot of the gangway of my second ship, the *Coulgarve*, when I arrived in Swansea to sign on. It was the smell of the sulphur being loaded aboard the small tramp steamer that chiselled the moment into my memory.

When I think of my childhood during the war, I have some vivid individual memories, but no clear overall scenario. The things I remember most about high school are the school bus, playing football during recess and playing truant whenever I could. Perhaps my best memory now of Sharpness is as one of the most valuable milestones on my life journey. It taught me respect for others, how to think outside the square and, above all, it gave me my first career opportunity.

Standing near the Time Ball tower, it is easy to visualise *Arranmore* riding at anchor off Semaphore Beach. It was from here that she would learn of the capture of one of her crew who had jumped ship in Port Adelaide. As one of thousands of merchant seamen who have jumped ship in Australia, I wonder how many of them, like me, got away with it, married and had a family. How many of their families would have watched the Anzac Day parade without realising the connection with that banner. I also wonder how many Australians are related to merchant seamen who jumped ship. When I spoke as a 'new chum' at the Seafarers Centre, I was asked what my mum thought about me jumping ship. I said she was not very happy, but she had eventually decided that if I wasn't coming home then the family would move to Australia, and they did.

As I walked from Semaphore to Port Adelaide that Sunday morning, I thought back 54 years and wondered if I would be stood under the clock if I got there late. My apprehension was brought about by the fact that it was the Birkenhead Bridge and 'scouses' have always had a thing about Birkenhead. Built 67 years earlier the bridge serviced road and shipping traffic and can be closed to pedestrians at times that can be inconvenient.

If you were caught at the Port Adelaide end you could slip into the British Hotel for a quiet beer, but after 158 years, and no doubt holding many memories for thousands of mariners, including Vindi boys, it had finally closed down.

Unusual for Australia, the bridge is a twin bascule type, a reference to the see-saw lifting action that enables the two 360-tonne leaves to tilt upwards, allowing ships in the Port River to pass through.

Fortunately, the bridge was open to road traffic; I arrived on time and was welcomed warmly by several Vindi boys who were keen to know what year I was at Sharpness. While making the mandatory introduction speech, I mentioned *Athelknight* and, to everyone's surprise, I found that Supply Officer Keith Withey had sailed on the same vessel, but at a different time, from October 1948 to May 1949.

Most of the meeting was devoted to progress reports on the staging by 12 the *Vindicatrix* SA branch of the Vindi Down Under Reunion in November 2005. It soon became obvious that life after the Merchant Navy had unearthed a wealth of talent and expertise across a broad field of endeavour.

It was also obvious that distant memories of the rough and tumble of life at sea were just that. When the bar opened there were few drinkers, most opting for coffee and biscuits. On the steps outside there were only two smokers, one of them being me.

It's a far cry from those early days, but let's face it, many of those present were in their seventies, including me. I expect the reunion right in the heart of South Australia's wine growing region the Barossa Valley may see some of us let our hair down – what's left of it.

In 2004 jumping ship was recognised as another weak security link in the war against terror when it was revealed that since the September 11 attack in New York, 101 seamen had deserted from their vessels in Australia. Of course, many would be doing it for a better life. During the Cold War when many more would have been escaping Communism I don't think the authorities did a head count. What makes it different today is that many have jumped off vessels flying flags of convenience. Reports that Al Qaeda and some international drug cartels actually own or control a number of merchant vessels are alarming.

*

Anyway, I digress. The reunion with the Vindi boys got me back on the Apple computer and rewriting the *Seventh Wednesday*. And, in due course, the book was re-released in print and on Amazon in 2005 as *The Fortunate Life of a Vindicatrix Boy*. By putting *Vindicatrix* in the title, I thought that I would appeal to that world wide network of Vindi boys.

By then, I'd turned 71 and it was only later that a realised I'd missed the boat with the Vindi boys as many would have passed on by then. The book sold well locally and initially, but I failed to get any real momentum. I have received small cheques from Amazon each year, but not enough to really make a difference to someone surviving on welfare in Australia these days..

I turn 84 this year and, even though I have aches and don't move as well as I once did, I wake up everyday and look forward to a good walk and a chance to have a chat with the many friends I have made here in Cairns, Australia.

After my sister-in-law, Madge Williams, passed in 2014, I reunited with Christopher, Madge's son, and my nephew. It was good to chat to him again, despite the sad occasion of Madge's passing. I was living in a hostel in Adelaide by then, with very little money once my food and accommodation were sorted. Christopher appeared to have settled well in a warm part of Queensland and he undertook to sponsor my trip up there and help me into a flat.

Christopher has helped me immensely with this new release of my story. I lost access to computers and email addresses in Adelaide. I think it was shortly after that disastrous trip to Sydney where I'd travelled so that could enjoy a reunion with Maggie, Madge and Joe. So Christopher scanned the book so that he could recreate the manuscript, including finding all the photos and so much more.

*

Christopher here again: Even so, John recently penned a piece about the first flat we got him into in 2014, a bright little bedsit, just down from our place in Edge Hill, inappropriately called the *Penthouse Apartments*. Of course, John being John has a different name for it.

Bathrooms can be funny places at times

The Pentagon (White House), one of the first flats I lived in in Cairns. It was on the third level of a white, oblong, block of flats, with staircases and no lift. Whenever I wrote to family and friends down south, where I'd lived for most of my time in the cities of Melbourne, Sydney and Adelaide, I used to address for return mail, John Williams, The Pentagon, White House, ... Cairns etc.

One day I was in the small bathroom, which had wooden planks and an aluminium, small bath (all square). I had just started running the taps, when the floorboards began to collapse. I put my feet on a ledge which remained as the rest of the floor just collapsed beneath me and into the flat below.

Suddenly a voice came up from below and I saw my neighbour sitting on the floor with him floating in a river of water. I leaned across to the opposite wall of the shower and turned off both taps. I then rushed downstairs where I helped him to his feet.

Christopher: This event did happen, even though I suspect some embellishment, and I am sure that 'Uncle' will continue to tell stories and write them down until his last moment. To John for the final word.

*

Since coming up in 2014, I feel like I have started on yet another chapter in my life. Everyday in Cairns is warm and the people I meet, whether indigenous, overseas born or locals, are always friendly and like to have a chat. I'm a regular at my local pub, the Edge Hill Tavern, and a number of people there have supported me in my book writing including Eugene, Declan, Mick, Steve, Fred, Mark and many others, including Heather, Christopher's partner.

Thank you for reading my story and I wish you the very best to you, your family and your friends.

And, I'd love to hear your thoughts and comments and you can write to me care of Christopher at chrisjw61@gmail.com

I'd be honoured to return any and all messages.

John Williams, January, 2018

JOHN WILLIAMS

A FORTUNATE LIFE

www.ingramcontent.com/pod-product-compliance
Lightning Source LLC
Chambersburg PA
CBHW071900290426
44110CB00013B/1226